ZEPHYR

Zephyr's
EXTRAORDINARY PEOPLE

First published in 2001
by Zephyr Books Ltd
PO Box 110 Hitchin SG4 OBB

A catalogue record for this book is available from the British Library

ISBN 0-9541098-0-5

Printed and bound in Great Britain by
Bookcraft, Midsomer Norton, Bath, a company of the CPI group

www.zephyrbooks.co.uk

For Eileen, Liz, Jim, Chris, Rachel and
La Porcherie

Acknowledgements

Without the help of our subjects we should have been in great difficulty and we thank them warmly. Gratitude is also due and given to those who helped us with memories and comments and to librarians in many parts of the country who remain ever helpful.

Liz Wallace, Louise Fletcher, Jim Meacock and Eileen Wallace read some chapters, and Gill Riordan read them all. Their valuable comments and suggestions were much appreciated and almost always adopted.

The photographs, including those on the jacket, are by Jim Meacock, except for the following, where the owners have given permission for their use: Willard White by Ken Loveday, BBC Picture Archives; Margaret Tyzack, BBC Picture Archives; James Dyson, Dyson Ltd.

Contents

Introduction

Many people are interested in ideas. Most people are interested in events. We are all interested in people.

The autobiographies of politicians and writers are often serialised as extracts in newspapers. The activities and antics of the celebrated ensure consistently high circulation figures for tabloid newspapers. Full-page profiles in broadsheets provide insights into what motivates people in the news. Obituaries reveal little known aspects of the lives of the great. Weighty academic biographies provide definitive accounts, for a time at least, of the influences on their subjects' work, often attempting to link lives and artistic achievement.

This book, the first of an annual series, tells the stories of twelve important people. Each of them has achieved something of substance. What are those achievements? How did they become what they are? Why did they choose a particular route? What and who were the influences upon their careers? What hurdles and setbacks have they overcome?

Our twelve subjects are very different kinds of people. Some, like Willard White, have risen from humble beginnings to international fame. James Dyson and Tony Benn had comfortable upbringings but then spent much of their lives struggling against the odds. The Younge brothers were brought up by a single mother in considerable hardship but with strong guidance and sound education. A particular school experience took Bill Alexander from a shopkeeping Norfolk family to directing plays in London, Stratford and Birmingham. Tasmin Little's gift was recognised early by a close and supportive family, yet she still had to make her mark in the fiercely competitive world of solo musicians. Born and educated in the East End, Margaret Tyzack went on to play a wide variety of grand and formidable women. Jeremy Dixon and Edward Jones both took their interest in art from their parents and flourished in the unique environment of the Architectural Association School at a time of social upheaval.

All have reached high and low points in their careers, experienced failures and setbacks as well as success. The distinguished theatre director, Bill Alexander, found that worldwide acclaim did not eradicate problems such as filling the large theatre of the Birmingham Rep - in an echo of the plight of London's Royal National. Even though she was at the most prestigious music school for string players in Britain - the Yehudi Menuhin School - Tasmin Little did not learn much for three years and then needed corrective tuition to get back on course. At one point in his career, James Dyson, the most determined of men, almost gave up, but was persuaded by his wife to persevere.

Often a gift recognised early and nurtured is the most fundamental element of a successful career. The stories of the thriller writer Robert Harris and the actor Margaret Tyzack show this. In both their cases, comprehensive schools and teachers were the key motivating factors. For Bill Alexander an English teacher at his public school helped to guide him towards success.

The importance of chance in influencing the careers of these talented people is another theme running through their life stories. The most notable example of this is the reunion of the architects Jeremy Dixon and Edward Jones after a long interval and the birth of their highly successful partnership.

In one way, the lives of the talented are not very different from those of the rest of us - neither a "bowl of cherries" nor "a bitch", but an unpredictable mix of the two. If there is one strand running through the stories it is this: we all need to discover something that we can do well and then to develop our skills and talents, using the confidence this brings to overcome the obstacles. The stories that you are about to read show how twelve people did this.

Ron Wallace, Editor

TASMIN LITTLE

London, September 1995: the Last Night of the Proms. Every seat in the Royal Albert Hall is occupied and down in the arena, stripped of its plush chairs for the annual series, the promenaders are waving banners, flags and rattles, wearing the obligatory silly hats and ready to sing along for all they are worth to 'Land of Hope and Glory'. But first, they are listening raptly to the evening's star violin soloist. This blue-eyed, brown-haired young woman at the centre of the stage holds everyone enthralled. She has already played Vaughan Williams's *The Lark Ascending* in the first half; now, clad in a slinky, red gown for the evening's party mode, she swings into the Saint-Saens *Introduction and Rondo Capriccioso*. Her fingers dance around the violin's fingerboard, the bow flashes, zestful and assured, across the strings. Best of all, she seems to be enjoying every moment of the performance, now and then catching the conductor's eye with a wicked gleam from her own, or flashing a bright, beaming smile across the 7,000-strong audience - who are just a fraction of the number watching and listening to the international live TV broadcast. The eyes of the world are upon her, but she does not appear nervous, insecure or in any way uncomfortable. She was born to perform and to communicate her love of music to her audience - the larger, the better. She is, of course, Tasmin Little.

Now 36, Tasmin Little has been called 'Britain's First Lady of the Violin'. Her meteoric career has taken her to every continent except Antarctica, winning plaudits from the most notoriously hard-to-please orchestras and conductors in the world's musical capitals, including New York and Berlin. She is certainly popular with a wide audience, but she has also played the most challenging new music; in 2000 Simon Rattle sought her out to be his soloist in the complex and highly demanding violin concerto by the great Hungarian contemporary composer Gyorgy Ligeti. Little has never sold her soul to 'crossover' or her image to the insidious skin-baring demands of marketing photography. With her, what you see is what you get. She is phenomenally gifted, but remains, all the same, just like the classic girl next door: lively and sociable, with a natural and unpretentious charm mingled with the strength and resilience to tackle the hefty demands of her increasingly hectic lifestyle. Now she is also balancing her professional life with a happy marriage to the recording engineer Mike Hatch and raising their young daughter, Chloe. And while her life has moved into a new gear, so has her playing, with the recent loan of a Stradivarius violin, which would be a dream come true for any violinist. Adjusting - whether to motherhood or to a new instrument - is not always easy. But if anybody can do it, Little can.

It is not often that a musician seems quite as comfortable on stage as Little does. But this assurance is not coincidental. She is the daughter of the well-known actor George Little, who made her aware of the importance of stagecraft from the very beginning. George - who has performed in a number of musicals including the leading role in *Fiddler on the Roof* and most recently Colonel Bellowes in *Doctor Dolittle*, as well as appearing in popular TV series such as *Emmerdale, All Creatures Great and Small* and *Peak Practice* - was the first to teach Tasmin that the art of performance begins well before the music itself.

"He used to say, 'Your performance starts from the moment your nose peeks out of the curtain and you walk on stage to the moment that the back of your dress disappears off stage'", Little recounts. "He's absolutely right. It's very important that your audience should see that you want to be there. They need to see that you want to communicate something to them, that you're there to play to them, that you're involved in it together and that you need them there. This was something I learned from him: the whole business of literally taking walking on stage in your stride." George also taught her the vital art of nerve management. "He always said to me, 'You must use the nerves - don't let them destroy you, but use them to create an exciting performance'. Of course it's the same for an actor. You mustn't get stage fright. It's all right to have butterflies, but that must be from excitement, not crippling nerves. I think you can only do that if first of all you're the kind of person who responds to that situation in a positive way, and secondly if you've prepared yourself well. If you feel you don't know the piece, that's when your nerves will not work for you. But if you have done your preparation properly, you can walk on stage and just let it happen."

Stagecraft is certainly vital, says Little, but she acknowledges that all too often the demands of modern presentation place appearance ahead of the music itself - something she has never wanted to do. "Music is the most important thing, but there are other areas as well that need to be considered. Yes, today image is in danger of taking over, but I still think there's a middle line to be found: good presentation of what hopefully will be a fine performance. People like to see a performer's face; they don't want it to be covered up by your hair, or by a shadow from lights that have been poorly positioned. The lighting is important and what you wear is important - and if you get this kind of thing right, the performance will be enhanced. Like the cover of a book, it's got to give your audience a taste of what's to come. Then you want to open the book, but hopefully you won't keep closing it to look at the cover!"

❖ ❖ ❖ ❖ ❖

George Little was born in Bradford and came to London to pursue his acting career in the mid-1950s. Working with the Royal Shakespeare Company in Stratford-upon-Avon, George Little noticed that the theatre's box office assistant was a more than usually pretty young woman and asked her out. He and Jilly were married in 1956 and settled in West Hampstead soon afterwards, where their first daughter, Sharon, was born in 1962, and Tasmin three years later. George and Jilly invented Tasmin's name: liking the flower jasmine and the name Tamsin, they combined them. It was only ten years later that a family friend told them that in Tamil the word Tasmin means 'a rare and precious jewel' - and that a traditional Muslim name, Tazmeen, means 'a fount of knowledge'.

"As my father was an actor, life at home was always quite colourful," Little recounts. "My parents have always been very sociable people, so a lot of very interesting guests used to come to visit and we went out a great deal. Because my father was frequently performing in musicals, there was always singing in the house and music on the record player. So I definitely grew up in an environment that was musically and verbally orientated. We were not a quiet household at all! And I'm sure that in many ways that has affected the people I seek and like to be with; it was also perhaps a background to what became my own musicality."

Tasmin's sister Sharon was also artistic, but gravitated towards painting rather than music. Sharon had started to play the violin, but had soon given it up. Consequently, their parents did not at first think of starting Tasmin on a musical instrument, assuming that, as it had not worked for Sharon, it would not do so for their younger daughter. But in fact signs of musical aptitude were there much, much earlier. Tasmin, according to her parents, had been singing quietly to herself in her cot at the age of six months. And then, when George was starring in *Oliver!*, little Sharon went to see the show with Jilly, adored the music and played the recording at home over and over again. The story goes that baby Tasmin began to sing "O-i-er, o-i-er" in tune. "I can't sing it in tune now!" laughs Little. "At the time, my parents just said, 'How sweet,' but didn't think anything more of it."

Six years later, Tasmin went down with chicken pox. Though not particularly ill, she had to stay home from school in quarantine - and was bored. "My poor parents were trying to find ways of occupying my time. It was my idea to learn the recorder because a friend at school was having lessons, so I asked Mum if she'd buy me a recorder and a book to help me get started. She gave them to me and said, 'Please don't disturb me now for half an hour, I'm going to do the washing up'." Tasmin did disturb her within the half-hour. She had apparently taught herself to read the treble clef and play the recorder in less than half an hour and had finished the entire book. As soon as she was better, she wanted to go to recorder classes. Around the same time, an old friend of the family, Gertrude Macauley, lent them a piano and Tasmin and Sharon both started piano lessons. Sharon did not enjoy it much, but Tasmin did. Soon afterwards, she decided that she also wanted to learn the violin.

There was a snag, however. At Tasmin's school, New End Primary School in Hampstead, children under the age of eight were not considered old enough for violin lessons. Tasmin, not yet seven, was desperate to begin. "My mother badgered the teacher and told him that I'd taught myself to read the treble clef and play the recorder. Finally he gave in and said he'd give me an ear test. And he found that I'd got perfect pitch, at which point he became very keen to teach me." The teacher arranged for the local borough to fund fifteen minutes of violin lessons a week, which rapidly increased to half an hour a week. Tasmin made such quick progress that only a few months later she was able to play the Bach *Double Concerto* with her teacher in a concert. It was apparent that she was learning unusually fast; her teacher soon suggested that, much as he wanted to have her as his pupil, it was in her best interests to seek a specialist musical education. "I think this was very magnanimous of him because often teachers want to keep hold of star pupils," says Little. "He suggested that I should audition for the Yehudi Menuhin School, amongst others. But I never got around to auditioning for the other schools because I was accepted into the Menuhin School. I'd been playing just about a year when I started there and I stayed for ten years."

❖ ❖ ❖ ❖ ❖

TASMIN LITTLE

The great violinist Yehudi Menuhin had been inspired by specialist musical education overseas, especially in the Eastern Bloc countries, to found a high-level music school for exceptionally gifted young string players and pianists, aiming to provide an environment for intensive training free of charge that was not otherwise readily available in Britain. Set in secluded and beautiful grounds at Stoke d'Abernon, Surrey, the boarding school had only thirty-five pupils, the creme-de-la-creme of many hopeful applicants, each of whom it was able to provide with a full scholarship. At only eight years old, Tasmin was the youngest pupil at the school.

After living in her lively home with a wide circle of friends her own age and enjoying a continual round of ballet classes and tea parties, going away to a boarding school of this nature so young cannot have been easy. "I was quite lonely and homesick at first," Little remembers. "But I did enjoy myself. My teacher, Jacqueline Gazelle, was particularly kind to me." Jacqueline Gazelle was the widow of Marcel Gazelle, one of Yehudi Menuhin's accompanists, who had been the school's first Head of Music. "She was a wonderful teacher and a very strong-minded, passionate woman. She had a temper and I was partly scared of her, but absolutely adored her too. I think she was a very strong influence on me, because obviously this was very good teaching I was receiving at the tender age of eight and I was lucky to have that. She believed in playing with passion and attack and fire; I'm glad I had that at such an early age. It was important that instead of teaching children in a rather precious, unemotional way, she took the emotion for granted. I think it's important not to assume that children don't feel the emotion. Sometimes people think they're too young to understand it. Yes, at that age you are too young to understand it - but that doesn't mean you don't feel it. It was wonderful for me to have a teacher who wanted me to play with huge amounts of character. I will always be grateful for the amount of time I had with her."

But, after just three years, Jacqueline Gazelle died. Replacing her proved difficult and Tasmin, aged eleven and studying at the UK's top music school, found herself without a permanent violin teacher for three years. "Pauline Scott, who was also teaching at the Guildhall School of Music and Drama, came to the school when I was 14. By then I had got into so many bad habits in my playing that I was having to go to physiotherapy for my arm muscles - I was misusing them and had recurring problems. So at the age of 14, when I began to study with Pauline, she made me go right back to the beginning. That was slightly frustrating because the school made a point of enabling the pupils to go out and play concerts - you wouldn't do a whole concert, you'd play ten minutes of a piece that you'd been preparing. I didn't do any of that for a year. I could see all my friends doing concerts and meanwhile I was stuck with scales and studies! I was upset, but I understood that if I did this work now I'd never need to do it again. That was what saw me through. For one whole year I just practised scales, studies and an occasional piece. But it paid off, because all of the technical problems I'd been experiencing were ironed out. I am now working and living, using that technique that I built up when I was 14. At first it was pain - but now it's all gain."

Yehudi Menuhin himself would visit the school four or five times a year to give masterclasses. These proved a valuable source of inspiration for his young students, Tasmin included. "Funnily enough, we were very rarely scared to play in front of him. He never lost his temper. You would worry that you would disappoint him, rather than that he would get angry with you. We all wanted to play well because we wanted him to be pleased with us."

Menuhin's ideas on violin technique - and, indeed, on life - were often original, sometimes even eccentric: "I remember one lesson when he talked about nothing to do with the instrument. We'd put the instruments down and we were waving our arms in the air, because he was very interested in the body moving as a whole and the harmony between the arms and the rest of the body. In a way he was quite into the latest fad, so there was yoga and there were interesting things to eat. He was someone who liked to try all sorts of ideas and different ways of living. Some of them he would bring along to the school and some would be interesting, but at other times you'd quietly wish he'd help you learn to shift your arm position smoothly instead!" But his influence was deep and lasting nonetheless. "I do remember some really wonderful, inspirational lessons I had with him, in particular on the Bartok *First Rhapsody* and another fantastic lesson on the Bach *Chaconne*, when I was 16. I'm still grateful for those lessons."

Little's connection with Menuhin later strengthened as her career developed. When she left the school at 18, she had to return the violin that it had lent to her for the duration of her education and needed to buy her own instrument for the first time. Good violins do not come cheap and Menuhin's assistance in helping her to raise the necessary funds proved crucial. "We'd found a violin - a Henry Lockey Hill - but we needed to find £5,000 to buy it. That was an enormous amount of money in the early 1980s and my parents just didn't have it. I had no violin of my own and it seemed that I was going off to the Guildhall School of Music with no violin to play. We were desperate." Gertrude Macauley, who had given the family the piano all those years ago, came to their rescue once more, organising contributions from her friends. The Littles put on a concert to raise money, while Menuhin wrote a wonderful letter of support which was sent to various funds to see if they were able to provide grants. Few funds at that time were dedicated to help young musicians to buy instruments. Today the number has increased because the importance of having a good instrument as a student is more widely recognised - and perhaps also because the prices of such instruments have rocketed. "But in those days," says Little, "everyone would give money to help you study but not to help you buy a first instrument - it was extremely difficult. One particular trust gave about £2,000 and then by various other means we managed to cobble together the rest of the money and buy this instrument. I was very grateful for Menuhin's support because, without it, the various trusts probably wouldn't have helped me."

Near the end of Menuhin's life, Little met him again when her husband, Mike, was asked to engineer the sound on some recordings which he was to conduct. "We all went off to Warsaw where he was recording with the Sinfonia Varsovia. I remember him rehearsing the Elgar *Introduction and Allegro* for strings. The orchestra didn't know the piece at all to begin with and it was fascinating to watch the rehearsal. Although Menuhin's conducting technique was not particularly good, he had an amazing knack of inspiring the musicians. He would sing what he wanted and they were able to take it on board immediately. Eventually, through his gestures, they would come to perform it in a marvellous way. That performance was superb, as good as any we'd heard anywhere, and it had started out being a complete mess!"

On this trip Little and her husband also spent time with Menuhin socially. They would go together to the studio in the car and chat on the way, and on one occasion Menuhin invited them and the record producer out for dinner in a hotel restaurant. "What utterly impressed me," says Little, recalling the evening, "was that he was talking to Mike about the latest digital technology. He knew words and phrases that even I do not know although my husband works in this business! He also came up with some hilarious stories - he was a brilliant raconteur. He had a very quiet way of speaking. He never raised his voice; he was the sort of person who would draw you in. You would draw closer to him because what he had to say was so fascinating and you just wanted to hear the latest pearl of wisdom. He was at home everywhere he went and he had a knack for making everyone feel at home and relaxed in his company. He never put on airs and graces - I'm always impressed with that because he really did move in amazing circles. He was always doing good deeds and writing letters. I remember on the plane going over to Warsaw he was scribbling his idea for resolving the Northern Ireland problem on the back of an airline sick bag! He was really a man of broad ideas and, yes, some of them were a bit far-fetched, but he was an incredible person."

❖ ❖ ❖ ❖ ❖

After Tasmin, now 16, had worked on correcting her technique for a year and a half, her teacher, Pauline Scott, suggested that she was now ready to enter her first competition, the 1982 BBC Young Musician of the Year. She shot straight through to the string section finals. The youngest player in the last round, a smiley teenager in a pale pink ballgown, she wowed the entire audience with her performance of the Delius *Third Sonata* and Ravel's *Tzigane* and was ultimately awarded third prize in her section. It proved one of the most crucial events in the launching of her career. "Although I didn't know it at the time, not winning the BBC Young Musician of the Year was the best thing that could have happened to me!" she explains. She received innumerable comments and letters from viewers who felt she should have won, and soon found that organisations wanted to book her to give concerts because they thought she should have been given the first prize. The man who later became her first agent was watching on the TV and would one day tell her that he'd thought: "That girl's good. She won't win."

George, even more disappointed than Tasmin herself that she had been awarded third prize rather than first, talked to some of the judges and was told that most of the jury had wanted to give her first place but had been strongly opposed by one member. There, explains Little, lies the general problem with musical competitions. "I've never been that fond of competitions because I think that the requirements are not always the same for a competition as they are for a concert and a professional career. Quite often there's a big discrepancy between the judges' opinions and so often someone who is neither one thing nor the other will take the first prize: it will be a player about whom nobody disagrees, rather than one whom everyone agrees on."

In retrospect, she was glad not to have won the BBC competition. Having concentrated almost exclusively on technical work for so long prior to the contest, she had not yet learned enough concertos and recital repertoire to support the demands of the winner's instant career opportunities. "I desperately needed to spend some time learning some important violin works, and that was in fact what I did for the next few years." The benefit of the competition had been that it armed her with a new yardstick by which to measure her progress. Realising that her hard work was paying off and that in national terms she measured up well against her peers, Little set to with a will.

After leaving the Menuhin School, Little went to the Guildhall School of Music and Drama in London to continue her studies with Pauline Scott. She competed in the Shell/LSO Young Soloist Competition, taking the silver medal, and twice in the Yehudi Menuhin Competition in Folkestone, first winning the third prize and subsequently the second prize. She worked hard, enjoyed college life, led the college orchestra - valuable and enjoyable experience, even if not ultimately her chosen musical direction - and in her third year she won the prestigious Gold Medal, an award previously given to the cellist Jacqueline du Pré, among others. "I was very pleased to have won that. I'd worked extremely hard for it, playing the Brahms *Violin Concerto*. I thought to myself, 'Right, I've won a competition now, so I'm not going to do any more!' I realised I probably wasn't the kind of violinist who would tend to win competitions. I think that my style of playing is probably one that judges will not agree on; some people will love it and others won't."

In 1985, during the summer holidays after her second year at Guildhall, Little went to the famous summer music course at the School of Fine Arts in Banff, Canada, where she played in masterclasses given by the veteran Hungarian violinist Lorand Fenyves. Feeling that she would like the chance to study abroad for a while before starting her career, but not wanting to put the latter off for too long, Little decided to leave Guildhall a year early, applied for - and won - funds from scholarship trusts for the money she needed and went to Toronto for six months to study full-time with Fenyves. "It was very important for me to learn to stand on my own two feet as a musician at that stage, and Mr Fenyves's teaching was marvellous for that. He always encouraged me to search for my own individual 'voice' and my own interpretation of a work. In those six months we worked tremendously hard. I threw myself into learning repertoire: I learned six concertos, six sonatas and five major pieces and Mr Fenyves used to joke about it, saying 'Tasmin is eating a concerto a week'! And he was right - I was devouring them. It wasn't quite one a week, but I got through a huge amount of repertoire, which stood me in very good stead for beginning my professional career."

Not long before that, Little had been offered an engagement which also stood her in excellent stead. She performed the Delius *Violin Concerto* with the Royal Philharmonic Orchestra conducted by Kurt Masur, the great German conductor who for many years was doyen of the Leipzig Gewandhaus. Her second prize, aged 20, at the Yehudi Menuhin Competition, had attracted the notice of several orchestras who offered her opportunities to perform with them, including the RPO. Delius had long been a special passion of hers - inherited from her father, who was born a few streets away from Delius's own birthplace and had loved his music all his life - and Masur was impressed with her performance. "He invited me to play the concerto with him at the

Gewandhaus. I did that just before I went to Toronto." The German orchestra immediately invited her back for a tour, her manager signed her up and, on her return from Canada, the stage was set for Little to begin her climb up the perilous musical career ladder.

Although by now she had a distinct head start in the fiercely competitive world of young would-be solo musicians, Little's career began slowly. For a couple of years, dates were few and far between, although she performed with the RPO several times. "Nobody particularly knew me; it was a question of people making a leap of faith and asking me to do things. Astonishingly, people still remembered me from the Young Musician of the Year, so in a small way that was a help." She also played concertos with numerous amateur orchestras, which proved valuable experience. "That was very helpful because I needed to get used to playing some of the repertoire I'd learned, rather than going instantly to perform it at the Gewandhaus. I'd had very little experience of playing the Sibelius concerto, for instance, so it was better to do that and find my way of interpreting it with an amateur orchestra. So I had engagements with amateur orchestras all over the country, I did recitals in music clubs and every so often a very nice date with the RPO would come along. And so it continued for a couple of years, with not a great deal of progress, particularly not abroad."

The turning point came in 1989. "Two major things happened which were definitely the beginning of the beginning." Little's manager called her one morning and asked her whether she knew the Janacek concerto. She didn't. Would she be willing to learn it? She said she would. Which orchestra and conductor would she be working with? He told her it would be the orchestra of the Welsh National Opera and Charles Mackerras. Fine, she said, she'd do it. And - by the way - where was the performance? "Oh," came the response, as the agent revealed an important bit that he had held back, "it's at something called The Proms!"

TASMIN LITTLE

The BBC Promenade Concerts are often called the world's greatest music festival. What is it like to play there? "I remember walking out into the Royal Albert Hall for the first time to play the Janacek at the 1990 Proms and that was extraordinary. I've never had an experience like it," Little enthuses. "You come up from the depths of the earth, as it were - you've got to walk up a ramp from below the level of the stage - and at first you can see all the people up in the top balcony. Gradually as you walk up the ramp you see more and more faces until finally you see all the promenaders in front of you - and it is quite amazing!" Later, of course, there was the occasion on which she played for the 1995 Last Night. "You can multiply the usual Proms atmosphere by ten for the Last Night! It's a party, basically - it's not like a normal concert at all. The atmosphere literally hits you when you walk into the hall and it gives you such a buzz. It was fantastic. After I'd played *The Lark Ascending* by Vaughan Williams in the first half, there were sixteen seconds of pure silence before anyone started applauding. Nothing happened; nobody moved. It was televised live, of course, and the cameramen didn't know what to do! There were shots of the ceiling, shots of the ground, shots of the audience - on TV, sixteen seconds is a long gap. I was aware at the time that there was a very special atmosphere, and watching it back on the videotape afterwards I counted the seconds! I played the Saint-Saens *Introduction and Rondo Capriccioso* in the second half and by that time the party was in full swing. I entered into the party atmosphere by coming on for a bow with a rose between my teeth, and I presented the rose to Andrew Davis, who was also in the party spirit and kissed my arm! It was all very funny."

The only comparable event at which she has performed, says Little, was the Proms in the Park, in 1998, when 40,000 people gathered for a concert in London's Hyde Park. "I'd never played to such an enormous number of people who were physically present! When you do a live broadcast, especially a live televised broadcast, you're aware that you're playing to an audience of probably more than 100,000, but you can't actually see them. But when you walk onto the stage and you see 40,000 people, it's quite something. And I really did enjoy that."

Thousands would be daunted by the idea of playing to five- or six-figure audiences, but not Little. "I've always enjoyed the Big Gig, the big, prestigious dates. My husband always says that the more important the date, the better I play, and I think by and large he's right - I respond well to a challenge and to the adrenaline. That's very important for any performer. As my father used to tell me, you must use your nerves to help create an exciting performance."

❖ ❖ ❖ ❖ ❖

The second major event of 1989 came when Little was asked to make her first recording, a CD of the violin concertos by Bruch and Dvorak for Classics for Pleasure - a disc that is still a perennial favourite among critics and public alike more than a decade later. The most usual pairing for the famous Bruch is the Mendelssohn concerto, but Little decided, characteristically enough, that she wanted to do something different. The Dvorak concerto, a work she had played several times and in which she felt very much at home, presented itself as both suitable and original. "I was terribly nervous because it was my first recording," Little recalls. "I didn't know how I was going to react. I was used to doing concerts, used to having one shot at a piece that would then go away and never come back to haunt me. And I realised that in ten years' time people might listen to the Bruch and Dvorak and if I'd played something wrong then they'd hear it and think I wasn't any good. The funny thing was that the moment I settled into the recording session, I loved the whole process; I found it fascinating. I learned a huge amount because when we stopped and replayed a take, I'd listen to it and hear everything I was doing wrong - and I knew I could go back and do something about it! I've always found that my performances of works have come on tremendously when I've recorded them. I've made more progress in that short time recording than I often do in two years of playing something in concert, because you don't always have that opportunity to listen back to what you've done and progress from it."

Recording has remained a vital part of Little's career. To date she has made nineteen records, several of which have been nominated for *Gramophone* awards. Among her most recent recordings, the four Delius violin sonatas with the pianist Piers Lane (one of her three regular recital partners) has been particularly highly acclaimed, winning the Diapaison d'Or. Among her other recent discs are the Finzi concerto with the City of London Sinfonia under Richard Hickox, on Chandos, and recordings of sonatas by Bax and Elgar with pianist Martin Roscoe, for the internet-based Global Music Network and on CD.

Back in 1990, the happy result of the Bruch and Dvorak recording was a number of excellent reviews that coincided fortuitously with Little's Proms debut that summer; the combination of the two threw her well and truly into the spotlight. That was not all that emerged from the recording, however. Trish Byrne, label manager for EMI's Classics for Pleasure series, had spotted a likely affinity between her violin soloist and Mike Hatch, a particularly likeable and able young recording engineer who had started his own company, Floating Earth. She had invited him to engineer the Bruch and Dvorak disc and arranged a lunch in Notting Hill for the entire team. Sure enough, Hatch and Little got along rather well.

In 1993, they were married in the church of St Giles, Cripplegate, in the Barbican. The event was naturally a feast of fabulous music-making. Tasmin and Mike invited many of their musician friends to perform. With organ music from Wayne Marshall, glorious singing from The Sixteen conducted by Harry

Christophers, Piers Lane playing Chopin piano music, and the day culminating in a grand reception and ceilidh, it was an occasion that everyone there would remember for years to come.

After dividing their time for a while between Little's flat in north London and Hatch's cottage in Buckinghamshire, the couple settled eventually in a spacious apartment in Ealing - handy both for Hatch's Floating Earth studio along the M40 and for easy access to Heathrow Airport. The flat, with a spacious garden and, most unusually, an outdoor swimming pool, was soon swinging with what became an annual summer party for their wide circle of friends - some of the rare occasions when both Hatch and Little were at home at the same time.

❖ ❖ ❖ ❖ ❖

By now Little's career was gathering considerable momentum. Important engagements were piling up, but still certain events stand out in her memory. "There are important concerts that were unforgettable moments, things I'd always aspired to - for instance, making my debut in America." The first concert that she did there was with the Cleveland Orchestra, playing the Brahms concerto with Leonard Slatkin conducting, in 1997. "That was a wonderful and very important concert," recalls Little, "not least because I felt I played the Brahms better than I ever had before." She had a marvellous response from the audience and two wonderful reviews, and felt that it had been a very exciting debut. Three months later, Little played for the first time with the New York Philharmonic, conducted by Neeme Järvi. "I gave four performances of the Tchaikovsky concerto. Again it went very well, with fantastic responses from the audiences, and the first concert was broadcast live all over the USA! That was quite a concert to go into New York with, but I thoroughly enjoyed it, and I had a lovely response from the orchestra as well as the audience."

But perhaps most of all, Little has been thrilled by her recent musical partnership with Sir Simon Rattle. She first met the conductor when they participated (with Rattle as pianist) in a performance of Messiaen's *Quartet for the End of Time* in a charity concert in Islington, together with clarinettist Antony Pay and cellist Lynn Harrell. "After that, he invited me to play the Ligeti concerto with him and the City of Birmingham Symphony Orchestra in four performances which we gave in 2000." The concerts took place in Cambridge, Vienna, Birmingham and lastly at the Royal Festival Hall in London, in the final concert of the major ten-year-long series Towards the Millennium.

A few months later, Little joined Rattle at the Aix-en-Provence Festival for an outdoor performance of the Brahms concerto. "Again it was one of the best performances of the Brahms I've ever done, although the outdoor acoustic was far from ideal. I loved playing the Brahms with Simon - he's a dream dance partner! It's a real partnership. I felt that my inspiration was coming from him and in a sense I think his ideas were bouncing back from me. He conducted from memory, I was playing from memory, and his eyes almost never left me. Of course he was working with the orchestra, but I knew that his eyes and ears were always on me as well. It was a tremendous evening, one of those really unforgettable occasions."

"I think Simon Rattle is not only one of the greatest conductors living today, but he's also a wonderful person, warm, charismatic and kind. Like Menuhin, he never puts on airs and graces; he just is himself. He doesn't talk down to anybody, he doesn't patronise, he treats you as an equal, he's interesting company and has a marvellous sense of humour. He's a coffee lover like me - the first thing that happens when I go for a rehearsal is that he puts the coffee on! He is a very down-to-earth, normal person who happens to be a great conductor and a wonderful, all-round musician. I think he's somebody who's quite prepared to take chances and I was very flattered that he asked me to play the

Ligeti when he'd never done a concerto with me before. The Ligeti is such a hard piece, you've really got to have confidence in your team. So I was bowled over that he entrusted it to me for these very important concerts and I wanted to do my utmost not to let him down in any way. Afterwards he was full of praise and said how much he'd enjoyed it. I was so pleased - not only for myself, but also that his faith in me had not been disappointed." The critics were not disappointed either. John Allison wrote in *The Times,* "Both as a commanding soloist and part of the virtuoso ensemble, Little was in total control, right from her opening motif which spread like tentacles through the orchestra. She caught the deep melancholy of the melody that uncoils throughout the second movement and is picked up by wailing ocarinas and recorders. Under Rattle everyone evoked the mysterious allure of this score, and played through to the spiky close as if their lives depended on it."

Little describes the Ligeti as far and away the most difficult concerto she has ever learned. How does she tackle the process of preparing such a piece? "Very slowly! It's just a question of plugging away at it. There are no short cuts; it's hours of work. You literally start at the beginning and you tick off a page after you've got it under your fingers. There are pages that you have to come back to time and time again - whenever I was practising before the concerts, I'd always go to the same bits that needed to be done over and over again. Some of them never got any easier! It's not a piece to take on lightly. It is extremely difficult for the whole orchestra as well, and of course for the conductor who has to keep all these disparate elements together." As if learning the work was not hard enough, Ligeti also demands that the soloist should provide an original cadenza. He is quite specific about what he wants from the cadenza - certain thematic material, how long it should be, that it must get faster and faster at the end until the orchestra interrupts with the final four bars, which is the end of the piece - but he expects the soloist to write the cadenza herself. "It's a very dramatic ending and quite daunting," says Little. She was very pleased that Ligeti's assistant came to the concert and told her, "It was an excellent cadenza and Ligeti would have been very happy with it." She has now been invited to perform the concerto with Rattle and the Berlin Philharmonic Orchestra in 2003.

Another concerto with which Little has been associated - a work of a very different nature - is that by Frederick Delius, a composer Little has consistently championed throughout her career. This was the work that she performed in her early twenties with Masur and the Leipzig Gewandhaus Orchestra. And, while a student at the Guildhall, she had written a paper on it that was later published in the Journal of the Delius Society. "I wanted to play Delius because I feel his music is unjustifiably neglected and also that people, when they do play his music, have often played it devoid of any passion, bravura and romance. It was as if they'd seen the Ken Russell film that shows the ageing Delius pathetic and paralysed in his wheelchair and decided that his music needs to be pathetic and paralysed in timbre and character! So I felt I had a bit of a mission to persuade audiences that Delius was not merely this pathetic figure." Little has done a good job: today interest in Delius seems far more widespread and she is often asked to include a piece of Delius in her recital programmes, something that did not generally happen ten years ago.

In 1997, Little's interest in Delius took her in a new direction when she organised and presented a television documentary about a mysterious episode in the composer's youth, at the time when he lived in Florida. "I'd known that Florida was a big influence on him musically because he loved the old spirituals and slave songs and heard a lot of those while he was living there. But through doing a bit of delving, I came across the theory that he had had a mistress out there - a black sweetheart - and she had borne his child. I wanted to find out more about it by going to

Florida to see if there was any evidence. I met some fantastic people, but there were also some who did not want this idea talked about at all because they found it offensive to think of a white person, particularly a marvellous composer, having a torrid affair with a black girl. That was not something that was considered acceptable. But I still wanted to pursue it, and I think we found enough evidence to support it. Unfortunately many of the birth records were destroyed when a number of the churches were burnt down at the beginning of the twentieth century. We weren't able to prove it conclusively and I don't suppose we ever really will. But I felt I'd learned more about Delius just by having been there and seen the rather basic but lovely wooden house where he lived, near the St John's River. At the time I was preparing to make my recording of the violin sonatas and I was learning for the first time the *Op Posth Sonata*, a beautiful early work that was unknown until very recently. And I was immersed in this luscious scenery learning this luscious piece. That was inspiring."

Little's interest in contemporary music was spurred on by her husband, a great enthusiast for many of today's composers. Over the past ten years she has acquired a strong reputation for performing new works by a wide range of composers, from the most famous, like Ligeti, to those who are still trying to become established. A highlight of 2001 was her world premiere at the Proms of a new violin concerto by the young Scottish composer Stuart MacRae. "I do think it's very important to put your expertise and enthusiasm at the service of the composers themselves, because they get a pretty raw deal most of the time and it's very hard for them to make their name," Little emphasises. At the time when she was interviewed, she was looking forward to seeing MacRae's new concerto, which was nearly finished - and had been inspired partly by hearing her play the Ligeti concerto. Learning a newly written concerto from scratch (so to speak) is no easy matter. "You always have to put your own ideas on hold. You can think you might know how a musical line will be shaped, but then you play it with the orchestra and it turns out to be totally different! Sometimes it's not even clear from the score what will be the dominant factor in a particular passage; it's really only when you play something with the orchestra for the very first time that you can make sense of what's going to work." In the event, both the work and the performance were very well received by the audience in the Albert Hall and by the press.

Nevertheless, Little is eager not to be hemmed in to one particular type of repertoire. "Once you start to play contemporary music, composers start to send you pieces and you could very easily spend your entire time playing new works. I've always shied away from being pigeon-holed. I don't want to be the British violinist playing British works, I don't want to be the young violinist playing contemporary works; rather, I want to have a wide range and balance of repertoire. That's always been very important to me. I'd like people to think I'm an overall musician who can play Bach as well as Ligeti; that's something I've been striving for."

❖ ❖ ❖ ❖ ❖

The voice of the violin, of course, has to emanate from a good instrument. And the finest violins today can cost more than London houses. For Little, the matter of raising the money to buy her first violin, the Henry Lockey Hill for which she had to find £5,000 as a student, later paled beside the funds she needed to progress to a more refined and powerful instrument when her concert career began to develop. Italian violins of the seventeenth and eighteenth centuries, especially those by makers of the Stradivarius or Guarneri luthier dynasties, are the most sought-after instruments in the world, the most important examples selling for around £1m. Consequently, few musicians can afford to buy them and many depend on the loan of an instrument by a wealthy collector or institution. Even more tragically, a number of the greatest instruments end up lying unplayed in glass cases in museums or in bank vaults, their monetary and historical value overtaking the purpose for which they were built: the making of music.

In 1990, after the success of her first recording and Proms debut, Little realised she had to upgrade her instrument to "something a little more glamorous". "I'd played my lovely Henry Lockey Hill until then, but I realised I had to buy something more in keeping with the kind of engagements I was starting to get." The London violin dealer Charles Beare came across a Guadagnini violin, made in Milan in 1757, that he thought would suit her - "a very beautiful instrument but obviously a bit more expensive!" - and also helped to find a sponsor who put up 90 per cent of the necessary money. "And through the sale of my Henry Lockey Hill - which I was sad to part with because it had been my first instrument - plus some extra money I'd saved, I began to buy the Guadagnini in instalments, over a period of ten years." She is now the full owner of the instrument. "I think my Guadagnini is my soulmate among violins. It has a beautiful, deep burnished tone with wonderful colours in it, which took a while to come out because it had been sitting in a bank vault for a few years before I played it. But after I'd been using it for about eighteen months, the colours really emerged; now I've had it for ten or eleven years and it's great. I think it's a wonderful instrument. If I had one criticism of it, it would be that it doesn't quite have the carrying power of Strads or Guarneri del Gesu."

In 2000, Little was loaned the 'Regent' Stradivarius, part of a collection housed at the Royal Academy of Music in London. Again, she says, it had not been played regularly for several years. Violins need to be played regularly to 'open up' their sound, and this instrument - the violin equivalent of an Aston Martin - is no exception. "It's been interesting to work on a Strad," says Little, "and I'd like to work more on it because it's an instrument I don't know very well yet. But I am getting to know it gradually and it does need to be worked in a little more. But it's coming and it's an incredible, fantastic violin. I'm glad to have the chance to play it." The Strad, says Little, has a greater power of projection than her Guadagnini and is therefore better suited to playing concertos in large concert halls. The Guadagnini, with its sweeter but rather smaller tone, is perfect for recitals at more intimate venues such as London's Wigmore Hall.

As the violinist's 'voice' is the instrument she plays, adjusting to a new and very different one is sometimes surprisingly tricky. In addition, players often become deeply attached emotionally to their violins. "Now," jokes Little, "I feel a bit promiscuous! Because obviously I have my lifetime partner in the Guadagnini and I seem to have taken another lover! So I feel slightly sad because it's as if the Guadagnini's nose has been pushed rather out of joint. Of course, at some stage I shall have to give the Strad back and when that time comes I'll probably feel sad to lose it. But at the moment I'm enjoying working on it; I've always wanted the opportunity to work on a Strad, but I've never had the means to buy one. I know I will part with it sometime because it's not mine and it will go to someone else. But it's a nice, enjoyable period in my life to try a different instrument - and then, a dutiful wife, I'll go back to my lifetime partner!"

❖ ❖ ❖ ❖ ❖

As Little's career grew ever more international, so did her husband's. Oftener than not, the pair found that Little would fly off in one direction to play a concerto or recital while Hatch flew off in another direction to check out various recording venues around the world or to engineer a new project in one of them. So their decision to start a family was complicated by time – or, more specifically, the lack of it. Little had always wanted to have children, but had not expected her career to become so far-reaching or even to find herself so continually in demand. At the beginning of 2000, she spotted a quieter patch than usual towards the end of the year and decided to take it as a providential sign. Mike and Tasmin's daughter, Chloe Liana, was born on 25 November, amid many jokes from family friends about the new little Little Hatch. She was named partly after the work that Little selected as her favourite record when she was the guest on BBC Radio 4's *Desert Island Discs* several months later: Ravel's ballet score *Daphnis and Chloe*. But Chloe, she says, was also the name of Delius's mysterious lost love in Florida.

Little kept up her performances and recording until just two weeks before Chloe's slightly earlier than expected birth. During this time, the unborn baby had already been proving her enthusiasm for her mother's music-making - especially Beethoven. "She always seemed to respond and become very active whenever I played Beethoven," Little recounts. One of her last concerts before taking 'maternity leave' was a recital in which she performed the *Kreutzer Sonata*. The baby kicked hard all the way through it. "And at the end a woman from the audience came up to me and said: 'You know, I was so enjoying watching your bump moving about during the Beethoven!'" Testing the theory, Mike knelt beside the bump and sang the opening of Beethoven's *Fifth Symphony* against it - and was rewarded by a direct biff on the nose from the baby within.

Combining any career with motherhood brings complications, and Little acknowledges that her particular situation would be impossible to maintain without her "marvellous nanny". Sarah joined the household shortly after Chloe's birth and travels with mother and baby whenever necessary. Meanwhile Little, with her ever down-to-earth practicality, has adjusted her work patterns to accommodate her new arrival as best she can. "I have to be very, very organised - it's lucky that I am usually organised about my career. But now, with less time to devote to it, I have to be more organised about when I practise, very concentrated on my practising when I do it and realistic about how much new repertoire to take on. In the past I've often played an enormous amount of repertoire in one season - up to twenty violin concertos in less than twelve months, which takes time to prepare. I won't be able to do that volume or variety of repertoire in such a short space of time any more, so I have to think carefully about how much to do at a particular time. Now I'll confine myself to offering eight to ten concertos in one season - which is still a lot but is do-able - and just a couple of different recital programmes rather than five or six, plus several new works."

But in the 2001-2002 season, Little seems to be almost as busy as ever. In December 2001 she performs the very challenging and powerful concerto by Nicholas Maw in its first German performances with the Stuttgart Radio Symphony Orchestra under Roger Norrington. In Britain, she plays the Tchaikovsky concerto in Liverpool with the Royal Liverpool Philharmonic Orchestra under Libor Pesek in November and, also that month, gives recitals with the pianist Martin Roscoe in Belfast and Bradford. At the Queen Elizabeth Hall, London, in March 2002, she takes part in a chamber music concert that forms part of a major festival of Walton's music celebrating the composer's centenary. Early in 2002 she tours with the St Petersburg Philharmonic and gives an important recital at the Chatelet Theatre in Paris.

Little's family has always been close and seems set to expand happily within that closeness. And Little is far too much of a *bon-viveur* to live for work alone. "I always think that my ideal day is to do some playing in the morning, have some time off in the afternoon and in the evening see friends over a wonderful meal," she says. "That sums up all my main interests: my friends and family are very important to me, music is very important to me, and I like cooking! And I enjoy trying out different wines."

Luckily she is also passionate about travelling, which has occupied more and more time as her career has developed. "I'm very interested in different lifestyles around the world - seeing the way people live, the different religions that they follow and what they consider important. I feel that travel is important because it shows you that there is more than one way of doing everything and that you must be tolerant of other people's beliefs, their customs, their food - sometimes people eat things you wouldn't dream of eating! But they like it, so what's the problem? I think if more people travelled and understood other people's ideas and beliefs, there would be more peace and harmony in the world. The problems come when people are dogmatic about religion and ways of living."

Intriguingly, Little says that, if she had not become a musician, she would like to have been a nurse. "I really like being with people and I like looking after people - perhaps that's why I'm enjoying being a mother. I feel quite caring towards a lot of people, particularly people I love. I liked the idea of doing nursing, to look after people and make them get better."

The link between music and healing goes back at least as far as Greek mythology. Mental or spiritual well-being is now often seen as linked inextricably to physical well-being, and music often plays a major part in the former. Little agrees. "Sometimes when I'm tempted to think I'm not doing something useful in life," she says, "someone will come up to me after a concert and thank me for having made their week better. And I've had lots of very moving letters from people saying things like they bless me every day when they listen to my records! It is very moving - extraordinary to think that you've touched somebody's life in such a way. So I'm very grateful. I feel lucky that I've been able to do that and happy that I've made a difference to somebody's life somewhere."

TONY BENN

Tony Benn lives politics. You walk up the short path from his front gate, ring the bell on the red front door, and the man himself emerges up the outside steps from the basement below – his den. It is his natural habitat. An amazing place. You have entered a world that is only yards from a busy, London main road, yet it is private and peaceful. Cluttered with books, papers, technology (some new, some ancient), a mug of tea, a rack of pipes, it is his work place. For decades it has been a power house of ideas, the command base of campaigns, the place for reflection. The telephone rings. Another request for his views that will be heard later in the day on radio or television.

Tony Benn left parliament in 2001 after fifty years "to spend more time on politics". It was a typical comment from Benn – arresting, flamboyant, apparently quixotic, but rational and profoundly serious. His point is that parliament no longer exerts itself to control and influence governments. He once revealed on the radio that Labour MPs receive faxes not only telling them what their view is on the topic of the day but already addressed as if from them to the newspapers in their constituencies, ready for onward transmission. He complained that he felt "more and more like an Avon lady than an MP", a remark that made Avon furious, although they did send him a large supply of male cosmetics. He quotes with a chortle, although to make a very serious point, the remark that, "There are so many planted questions in Prime Minister's Questions these days that it should be renamed Gardeners' Question Time."

He does not blame ministers for the weakness of parliament. "All governments will try to get away with as little scrutiny and accountability as they can," he says. "Parliament should not let them." Democracy is at the core of the beliefs that he promoted in the Commons from 1951 with a break of only a few months until he left in 2001. As a minister for eleven years, his record is unequalled by any current Labour MP or minister.

Benn has changed little as a result of his withdrawal from the

Commons. He has emphatically not retired, quoting Walter Cronkite: "You wake up in the morning with nothing to do and by noon you are an hour behind schedule." Sitting in his basement, he is lucid, sharp and enthusiastic about the future. Keenly interested in what is going on in the world, captivated by ideas and producing thoughts on ways forward, he speaks confidently about the possibility of change for the better. This is not a man of the past. His work is not done. With his understanding of history, such a notion does not arise.

The aphorism about spending more time on politics reflects Benn's view that an elected MP, representing thousands of people, no longer functions effectively through the House of Commons as an influence on government. His concern is also that political discussion is so trivial. "MPs are representatives of the people not managers of parties", he said recently before gently chiding a television interviewer with being "more interested in politicians - who is going up and who is going down - than in what concerns people." And that was months before the 2001 election, when the professional politicians were forced by the low interest in voting to acknowledge that they are losing their audience.

There is also, of course, disappointment with the destruction, as he sees it, of the Labour Party's own democratic and debating processes. Commenting in his own pithy style on the contrast between his early days as an MP and what was expected of him before his departure from the Commons, he says, "I was happy to stay up all night to vote for the abolition of the means test, but I will not stay up to introduce it." This is delivered with a rare anger. Benn couples his sadness at the decline of the Commons with enthusiasm for the power of ideas, and he is optimistic about new forms of democracy. His faith in the power of reason and argument is undiminished.

Excitement is what Benn feels about the rash of campaigns on issues initially ignored by the main parties. "The tide is turning," he believes. "It is all bubbling up again." Disillusionment irritates him. As he sees it, "The future is made by people, not governments." Whilst Benn is enthusiastic about direct campaigning – for example on pensions, global capitalism, war in Kosovo, the environment – as the only way to restore interest in politics, he has no truck with what he calls the 'sectarian left'. Retreat into theory-based splinter groups may be good for the soul of individuals, but goes in the opposite direction to what is needed. It is, in his view, a form of bigotry. For Benn, influencing governments has to be the objective of politics. If it cannot be done effectively in parliament alone, it must be done by direct public campaigning to influence ministerial decisions. Although this delightfully unpretentious man does not talk in such grandiose terms, his mission is no less than the revival of democracy in Britain.

There are two clouds. Caroline, his wife and collaborator for all of his adult life, is no longer beside him. The pain of parting is still with him. It is not on the lips, but it is there briefly in the averted eyes. He is immensely proud of her achievements. More easily borne is his formal separation from the establishment. There are a few things that he will miss there but, as he impishly speculates, a small link with Whitehall may remain if the security services forget to stop bugging his phone.

'Controversial', 'dogmatic', 'unprincipled', 'inflexible', 'divisive', 'turncoat' are amongst the less rude labels that have been attached to Tony Benn over the years. He has always ignored such attacks, despising the personalising of argument. In fact, his record shows remarkable consistency. Benn is essentially a free-thinker, not the dogmatist as which he is often portrayed. Indeed, he categorises ideology in with religion and money for its tendency to generate hierarchies and exclusion. The unswerving commitment throughout his career has been to democracy. The duty of government and parliament, in his view, is to represent the interests of the small guys against the big.

TONY BENN

Despite not achieving the highest political office of all in Britain, he has done much in his eventful life to turn aim into achievement. It is easy to dismiss Benn as a thinker, not a doer, one more interested in theory than in results. In a way he encourages that interpretation by emphasising the power of ideas, but his work in the Wilson and Callaghan governments of the 1960s and 1970s belies the judgement. He showed that ministers have powerful weapons to use against undemocratic forces, in which he includes international companies, if they choose to use them. He really did, as a minister, tip the balance in favour of the elected representatives of the people.

There are paradoxes aplenty in the story. The man of the left was born with at least a silver-plated spoon in his mouth. The alleged dogmatist was remarkably flexible and subtle when faced with the need to make ministerial decisions. The advocate of public ownership and the supposed scourge of capitalism accepted the Cabinet's sale of some publicly-owned shares in British Petroleum in 1976 to prevent further cuts in public services. The nationaliser tried to persuade a Labour government to introduce advertising on a BBC radio channel as a means of sinking the pirate radio stations of the mid-1960s. The charming, never discourteous and seldom overtly angry man makes as many enemies as friends. The opponent of dynasties is himself at the centre of one, with a father who was an MP and minister, and a son who joined him in the Commons for his own last session as an MP and became a junior minister in 2001.

Inconsistency is a charge made by his critics, but with little evidence to support it. Few people would wish to claim consistency over a long career, when consistency means sticking rigidly to positions irrespective of greatly changing conditions, but Benn's commitment to democracy has not wavered, however high his office. He acknowledges two major changes in his views: he regrets his acceptance of the justification for the Cold War and his early endorsement of the benefits of nuclear power, both of which he says he got wrong at first. The tension between principles and the need to solve daily problems in government is part of the politician's life. Accepting office is often accompanied by the dilution if not abandonment of beliefs. Benn thinks that the opposite happened to him. "I was radicalised by sitting in Cabinet meetings", he says. "The more I saw what was going on, the more I thought it had to be challenged." Perhaps the real anger behind this charge against him is that he was not what those who promoted his early career expected him to be. He looked as though he might be 'one of us', the establishment. He was not.

An upper middle class early life gave Benn an easy start in politics. The labels 'champagne socialist' or more recently 'sushi socialist' are often applied to Labour politicians who enjoy a high standard of living. A socialist has no obligation to remain personally poor, still less a retrospective obligation to make himself poor. Benn was born into a well-heeled family, but in his own adulthood has followed a simple personal life. His home, sometimes absurdly described in much the same way as was Peter Mandelson's famous house round the corner, is not luxurious or indeed even particularly well maintained. It is very much a working politician's base. Benn himself went to Westminster School, the private school next to Westminster Abbey. As advocates of comprehensive education, he and his wife Caroline sent their own children to Holland Park, the local comprehensive school, where Caroline was for many years a governor.

For those who think in terms of class, which many of his press critics do rather more than does the man himself, Benn may be considered to have voluntarily lowered his class in accordance with his emerging principles. In common with politicians as diverse as Clement Attlee and Joseph Stalin, but with few modern politicians irrespective of their creed, he leads a simple life without the need for ostentation and luxury. He is a teetotaller and a tea-aholic. Unlike some office-holders, Benn has not used his private income or the public purse to surround himself at home or in ministries with the trappings of wealth and status.

❖ ❖ ❖ ❖ ❖

Benn's upbringing was both very comfortable and very political. Born Anthony Neil Wedgwood Benn in 1925, his second name honoured his Scottish ancestry and his third the family's uncertain connection with the great Potteries dynasty. His father, William, was a politician from his student days at University College, London, when he opposed the Boer War, to his death in 1960 whilst waiting to speak against a new constitution for what was then Rhodesia and Nyasaland. Benn himself was by then an MP and was at the Commons end of the Houses of Parliament when news reached him of his father's fatal heart attack at the Lords end.

Benn senior had been the youngest MP to be elected in the Liberal landslide of 1906. The subsequent Liberal governments were in part dependent on the support of the first Labour MPs and therefore required to introduce the first 'Labour' social changes such as old age pensions and national insurance for health and unemployment. William Benn ostentatiously rejected Liberalism by crossing the Commons chamber and identifying with Labour, despising Lloyd George, particularly when he formed a coalition with the Conservatives. Twice a cabinet minister, he was Secretary of State for Air in Attlee's post-war government.

Tony Benn's mother, Margaret Holmes, was on the surface a more formidable person than his father. From a non-conformist and Liberal background, she was a Scotswoman who rebelled by smoking at the age of fourteen, attended women's suffrage meetings, and was an early advocate of the ordination of women in the Church of England. She became President of the

Congregational Federation, which elected its ministers as 'the priesthood of all the believers', rejecting hierarchies. The Benn children were brought up on the Bible by a mother who read the Old Testament in Hebrew and the New Testament in Greek. When Tony Benn's parents were married, most of the leading Liberals except Lloyd George were present. Asquith was one of the formal witnesses of the union.

There were three aspects of this highly political upbringing that were of the greatest importance to Benn's future. First, he never wanted to be anything but a politician, apart from a transient and achieved desire to be a pilot. The whole of his upbringing was dominated by his parents' political activities, with religion as a secondary influence. Second, he had witnessed the later stages of his father's career, not least the coalitions and divisions that preceded the Labour triumph of 1945. Third, he had mixed with the mighty from childhood. This feature of his life is particularly important, for Benn has never known political fear born of respect for office or apparent grandeur. He had met David Lloyd George, Ramsay MacDonald, Clement Attlee and Mahatma Gandhi whilst still a boy. He had watched the changing of the guard on Horse Guard's Parade from the window of 10 Downing Street at the age of ten. How could a child who had seen so many of the famous from such a young age be anything but matter-of-fact about them?

The source of the family's wealth was the publishing company Benn Brothers, run by Tony's uncle, Sir Ernest Benn, a man with strong capitalist views and the writer of right-wing tracts, such as *Confessions of a Capitalist*. Ernest was a very successful businessman, transforming the company from a small publisher of commercial journals such as *The Cabinet Maker* and *Nursery World* into a major house, publishing H G Wells and Joseph Conrad.

The family home throughout Benn's childhood was a large house in Grosvenor Road, now called Millbank, that part of the riverside road that leads to Parliament Square. Nanny was a valued member of the household. Next door lived the Webbs, Sydney and Beatrice, prominent founders of both the Fabian movement and the London School of Economics. Sydney is credited with having drafted Clause 4 of the old Labour constitution and served in parliament alongside William Benn. There was also a cottage at Stansgate in Essex.

This wealth enabled Benn to have a private education at two of the most exclusive places of learning: Westminster School, a boys' public school in the shadow of Westminster Abbey, and Oxford University. It was an established route for boys of high income and connections. Attending Westminster School as a day boy, Benn's early life took place within easy walking distance of parliament. Wearing the school uniform of top hat and high collar, he walked daily between the Houses of Parliament (dad's work place), Westminster School, Westminster Abbey (daily school prayers) and home on the Embankment, all within a few hundred yards of each other.

Benn's advantage was that the very exclusiveness of public schools in the 1930s and 1940s enabled intellectual debate to be valued, because the potential revolutionaries beyond the walls could not hear it. It was usual for conventional views to be challenged. There was an element of 'letting them get it off their chests' whilst still young, in the belief that healthy release as a teenager would encourage maturity, understood as a move towards respectable conservatism. This attitude was behind Harold Wilson's later jibe that Benn had become immature with age. It equates the holding of principles and a coherent set of ideas with youth, whilst bending in the wind and abandoning most of one's principles are indications of wisdom and maturity. In fact, no school of intelligent pupils could ignore the great questions of the day in the late 1930s and the 1940s. Social unrest at home, born of grotesque inequalities, and the rise of fascism abroad compelled attention. (The young Benn had met Oswald

Mosley when the latter was still a Labour MP before becoming the leader of British fascism.) Masters as well as boys openly declared their allegiances. It was not a time for fence-sitting.

Benn's time at Westminster School spanned the period of appeasement, the outbreak of war, the retreat from Dunkirk and the blitz on London. The school was evacuated several times, to Lancing College in Sussex, to halls of residence at Exeter University and finally to Bromyard in Herefordshire. It was a happy time. The young Benn took part in debates, although the records show rather low attendance, performed reasonably well at his academic studies, gaining his School Certificate (the 1941 equivalent of GCSE), joined the scouts, followed his elder brother into the Air Training Corps, enjoyed sport, especially rowing and boxing, and acted as assistant stage manager in a school revue by his fellow pupils, Flanders and Swann, who went on to success in the theatre.

In 1942 Benn went to New College, Oxford. He immediately joined the Union, the debating society that made itself even more exclusive than the university of which it was a part by charging a high admission fee and requiring debaters to wear formal evening dress. Despite his protestations, Benn was often referred to as 'The Honourable Wedgwood Benn', a title attributed to sons of peers. He also joined the university Labour Club, although he did not play a major part in its affairs.

His undergraduate career was interrupted a year later, when he reached the age of enlistment and volunteered for the air force, in which both his father and his elder brother were already serving. Basic training was at Stratford-upon-Avon followed by initial training as a pilot at Elmdon, now Birmingham's international airport. Early in 1944 he left on a troopship for South Africa, going on to Bulawayo in the then British colony of Rhodesia, now Zimbabwe, to complete his training. His stay in a British colony had a profound effect on him. Just as many soldiers learned so much during the war about British society and its command structures that they voted Labour in large numbers when the war was over, so Benn was able to see what Britain regarded as an appropriate way of life for black workers in British mines in Africa. He was appalled.

It was March 1945 by the time that Benn 'got his wings', as air force jargon puts it, and soon the war was over. By one of the legal inconsistencies of the time, Benn was not allowed at the age of 20 to vote in the 1945 election. Enlistment for war at 18 and voting at 21 were the rules then. His joy at Labour's victory was not diminished by this. Clement Attlee formed the first Labour government, with a majority of 146 over all other parties. Power at last.

Although not officially demobilised until the autumn of 1946, Benn resumed his studies at Oxford in January of that year, benefiting from the arrangement that allowed serving officers to retain their pay until formally leaving the service. The Oxford Union again became a major focus of his activities. Whilst he studied PPE (politics, philosophy and economics), he moved up through the main Union offices to become its President in 1947. The euphoria of Labour's victory had already given way to discontent as the hopes of the voters could not immediately be realised. Indeed, in many ways the post-war period saw more hardships than the war, although without the dangers. There was no honeymoon for the first majority Labour government. Benn found himself defending the government against hostile and often vituperative attacks.

Contact with people who would later sit in the same governments as himself and with whom he would later do battle were made during this post-war period at Oxford. His tutor in economics was Anthony Crosland, a future Labour Secretary of State for Education who would in 1965 require local authorities to plan for comprehensive schools. Crosland introduced Benn to Roy Jenkins, who was later to be Chancellor of the Exchequer and Home Secretary before leading the Social Democratic Party break-away from the Labour Party. Once the hopelessness of Jenkins' SDP cause was evident he returned to Oxford, as its Chancellor, having begun life in Wales and attended the local primary and grammar schools, climbing the social ladder upwards as Benn passed him climbing down.

During his education Benn had developed a consistent and coherent set of views that were very similar to those held throughout his later political career. It is quite wrong to believe, as some have suggested, that he was converted later in life. Despite his comfortable and indeed privileged upbringing his views were always strongly democratic, socialist and liberal. When there was a left and a right in Britain, Benn was in the middle. At his first speech from a Labour platform, whilst still an undergraduate immediately after the 1939-45 war, he argued for social democracy as the middle (perhaps we should say 'third') way between the American and Russian extremes.

It is perhaps because his views did not spring from loyalty to the class into which he was born that he has attracted so much personal animosity. The wealthy think of him as a renegade, perhaps even a traitor. Some Labour people think of him as from an inappropriate class. People who know him and have worked with him see him as a truly classless person. As a dissenter and one who challenged conventional thinking from a base of a coherent set of ideas, he was bound to offend many.

Apart from his mother and his nanny, Benn's life had until 1948 been largely with men. He had two brothers but no sister. His school, his Oxford College, his training as a pilot had all been in wholly male institutions. Nonetheless, his political outlook embraced from the earliest days the equality of the sexes. This was just as well, for he soon met Caroline de Camp, his future wife. Caroline was a very well-educated American, coming from a family with strong egalitarian credentials and a family history that embraced roles in the American War of Independence against the Britain of George III and running escape routes for freed black slaves at the time of the Civil War. She was in Oxford to take part in a summer school to promote international understanding before going on to France.

Nine days after meeting they agreed to marry, sitting on a bench that Benn later purchased and moved to Stansgate. Their resolve was unaffected by Caroline's return to Cincinnati to add an MA, earned by a thesis on the English poet John Milton, to her first class degree. They married in Cincinnati, less than a year after meeting. Caroline's death in 2000, when widespread press coverage emphasised her work to promote comprehensive education, ended their long romantic and political partnership. Caroline was, if anything, the more radical of the two. Writing his diary when they had been married for almost thirty years, Benn paid a warm tribute to her on her birthday: "We have had such a marvellous life together and her radicalism and support and determination have really kept me going. I couldn't have managed without her." At the end of the memorial service for her in St Margaret's, Westminster, next to the Abbey, the congregation sang *The Red Flag* and the *Internationale*.

Between marriage and his election to parliament, Benn worked at the BBC as a radio producer. He was much involved in political programmes and took a lead in ending the deferential style adopted by broadcasters towards politicians at the time, paving the way for the current John Humphreys and Jeremy Paxman approach where the interviewer sees himself as challenging national figures on behalf of the public. This work also brought him into contact with leading politicians.

Benn's entry into parliament for Bristol South-East at a by-election less than a year after the 1950 general election owed much to lobbying on his behalf by influential members of the Labour Party, particularly his Oxford friend, Crosland, who was now an MP, having entered the Commons at the general election of 1950. His local sponsor was Mervyn Stockwood, later to become the radical Bishop of Southwark, campaigner for nuclear disarmament and author of books such as *Christianity and Marxism* and *The Cross and the Sickle*. Stockwood was curate of St Matthew's church, Moorfield, in Bristol and a member of the committee to select the new Labour candidate. The vacancy in Bristol had occurred because Sir Stafford Cripps, the local member and the ascetic Chancellor of the Exchequer in the second half of Attlee's government, had retired through ill health shortly after the general election of 1950. Stockwood was a very close friend of Cripps, even having a room at 11 Downing Street.

Crosland, a rising star in the Labour movement, persuaded Stockwood to canvass for Benn. Support also came from a very influential Bristol councillor who transferred his admiration from Benn senior to his son. Tony Benn had never before visited Bristol. He had two rivals who had formidable local credentials. Both had already been Labour MPs, losing their seats in the 1950 general election; one had been a minister. Both also had disadvantages. The trouble with one was that Labour headquarters pushed his case too hard and stirred local resentment, a lesson that often seems lost on the current Labour leadership. The trouble with the other was that she was a woman, a major handicap in 1950.

Benn's selection by a very large majority was not diminished by the problems of his main opponents, for he displayed on this important occasion at the age of 25 the strengths that were to be the foundation of his political career – intelligence, meticulous preparation, clarity and honesty about his principles, and a fine oratorical style. He also tackled head on what he knew would be seen as the weaknesses of his candidature, his likely removal from the Commons when he inherited his father's peerage, his elder brother having been killed in an aircraft crash at the end of the war. (This was a handicap that he was later able to overcome in a successful campaign to win the right to renounce a peerage.) Above all, he was likeable. Surprisingly, he supported the war in Korea, which was technically a United Nations action, although in fact an American operation with British and Australian contributions to the forces. The by-election caused by Cripps' resignation took place less than a month after Benn's selection as candidate. He had the support on the hustings of Michael Foot and Barbara Castle. He won.

❖ ❖ ❖ ❖ ❖

A view has been fostered, for example by the shrewd political commentator Andrew Marr, that Benn is in the same category as Joseph Chamberlain and Enoch Powell - "mavericks, eloquent critics of modern times but who could offer no alternative world that was credible, and so failed," as Marr has put it. This view of Benn falls before the facts. It casually forgets that Benn held important office in Labour governments led by Harold Wilson and James Callaghan and was a very effective minister. He achieved much.

He was Postmaster General from 1964 to 1966, Minister of Technology from 1966 to 1970, absorbing the Ministry of Aviation and the Ministry of Power, Secretary of State for Industry from 1974 to 1975, and finally Secretary of State for Energy from 1975 until 1979. Whenever Labour was in power in the 1960s and 1970s, eleven years in all, Benn held office. The fact that Margaret Thatcher, with her zeal to "destroy socialism forever" and therefore all that Benn stood for, negated most of his achievements, does not detract from his success. Whatever we achieve can be destroyed by our successors without diminishing ourselves.

At the party conference in the year before the 1964 election that saw the return of Labour to power after thirteen years, Harold Wilson had made an electrifying speech committing a new Labour government to the creation of a new society "forged in the white heat of scientific and technological revolution." This was music to Benn's ears. He had always been fascinated by technology and throughout his life has been amongst the first to embrace the latest means of communication.

Benn saw at once that the General Post Office could become a publicly-owned, technological company, provide an opportunity to show how services could be modernised and made responsive to their customers, and be held up as an example of public enterprise. It fell to him, with others, to turn Wilson's speech into reality, when he was appointed Postmaster General, the rather archaic term for his position.

This was not simple. The GPO's responsibilities included all telephone and postal services and broadcasting. The Post Office Savings Bank, at that time the biggest savings bank in the UK and the bank holding the largest sum of money of any bank in the world, was run like a civil service department. Its own 'Sir Humphrey' took long lunches and did not expect his new minister, the youngest in the government, to make many changes or indeed to communicate with anybody in the office except through him. It was not a natural candidate for technological revolution. Another problem for Benn was that his potential friends and allies in the enterprise, the trade unions, were not soul mates but promoters of their members' interests against Benn the employer. All of this was compounded by a huge deficit on the postal services inherited from the Conservative government that had failed to raise the price of postage for fear of the electoral consequences. Above all telephone services were a disaster, with long waiting lists to obtain a telephone at all and then many calls misdirected. The political background was a Labour government with a majority of only four, soon reduced to three and not expected to last long. It was a bed of nails for the young MP's first ministry.

Like John Prescott at the Department of Transport in the late 1990s, Benn was expected to solve all these problems quickly when most of them required long-term planning and massive investment. Despite its great financial difficulties, Wilson's cabinet gave Benn the money he needed, but cash was not enough. As Benn put it in a speech in May 1966, "I must be the first Postmaster General in history whose expansion programme is not held back by Treasury policy but by the practical difficulties of turning capital authorisation into urgently needed new plant and equipment on both postal and telecommunications sides."

Despite these difficulties, when Benn left the GPO after only two years it was in profit. More commercial approaches had been introduced, such as a great increase in the number of commemorative stamps to increase revenue, although he failed to persuade the Queen to forego her portrait. Work had started by GPO engineers on new business ventures such as car radios - very forward-looking in 1966. The separation of the postal and telephone services and their establishment as trading corporations had been planned. The future improvement of postal services was ensured by the establishment of postcodes. Benn was clearly decades ahead of his time.

The Giro Bank, already a feature of many other countries and certainly not an innovation in international terms, was to be established. This was to use the Post Office Bank's branches, which were more numerous than the private banks' and open much longer. The opportunity to take over much of the other banks' business was understood by Benn. The Giro was, however, new and did not therefore attract the necessary capital investment from a government in financial difficulties. It was therefore slow to get off the ground, but it earned £112 million for Mrs Thatcher's revenues when she sold it some years later.

Benn's broadcasting decisions at this time included a 20 per cent increase in the licence fee to avoid a huge BBC deficit, the establishment of BBC Radio 1 to make the elimination of the offshore pirate stations politically possible, and co-operation with Jennie Lee to found the University of the Air that was re-titled the Open University. Benn, a constant pipe-smoker, succeeded in banning tobacco advertising on television. The important technical decision in favour of the PAL television system was taken during his ministry, with Benn showing at the time a natural preference for a European approach. A now surprising aspect of his thinking at the time was that he favoured the introduction of advertising on the BBC Light Radio channel.

In July 1966 Benn became Minister of Technology. He was a natural choice for a post that had been created by Harold Wilson to realise his technological revolution. One of the ironies of Benn's career is that the headquarters of the ministry was the Millbank Tower, built on the site of his birthplace and childhood home, and much later the home of New Labour's command post. The old Ministry of Aviation was added to his ministry. Now Benn was carrying out some of his father's previous responsibilities, sitting in an office block built on their former home.

The ministry was huge in its responsibilities. Its aim was no less than the government-led restructuring of British industry. This was not born of Benn's socialist idealism but of Wilson's pragmatism. Just as Edward Heath was later, as Conservative Prime Minister, to nationalise Rolls Royce (cars and aero engines) because the alternative of bankruptcy was unthinkable, so the Labour governments of 1964-1970 set about saving British industry, of necessity because industry was not saving itself. The need to invest and restructure was obvious, but it was not happening. Industries were dying, and not just those for which there was less demand, but also old industries which had a future and new industries in their early stages. Looking back to those times, Benn cites ship-building to illustrate the problem. Britain had 48 per cent of the world market in 1948, but, because the industry was successful and making money, no investment in the future was thought necessary. When it was doing well nobody bothered to invest. By the time it was becoming unprofitable, nobody wanted to invest.

Benn's was a brave attempt, partially successful and partially a failure, to modernise British industry and save the economy. The problem was similar to that highlighted by James Dyson years later - the failure to invest in research and the development of new or improved products. The answer in the 1960s was government investment to encourage restructuring of the old and the nurturing of the new. Government had to attempt it because nobody else was doing so.

During this time there were successes, such as the forced amalgamation of companies to create ICL, which still trades successfully, and failures, such as Upper Clyde Shipbuilders. There were rescues that succeeded for a time such as British Leyland cars (forerunner of Rover), the third largest European car-manufacturer when established under Benn and still surviving in 2001 as Britain's only home-owned mass car manufacturer.

A key feature of Benn's policies was the involvement of employees who, he says, desperately crave good managers. He never believed that nationalisation or any other form of ownership would in itself transform enterprises. At the end of Derek Ezra's time in charge of the National Coal Board, Benn asked the National Union of Mineworkers, "Who do you want to run the industry?" "Derek Ezra" was the response. Benn believes that workers respect good management. They are not its enemies. "All you have to do is show them that they have an interest in more than wages", he believes. Consultation of workers is now enshrined in EU practice. British workers in 2000 were still learning second-hand from continental colleagues when their factories were to be closed by multi-national companies. For Benn it was and is a question of practising democracy.

It was during this time that Benn formulated his view that many Labour politicians fail to give a strong lead to their civil servants and allow themselves unnecessarily to be intimidated by industrialists, not using the power that governments have. His view was and is that it is often weak ministers who are responsible for allowing industrialists to challenge democracy. He took on the industrial giants.

When he found out that Phillips had used transfer pricing to produce a deficit on its trading account with Britain and that this was having a significant impact on the country's overall trade figures, he demanded correction. No response. He flew to Phillips' headquarters at Eindhoven. They got the message that there would be no more orders for valves, made by their UK company Mullards, from Britain's armed forces if they did not put the record straight. Benn had no authority to do this, but he got his way. His point is that businesses have to get on with governments and only weak governments release them from this obligation. "It is not a question of trade wars or of being a little Englander but of democracy", he says. In practice Benn got on very well with industrialists, often making common cause with them against the financiers.

The final stage of Benn's ministerial career, as Secretary of State for Energy from 1975 to 1979, was in many ways the most important, for he secured a large proportion of North Sea oil for Britain. This was all the more remarkable for having been achieved from the position of a humiliating demotion by Harold Wilson. Indeed, many observers thought that Wilson, who sacked other ministers on the left of the party, wanted to get rid of Benn altogether, and Benn's resignation rather than his acceptance of demotion might well have been Wilson's hope. The humiliation was captured in *The Guardian*'s headline, "Wilson gives Benn's head to the City."

Instead Benn buckled down and made a success of energy, overcoming the opposition of the Treasury which was satisfied to have got an oil revenue tax but was not keen on public ownership of the oil. The prospect was of the multi-national oil companies having a free hand to exploit North Sea oil without any benefit to the nation other than tax. The oil companies were ready for wholesale, unregulated exploration of Britain's oil reserves, making huge profits, since war between Israel and the Arab countries had led to a four-fold increase in the price of crude oil.

Benn set about the partial nationalisation of North Sea oil. In this he had the support of both Prime Minister Wilson and. James Callaghan, the Foreign Secretary but soon to be Wilson's successor. Benn's method was to found the British National Oil Corporation, under a former ally, Frank Kearton. The two worked very well together, Benn with his political acumen and Kearton with his high reputation for having transformed the textile giant, Courtaulds. Benn liked the Conservative industrialist very much, recalling him as "a lovely guy". He saw how having a very distinguished industrialist by his side when negotiating with the oil companies strengthened his hand. As with Mullards earlier, Benn used the power of his office to call the oil companies' bluffs. When Amoco would not co-operate in the nationalisation plans, he awarded no exploration licences to them in the next round, and the company came to him, saying that they now wanted to participate. Together, Benn and Kearton got control of major oil reserves, keeping them out of the hands of the oil companies and of the European Economic Community (the Common Market), and dividing the North Sea between Britain and the other countries bordering it.

The basis of the new company was the exploration rights already acquired by Derek Ezra's enterprising publicly-owned National Coal Board five years earlier, which were already bringing in a large operating profit. The NCB was in partnership with two American oil companies, Gulf and Conoco, and Kearton negotiated the transfer of the NCB's interests and more than thirty of its oil experts to the new national corporation. A bonus for the government was that the NCB-American partnership had just discovered new reserves estimated to provide £200 million profits in the next few years. The government was already the majority shareholder in BP. Amazingly from today's standpoint, Burmah and three other oil companies accepted 51 per cent ownership by the British government in their North Sea oil activities. They saw the need to co-operate with Benn.

By the time the Labour government fell, Britain as a nation was the owner of a quarter of the oil in the North Sea. This remarkable achievement was later nullified by Margaret Thatcher. Benn was not to know that he was securing a large part of Thatcher's war chest.

Benn took another major decision in his final years in office. His growing concerns about nuclear energy resulted in his reducing from twenty-two to two the number of nuclear power stations to be authorised, and he initiated research and development into alternative sources of energy. He admits that he initially got the entire question of nuclear power wrong, regarding it then, as some still do, to be 'greener' than existing forms of energy and therefore a good thing.

These achievements during eleven years as a minister, usually secured against the odds, are belittled now by Benn himself. In conversation he will emphasise the importance of ideas rather than achievements, arguing that achievements can be swept away by your successors. That, of course, is only true if your successors have very different objectives. If Labour had not been replaced in 1979 by eighteen years of uninterrupted Conservative rule, it might have been otherwise. His successes show how much a determined minister could achieve in governments led by Wilson and Callaghan that were far from radical.

❖ ❖ ❖ ❖ ❖

Benn played a leading role in what is often portrayed, for good reason, as the battle for the soul of the Labour Party, raging throughout the late 1970s, the 1980s and most of the 1990s. This was a long and increasingly bitter struggle. The dilemma always for a non-conservative party is to decide what compromises are worth making in order to win an election, and what the point of winning an election is if, in order to do so, it is necessary to jettison most of the party's principles and aims? That was always the nub of the ideological debates within the Labour Party in the last quarter of the century.

Whilst Benn's approach was always a mixture of political objectives and tactics, it was above all one of reason. His simple argument for democracy in the Labour Party was that it is a good thing; that voters/delegates may get it wrong (although history suggests that they have a better record than company directors, military dictators, the combined wisdom of the civil service or tightly-controlled cabinets), but it is nonetheless right that they should have the power of debate and decision. Either we believe in democracy and practise it – in party, parliament or the European Community, or we do not. Benn's hostility to the EU is based on his belief in democracy. He would much rather see Britain as a strong partner in Europe than as an off-shoot of America, but wants European institutions to develop democratic processes first. He is very pro-European, but on the basis of rejecting the existing model in favour of what he calls the Commonwealth of Europe with an assembly and council. Handing the British currency over to a central bank that is answerable to nobody is anti-democratic.

The views that Benn consistently promoted before Labour lost power in 1979 as well as afterwards have always been essentially about democracy. He quotes Hitler as saying in *Mein Kampf*, "Democracy always leads to Marxism." He adds that, of course, Hitler was wrong, but it makes Benn's point that people need only to know and understand and they will inevitably finish up on the left. "Democracy is the most dangerous idea in the world," says Benn, "which is why Moscow and Washington do not like it."

"I have made a million mistakes, but I hope that I have never said anything that I did not believe when I said it," is Benn's assessment of himself. It is perhaps a recognition that his consistency has not always been matched by the caution that he knows is needed when offering comments which a hostile press might exploit. He speaks as if everyone shares his love of open debate. He is a mature democrat in a country which has been led to denigrate political debate and has become democratically less mature than it was. In many ways Benn would be more at home in France, where polemics and discussion are valued. He enjoys open, political discussion and sees nothing wrong in people amending their views without being accused of 'doing a U-turn'. The problem is that most politicians, party managers and newspaper editors do not share this view. Benn's confidence in the power of reason is sometimes too great. Nonetheless, his role in the Labour Party is as a genuine democrat, opposed to centralism which gives a vote to all party members once a year whilst degrading the party itself.

❖ ❖ ❖ ❖ ❖

The central problem for Labour during the debates that dominated the last quarter of the twentieth century was whether it would tackle entrenched wealth and establish a more democratic and equitable society. Labour lost power for eighteen years in 1979 but it had already lost all prospect of continuing in office following its handling of the financial crisis of 1976. That was the pivotal event, from which all later fissures in the Labour Party arose. Simply put by Benn, the question was, "Who is going to pay for the financial and industrial mess facing the country?"

Wilson had returned to power in 1974. His inheritance from Heath could hardly have been more daunting. The value of the pound was falling, big cuts in public spending had been made and more planned, the price of oil was rising at an alarming rate, and power cuts had reduced most of the country to a three-day working week. The public had known only strife and hardship for several years. They looked to the new government for solutions and relief, but had not given it a majority in the Commons, so that it was politically weak. Wilson held another election later in the year that gave him a majority of just three over all other parties, and then two years later suddenly resigned and handed the crisis over to Jim Callaghan.

Callaghan's arrival was ominous, with several sackings, notably that of Barbara Castle. Benn himself expected to be a casualty. Already, before the crisis came to a head, the government was struggling. Elected to solve problems, it had continued to inflict the same pain as its predecessor. The answer so far to Benn's simple question was that working people would pay for the solutions in rising prices and no pay increases.

The financial crisis was deepening. Despite all the cuts, the Treasury forecast for government borrowing in 1976-77 was so high that many economists felt that it could not be sustained. The result was a 'run on the pound', the selling of sterling. The air of crisis was confirmed by the action of Denis Healey, the Chancellor of the Exchequer. On his way to London's Heathrow Airport with the Governor of the Bank of England to catch a plane, he turned round and went back to the Treasury. There was no more certain way of confirming not only that there was indeed a crisis but also that he had been insufficiently aware of it only an hour earlier. It looked like panic stations because it was.

Within three hours of returning from Heathrow to the Treasury, Healey had decided to apply to the International Monetary Fund for a loan, with its foreseeable conditions. That was the point at which the Labour government's fate was sealed and Labour's turmoil that lasted until the 1990s was set in motion.

The charge against Benn was that he had no alternative, but he did. Benn is not mentioned at all in Healey's account of the crisis but, along with Anthony Crosland, Peter Shore and others, he opposed Healey, whilst Jim Callaghan at the helm wavered until late in the argument.

It was not until 29th September, two days after Healey's Heathrow panic and when already at the Labour Party conference, that Benn first heard rumours of the IMF loan from a delegate. The following day, before an unscheduled conference speech by Healey, the papers were full of the IMF story, but there had been no cabinet discussion and the conditions for the loan were unknown. It was not that they were secret. They did not yet exist. Healey's five-minute speech was pre-emptive of debate, itself anathema to Benn for its anti-democratic technique. The Chancellor began by saying that he came from the battle front and went on to say that all the unpopular actions taken by the government so far must continue. He would negotiate with the IMF on the basis of these programmes. Of course, all these programmes had already failed to avert the crisis and what he meant was that there would have to be even bigger cuts in public spending and even tougher pay restrictions in order to secure the loan. Benn was appalled and could not even attempt a clap, considering Healey's bruising style to be "vulgar and abusive".

On 7th October Benn put his alternative strategy to the cabinet. Before he spoke, Peter Shore (now Lord Shore) had made the case for what Healey had already dubbed "a siege economy". His position was that these policies, advocated by the Treasury for the two and a half years since Labour had returned to power, had failed. They had certainly not prevented the present crisis. There was no point in continuing with the same medicine.

Benn's argument was similar to Shore's, but went further. He agreed with Shore that Treasury policies had failed. He posed a choice: monetarism, the Treasury's favoured and failed policy, or protection for a period. He accepted the label of "siege economy". He had long argued that Britain's problem was not mainly one of wage levels and public expenditure, but was to do with its industrial structure, inadequate investment and inefficiency. Much of his work as a minister had been striving to change that structure.

The purpose of a limited period of import controls was to give Britain time to restructure its industry. At that time Britain was not industrially strong enough to survive economically in the world and needed a period of protection to put its house in order. It should follow a sequence of retreat behind a tariff wall, restructure then re-emerge as a strong industry-based economy. Benn and Thatcher have something in common. They both understand the need for wealth creation. They differ over how to achieve industrial efficiency and the use of the wealth once created. Benn's advocacy of temporary import controls was about creating a strong economy. It was strategic, not philosophical, except in its rejection of the monetarist approach. Benn regarded the financial crisis as phoney because the Treasury calculated the national reserves, the basis of confidence in the pound, only on their gold and dollar holdings. Our greatest reserves, he pointed out with that imagination that challenges the orthodox view, were our North Sea oil deposits. How could we be financially weak when we had reserves of such enormous value?

Benn was also concerned, as were few others around the table, with the electoral consequences of Healey's policy. Labour was already in a defensive position requiring drastic action. Benn repeated his question, "Who pays?" The answer, if Healey prevailed, was working people. It was they who were losing their jobs, paying ever higher prices and enduring ever worsening schools, health services and pensions. Would they take it lying down?

Callaghan challenged Benn to say what would be the price of his suggestions, noting, quite rightly, that there was nothing specifically socialist about them. Benn conceded, as Shore had done, that either way there would be hardship. All routes, including Healey's, would lead to a siege economy. The question was whether the government and the IMF were inside the citadel, with the public and trades unions outside battering on the walls, or whether it was the other way round. This analogy set out, albeit very simply, the choice for Labour for the next twenty years. It encapsulated the division in the Labour Party that was to come.

Benn expressed the choice in human and political terms by quoting to the Cabinet an industrialist whom he admired. Derek Ezra, chairman of the National Coal Board, had observed Edward Heath's miners' crisis as an insider. Ezra had said that you could not "get people to make sacrifices to appease those who are gambling with your currency, but you could get people to make sacrifices if they felt they were building up their economy again."

Later that day, Benn had more than an hour alone with Callaghan, in which he added other proposals to the general line he had taken earlier in Cabinet. He wanted industrial strategy to be taken away from Treasury control, because it was not at all a financial matter, harking back to his own previous policies when at the industry ministry. He also argued to Callaghan that the Governor of the Bank of England should be present at ministerial discussions on industrial strategy, so that he could both give his view to ministers, independent of the Treasury's, and hear their views. This was an early version of Gordon Brown's wish many years later to have independent advice from the Bank. The difference is that Benn wanted independent advice, not the control handed over by Brown in 1997.

Healey was not having it all his own way. Callaghan, like Benn, distrusted the Treasury and was discreetly attempting his own personal solution, which was to work with Helmut Schmidt, the West German Chancellor, to secure a long-term Common Market loan in order to stabilise the pound and thus reduce the dependence on the IMF. David Owen, at this time a junior minister, soon to be Foreign Secretary, agreed with Benn's assessment of the Treasury. Indeed, he went further and suggested to Benn that the Treasury was encouraging the IMF to demand the cuts that it itself wanted to impose. Owen did not, however, agree with import controls, so that, while he agreed with the nature of the problem and was hostile to Healey's response, he was not in agreement with Benn's solution.

Meanwhile, Benn was being publicly identified as an opponent not only of Healey but also of reason. *The Economist* referred to a Bennite party fighting cuts that the government had to make. Benn was making no headway and became "utterly depressed and dejected", thinking that it would be better for Labour to be defeated now, as it inevitably would be later if it accepted the IMF policies. Any open suggestion of this sort would lead to talk of treachery and result in the blame for failure being attributed to him and those who thought like him. He therefore kept his fear to himself.

In the end Healey saw that the financial crisis had been an illusion. The political consequences, however, were not. When it was all over, the Treasury issued its revised forecast of government borrowing required for 1996-7 and shortly afterwards the true figures were known. The original estimate, on which the crisis had been based, was much too high. The entire basis of the crisis was phoney. In the event, the government had to use only half the IMF loan and might well have been able to do without any of it. It was all repaid before the government fell less than three years later. As Healey wrote, "If I had been given accurate forecasts in 1976, I would never have needed to go to the IMF at all." The entire crisis had arisen because his Treasury officials had got the figures hopelessly wrong.

The only question is whether the Treasury officials were innocent and incompetent or already so wedded to the new monetarism that they were complicit, as David Owen had suggested. An interesting comment had been made before the crisis by Len Murray, the TUC leader, at a meeting which Healey had just addressed. Murray urged caution about making further drastic cuts in public spending, "because the figures will be different later."

The IMF medicine, based on a misdiagnosis and quickly shown to have been unnecessary, led directly to the collapse of the Labour government in the 'winter of discontent' in 1978-9, with increased unemployment, the breakdown of Labour-TUC relations, dead bodies 'piled up' because they could not be cremated, rubbish uncollected. This was how Labour acquired its reputation for economic incompetence. It was the cause of all the tensions and splits in the Labour Party for the next two decades.

Would Benn's alternative have worked? That cannot be known. It was well argued and offered hope. On the other hand, the economic consequences of Healey's route to the IMF were not only predictable; they were predicted, by Crosland, Shore and other Cabinet members, as well as Benn. Even Callaghan understood and feared the consequences. The failures were in the lack of courage to challenge the IMF and in understanding the political consequences.

Some people left the party to form the Social Democrats and then joined with David Steele's Liberals to form the Liberal Democrats. Others, including Benn, remained to fight for the soul of the Labour Party. Whilst Labour argued, Margaret Thatcher began her long reign, with the public memory of the 'winter of discontent' always there as evidence of Labour's economic mismanagement. The memory of it lingered into the 1990s. The price for it was paid not only in 1979. The final instalment was paid in 1997 to secure Labour's election victory, when Gordon Brown neutralised it by undertaking to follow the out-going Conservative plans on taxation and public spending for the first two years of a new Labour government.

TONY BENN

"Power no longer resides in parliament", said this great parliamentarian in 2000, announcing that he would leave the Commons at the end of Tony Blair's first government. Benn's announcement was greeted with an extraordinary outburst of admiration, some of it from the most unlikely quarters. He was hitting the right note.

Is Benn right to place his confidence now in the movements that are growing up around single issues throughout the world? His belief is that these will provide the political education that is now lacking, and that there are some common themes, linking the various campaigns. These themes, in his view, are forcing governments to challenge big business.

There is some evidence to justify his high hopes. It is public hostility to genetically modified foods, fostered by the green movement, that has influenced food retailers to reduce them. It is public awareness of Britain's exorbitant retail prices, encouraged by the consumer movement particularly in relation to cars, that has led the minister for trade and industry to follow, not lead, a 'rip-off Britain' campaign. It is the consequences of the foot and mouth farming crisis that has led to a review of food policy. It is a clear public preference for the continued public ownership of the London Underground that has forced some changes in the government's approach. It is the worldwide movement against the World Trade Organisation that is allowing people to see how big business is ruining many countries. Benn quotes the *Wall Street Journal*, "Marx may have been wrong about communism, but he was right about capitalism."

Benn thinks that these developments will engage more and more people. If policies are to be made not by party conferences but as a consequence of groups demonstrating what people think, governments have to listen. Benn's vision is that, when each of these questions comes to the fore, more people will understand a little more. He sees himself as contributing to the coming together of these ideas in an increasingly comprehending and sophisticated electorate.

The problem is access to the media. He strongly disapproves of violence. Yet he is not one to support outbursts against demonstrators, such as that from Tony Blair after the Gothenburg riots in June 2001. He has seen firsthand the work of *agents provocateurs*, those who turn peaceful demonstrations into riots in order to undermine them. At the Wapping demonstration against Rupert Murdoch's press he witnessed a man wearing a balaclava throw a brick at the police who then charged, but not before the brick-thrower had removed his balaclava and passed to safety behind the police lines. Second, he points out that law-breaking has preceded every advance in human rights, recalling that Margaret Thatcher denounced Nelson Mandela as a terrorist. When Benn addressed a conference of 2,000 pensioners, he ruefully remarked to the organiser, Jack Jones, that, unless Jones threw a brick through a McDonalds' window, the press would ignore the conference. Of course, Jones did not, and the press did. Violence is increasing, in Benn's view, because people do not have access to the media. He does not advocate it. He regrets it. But he understands.

Although he is personally optimistic about the future of politics in Britain, he is also fearful, seeing the danger of fundamental instability, what he calls a post-Titanic situation in which Labour, if it stumbles, has no philosophy, no bulwarks to prevent disintegration. "Blairisim has an unstable base," he says, "and is increasingly out of step with what people are thinking." He fears that, if there were an economic crisis, Blair could turn out to be "the midwife of a very right-wing government." The danger for Blair, as Benn sees it, is that his 'big tent' is in fact a 'little wigwam', with an ever smaller coterie inside and the majority outside. Yes, more money for schools and hospitals, but only if it is channelled through business. Objections to subsidies from tax-payers to nationally-owned industries have been replaced by admiration for loss-making companies such as those running the railways that are kept afloat only by huge subsidies from the tax-payer. "Mandelson made the Tories electable by calling them New Labour", is how he puts it.

Benn is now a political educator and campaigner outside parliament only because he regards parliament at present as powerless. But it is entirely wrong to believe that Benn has only ever been just an agitator - the great dissenter who could not cope with office, as he is sometimes portrayed. It remains to be seen whether the achievements of New Labour ministers, backed by huge majorities and two terms of office, will match Benn's in much less favourable circumstances. The indicators so far suggest that history will take the more favourable view of Benn.

JAMES DYSON

James Dyson's fondest wish is to be a verb, as in "to dyson the carpet in the living room." This would proclaim the triumph of his major product, and at the same time remove his sluggish – and unmentionable - rival from the dictionary. Having conquered the vacuum cleaner market, he wants a place in the dictionary. The ambition is, of course, light-hearted, but can we be sure? Dyson is an odd mixture of a driven and a relaxed and happy man. Perhaps it is better that Dyson himself is a well-known name than that he should enter the dictionary or become a set of initials. After all, Joseph Cyril Bamford, an earlier British inventor, conquered the world with his mechanical excavators and his initials are now part of the language, but who remembers the man?

His career has been extraordinary, even epic, in its struggle against indifference, financial conservatism and business corruption. It must also be admitted that often he struggled on when reason suggested abandonment of his projects. The time and money spent on defending his patents in the law courts have been enormous. For much of the time the money being spent in this way was borrowed. On other occasions litigation was gobbling up his profits. Yet in the end he was right. He now heads a huge enterprise, features in every year's list of the most wealthy people in Britain, remains as excited as a child about new things, thinks about invention, design and product development all the time, is something of a crusader for technological and design education, and enjoys a rewarding and happy family and social life.

The world of James Dyson is at Malmesbury in Wiltshire. Home is a large, river-side converted mill house by the Avon, formerly owned by David Puttnam, the film producer. Work is six miles away in the futuristic building where the machines are made and the next products are being developed. Most days he moves between the comfortable old of home and the exciting new of manufacturing. There are, of course excursions to London – a second home in Chelsea, the Design Museum, founded by his friend Terence Conran and of which he is now himself chairman, and many other engagements. He also travels the world. But, born and raised in Norfolk, he remains a country boy at heart.

Dyson carries his ideas into effect at all levels at the Malmesbury base. The 1,800 employees, a fifth of whom are engaged on research and development, have excellent, modern working conditions. In their cafe they eat meatless, organic food prepared by antique dealers. Why antique dealers? Because, before the need for a café, sandwiches were obtained from a combined deli/antique dealers. When the factory needed a cafe, the deli/antique dealers were asked if they could run it. They could. Dyson, a regular visitor to France, saw the virtue of this. "If you ever go to antique stalls in France, you see them stop at lunchtime, spread out their table cloths and bring out a wonderful array of food. Antique dealers are good at food. The two things seem to go together." It is a clever combination of weekday food and weekend antiques. There is an analogy here with Terence Conran – Habitat and smart restaurants. Staff are encouraged to arrive by bicycle, with the carrot of excellent facilities, including showers and stylish bike storage next to the front entrance, not out of the way round the back.

The initial training of design and development staff begins with taking a machine apart and re-assembling it, not 'training' in the formal sense. They then have the machine for £20, an incentive to get the re-assemblage right and to use the product that they are developing. You are more likely to be taken on at Dyson Research if you are young, not as an act of discrimination but because you will not have been contaminated by the bad practices of other companies. It all sounds paternalistic – Dyson in Wiltshire as a latter-day Robert Owen with his New Lanark Mills – but it succeeds. People like to work there.

The make-up of the man is superficially easy to see. The themes of his life, and now of his aspirations for the country's economic well-being, are consistent and clear. They have emerged from battles that needed the confidence and risk-taking that he advocates and the virtues that he exemplifies. It all came right in the end. It has taken a long time, with many years of teetering on the edge of disaster and more than once of falling over it.

Dyson is known mainly for the dual cyclone vacuum cleaner, although there are other products which have succeeded commercially. It is the machine that has made him something of a folk hero in modern business. He is the man who took on big business, wherever it chose (often the law courts), and won. He is still fighting and mostly still winning. He remains at heart the inventor and developer of products that people need and are willing to buy at a price and in such volume that the company will flourish. He extends this approach to Britain, seeing it as the country's only way forward – manufacturing quality products that are innovative and well designed and will sell in volume at a premium price.

The success is truly great. With the first cleaners produced by Dyson's own company coming on to the market only in 1993, the cleaner had by 1995 taken half the British market, out-selling all the well-known makes. Within these two years the company had achieved an annual turnover of £35 million and was exporting to Japan, reversing the usual one-way traffic in consumer goods. By then, Dyson was 48 years old and had been struggling in business for almost two decades, making enough money most of the time to continue his work and to have a reasonable standard of living, but not much more. The man has the right - greater than those who do it with aplomb if not always with a record of success - to offer advice to the nation on how to plan its commercial future.

Dyson is dogged, persistent and, by his own account, sometimes difficult. He is passionate, not least in his denunciation of the short-sighted and corrupt. These are what he calls his "manic diatribes", that exist aplenty. He is also a charming, unpretentious and thoughtful man who values and delights in his family and friends. The story of his life is not only about his quality of self-belief and perseverance, it is also about his way of thinking. "Iterative" is a word that he uses often to convey the benefits of thinking a problem through, with small incremental gains in understanding and, in the case of a product, in performance. He also makes frequent references, which are puzzling until you begin to share his way of thinking, to the need for an inventor and developer to "have a relationship with his product."

The American, Buckminster Fuller, was a major influence on Dyson's way of thinking. Isambard Kingdom Brunel, based at the nearby Wiltshire town of Swindon, is his hero – an engineer, a man who thought in terms of big schemes, a fighter against the odds. Dyson's progress during the early years of struggle was also influenced by people whom he met, often by chance, as well as held back by the rogues and the dullards who thwarted him. It is at the same time both an involved and a simple tale that needs to be unravelled.

❖ ❖ ❖ ❖ ❖

The search for financial backers of ideas that are not yet complete and have not yet become merchantable products is one of the themes of his life. His experience was sometimes encouraging, but often dispiriting.

The first of these backers, and an associate throughout most of his struggling years, was Jeremy Fry. Fry was the founder and managing director of Rotork, still one of Britain's biggest engineering companies, and he gave Dyson work during his final year as a student at the Royal College of Art in London. Fry had had the idea of a shallow draft boat that would move quickly over the water, carrying people or goods in bulk, and that could be beached, eliminating the need for quays, ports or cranes. He provided Dyson with the facilities to design the boat, which was named a Sea Truck to indicate its use. Fry patented the truck, set up a subsidiary company, and paid Dyson £300 to develop, make and sell it. This was the only link experienced by Dyson that provided, without catches, the capital necessary to take a product from idea to commercial success. The idea and the capital were Fry's, the development was Dyson's. Dyson has warm feelings for Fry, who taught him much whilst he in turn was gaining from the young designer's embryonic skills.

From then onwards, raising capital, which often included selling partial rights to production or partnerships with people who lacked Dyson's determination and long view, was full of problems. Most importantly, it was a distraction. In the end it was only by selling specific licences that Dyson gained enough income largely to finance his own production. Then it was not so much a question of 'with one bound he was free', more a question of many years of hard slog, uncertainty and potential disaster providing at last enough capital to do what he could have done many years earlier. Success story Dyson may now be, but there were years of borrowing, saving and doing without. Deirdre, his wife, went for years without wardrobes in which to put her clothes because they had no money.

When his ideas about a ball to replace the wheel on a wheelbarrow were formulated, he was not in a position to finance it. He had left Rotork to set up his own company, having agreed to work with a friend in the building industry for which the ballbarrow was originally intended. The friend then himself ran into financial difficulties and had to withdraw. Dyson's first thought was to sell the idea to a big manufacturer. "Not feasible", was the response of Imperial Chemical Industries (ICI) at Welwyn Garden City. Contrary to his instincts, he was therefore forced to seek capital by sharing control. His sister was married to the son of a former chairman of Rio Tinto Zinc, the mining company, and had money. They started with £24,000 of borrowed capital, which they jointly guaranteed, and Dyson assigned the patent to the company. Within a year they had almost half the British market of barrows, selling 45,000 a year with a turnover of £600,000. Within another year, and having expanded to make a water-roller (a garden roller filled with water rather than concrete), they had an overdraft of £150,000 and needed more capital. The inevitable but, in the event, disastrous move was to bring in a new partner with additional capital. Disagreements about the expansion (and the dishonesty of an employee) exposed the weakness of Dyson's position. He was now a minority shareholder. The disagreements increased. He was sacked. 'His' company was no longer his. The patent on his invention was not his. He and his sister were not to speak again for a decade. Commercially he was "alone and a little wiser".

Once he had formulated the idea of a bagless vacuum cleaner using a cyclone (the need for a dual cyclone came later), the problem again was the lack of capital to develop it. Capital to establish the Air Power Vacuum Cleaner Company came from a loan made by Jeremy Fry, the sale of the vegetable garden from Dyson's own house and a loan taken out by Dyson with his home as security. Fry and Dyson put up equal sums of money, but with Dyson owning 51 per cent to ensure control of the company. The difficulty now was that it took three years of work to turn the idea into a marketable product, by which time they had no capital to invest in production. Their solution was to sell licences so that others could take over the manufacturing and selling. With a heavy heart, for he knew that this was not what he wanted to do, Dyson set out to "tackle the fire-belching giants of British industry". He had already learned the hazards of this approach and had a quite specific intent. It was to sell exclusive rights to the patent for a limited period, in particular places, for an up-front fee for his continued services as designer and 5 per cent of the profits. In this way he would not suffer the total loss of his invention as he had with the ballbarrow. It was a compromise with his ideals. He knew that. But he needed the capital.

He was rejected by Hoover, Hotpoint, Electrolux, Goblin, AEG, Vax and Black & Decker. Support came through Jeremy Fry's influence with Rotork, although Fry was no longer its managing director. The company paid him £20,000 with a 5 per cent royalty, although the manufacturing was eventually done by Zanussi and the direct selling by Klene-eze. The main features of the eventual machine were in place and working. It was named the Cyclon. 500 were sold.

For a time Dyson had higher hopes of America, and often contrasts the enterprising attitudes there with those in Britain. What he was to learn from his American experience, however, was the ruthlessness with which powerful companies operate. By now Jeremy Fry, Dyson's most consistent supporter for some years but close to retirement, had no more stomach for the battle ahead. When a major American corporation decided on litigation as the means of resolving a dispute, Dyson had to do a deal which left him very short of cash, but at least still owning his patents. Worn down by 'dealing', exhausted and depressed, he nonetheless rejoiced at still being in possession of his product.

Next it was Japan. A relatively new import company, dealing mainly in Filofax, had seen a reference to Dyson's cleaner in an American magazine. The result of negotiations was that the cleaner was made in Japan and went on sale as the G-Force. In a country that prefers mats to fitted carpets, sales of £12 million a year were being achieved after three years. The catch was that, because of the way in which the deal was done, Dyson received at best the guaranteed minimum of £60,000. The mark-up to the retail price, from the manufacturer's price on which Dyson's own percentage was based, was 600 per cent.

A return to North America involved more litigation about patents and contracts but also two deals. One deal resulted in the cleaner being marketed as Drytech, a dry shampoo carpet cleaner. The other deal was with Johnson's Wax, which wanted a commercial tank (not upright) cleaner. This was on the market within a year, was called the Rocket-Vac and provided Dyson with £120,000.

By 1990 there was enough income from the G-Force in Japan and the Drytech and the Rocket-Vac in the USA to keep the Dyson family afloat. Importantly, Dyson was now free of debt, although still paying huge sums for the litigation in America.

He seriously considered giving up any hope of manufacturing his product himself at this time, but decided to try the banks. Merchant banks exist in order to provide capital for enterprise. Venture capital organisations, not least the most famous such as 3i, support the more risky enterprises. The Welsh Development Agency is keen to get employment into Wales. All turned him down. In fairness to these money-lenders, the American litigation might well have been a major factor in their decisions.

The less likely but eventual source of capital was a branch of Lloyds Bank, and even then no thanks to head office. It was the local branch manager who persuaded head office to change its mind and reverse its rejection of Dyson's application. The Dysons owned houses in Bath and at Chelsea in London, which stood as collateral for a £600,000 loan. This loan was the basis for the company that was to be so successful a few years later.

❖ ❖ ❖ ❖ ❖

During these years of struggle to get from ideas to products and income, Dyson had learned much about the ways of business. Most of it was about how easy it is to be shafted. From individuals to large corporations, there were people and organisations willing to exploit his skills without rewarding him and often stealing his ideas. His initial experience with Jeremy Fry was an innocent's paradise. The two men were essentially the same - thinkers, inventors and developers of products. Fry had already established his successful company, Rotork, and he was a crucial supporter of Dyson at key stages in his growth. Some of the other people and companies were ruthless and sometimes corrupt.

One of the worst examples of this was when Dyson lost control of the company set up to make and market one of his earliest inventions, the ballbarrow, because of the need for more capital. The decision of his board was to appoint a sales director and then to expand into the American market. Dyson drew up a list of five companies that were worth approaching as potential US licensees of the ballbarrow. The sales director was sent to visit them. After a shorter period than expected he returned from the USA, having visited only two, saying that the second one was the ideal partner. Moreover, that company had offered him a job. Dyson smelled a rat, although not as large a rat as it turned out to be. He rejected the salesman's advice, made the remaining visits himself and decided that another company should be the one to be licensed. The salesman left the company, for a job in the UK, it was thought. At an advanced stage in the negotiations with Dyson's chosen American company, it suddenly emerged that Sears, the huge US retailer, was already selling the ballbarrow. Dyson's salesman had not gone to a UK job. He had bought a ballbarrow in the UK and gone to the company that he had recommended, which was now manufacturing the barrow behind Dyson's back. The pirate company had even used the same selling slogan, the identical design and colours (green body and red ball) and some of Dyson's own publicity shots. The only thing that they changed was the woman operating the barrow in one of their marketing photographs. In Dyson's publicity material the woman was his wife, Deirdre. That was too blatant even for the pirates.

His Japanese link was put under pressure by a lesser trick, but one that was equally underhand. The joint plan with the Japanese was to sell a licence for the G-Force in the USA. Part of the deal was to be that the Americans would put £100,000 up front. Dyson did the negotiations in the US - they were conducted on a large circular bed in a Las Vegas hotel - and made good progress generally, but none at all on the £100,000. He was about to break off the deal, when he had a telephone call from the Japanese company advising him not to press the point as they had had personal guarantees from the Americans that the £100,000 would be paid. It was only just before he was about to sign that he learned the truth. The Americans had already paid the £100,000 direct to the Japanese. The Japanese were the manufacturers, but had no rights to sell the cleaner anywhere except in Japan. The money was for Dyson's rights, not theirs. Dyson cancelled the deal and negotiated with other North American companies.

Outrageous though these tricks were, they were nothing compared to the action of another US company. Negotiations were advanced for the licence of a vacuum cleaner in North America, with the Canadian company that was already marketing Drytech. The deal was about to be clinched when an appalled chief executive telephoned Dyson from a public call box outside the Sears offices in Chicago. He was there to win over this huge retailer, the key to volume sales in America. As he had gone into his pitch, the Sears executives had produced a cyclone vacuum cleaner, very similar to Dyson's. It had been made by a company that had earlier signed a deal with Dyson but had then sent a lawyer's letter, saying that his drawings were not sufficiently advanced to be used for production and accusing him of deception. Meanwhile, and unknown to Dyson, they had proceeded to manufacture the cleaner and were already selling it to Sears. "It's just like yours!" was the anguished and incredulous outburst from Dyson's potential collaborator. Indeed, it was.

❖ ❖ ❖ ❖ ❖

This long 'apprenticeship', before Dyson became the successful entrepreneur that he now is, also included enforced training as a salesman. Selling is a crucial part of all business, but Dyson's view of it is not the usual one. When he went to a potential customer, he was the designer of the product that he was offering. If what he offered was not quite what the customer wanted, he was in a position to understand their needs and to make design changes to satisfy them. He often had a good time doing so. His experience selling the Sea Truck illustrates how his approach is best suited to a customer who is willing to work with the product developer. It worked with the Egyptian navy and failed with the British navy.

The Sea Truck, designed by Dyson as a student, was a flat-bottomed, fast-moving boat, intended as its name implies to move goods across water and land on beaches. For some time the main customers were Scottish sheep farmers, who needed to move flocks between islands.

It seemed to Dyson that navies could find the Sea Truck useful. With the Royal Navy he had a response which was typical of those that he would later encounter with his other inventions. They ignored its chief virtue and wanted to load it with armour-plating and heavy diesel engines so that it could travel at only 10 mph. It was as though they had a vehicle designed for one basic purpose and were trying to adapt it to something quite different - the antithesis of Dyson's approach to design. They had their own preconceptions of what a military boat needed and ignored the essence of Dyson's basic design.

By contrast the Egyptians used the trial-and-error approach that Dyson favoured. They bought and tested one, and asked Dyson, then a young man of 25, to join them on the Nile for a week. He helped them to get the speed up to 58 mph. The Egyptians saw that the boat's chief virtue was that it could carry bulk at speed. Two weeks after Dyson left, the Egyptians attacked Israel across the Red Sea with five Sea Trucks in the vanguard, firing a rapid-drying cement that disarmed the Israeli napalm positions and allowed their army to land on the Sinai Peninsula. Surprise, born of speed, and ease of landing were the Sea Truck's virtues for the Egyptians. For the record it should be noted that Dyson had also sold four of the vessels to the Israelis for use by divers.

The Royal Navy, however silly its approach, did at least give Dyson a chance. Other companies barely gave him the time of day. The companies in the vacuum cleaner business that could have bought the right to manufacture his design have already been noted. All of those have lost business as a result of their miscalculation in not responding to his overtures and some have spent huge sums on litigation to try to crush their unwelcome rival.

Dyson was, of course, selling his ideas and his products to potential backers and licensees, not direct to customers. Nonetheless he was acquiring an understanding of salesmanship and, as might be expected, developing unorthodox views.

His first major success at making money for himself from sales was with the ballbarrow. It will be recalled that this was conceived as being of greatest use to the construction industry. Typically, Dyson identified nine faults in the existing wheelbarrow and was unimpressed with the idea that the wheel did not need to be reinvented. The ball would run more effectively over the mud of a building site and its barrow should be made of a material that would not allow concrete to adhere to the sides. The difficulty was that builders are among the most traditional of craftsmen. In the event the ballbarrow found its market not with builders but with gardeners. Having failed in a rather ludicrous way to sell the ballbarrow to garden centres (he had employed a former Miss Great Britain for the purpose), he turned to direct selling through newspapers. The result was, for an operation of his size, a sales explosion. Cheques totalling £600 a day started arriving from people who, unlike the garden centre managers, were buying the ballbarrows unseen. Before long he was selling through a new direct sales organisation called Scotcade, which took out whole-page advertisements and issued newssheets for a range of products that they judged would shift quickly. This took the annual turnover of the ballbarrow operation to £600,000, with 45,000 being sold.

What got the market for the ballbarrow moving quickly were articles in *The Sunday Times* and in *Homes and Gardens*. Dyson was scathing about the advertising industry. Along with financiers, advertising agencies were his devils. He saw them at the time as spivs and as part of the British commercial disease, for taking huge sums of money whilst research and development are starved of cash. He learned from this experience with the ballbarrow that editorial matter is far more valuable than paid-for advertisements. Later, it was articles about the dual cyclone in publications such as the *TWA Flight Magazine* that enabled potential collaborators to contact him. Until a couple of years ago, Dyson did not advertise his appliances. More than two-thirds of his machines are still bought on the recommendation of existing users. He does now advertise, saying that manufacturers need to reach their customers, but sees it primarily as a means of giving information. "It's something that you do when you've got your product right. I am sad that advertising agencies have had such a high profile, especially in the 1980s. It is a peripheral activity, the last stage. Advertising cannot be a quick fix to save a poor product." For Dyson, getting the design, manufacture and price right are the big things.

Another important lesson was to be learned from the next venture into gardening, the water-filled garden roller. The lesson was that the money that will sustain a business and repay investment cannot be made unless the market is large enough, however good the selling. The water-filled garden roller destroyed the existing market for concrete-filled rollers, but did not replace it. Since rollers are not needed very often and Dyson's was designed to be portable (emptied and filled with water whenever needed) and also easily fitted into the boot of a car, people borrowed rather than bought them. After the initial sales, market saturation was reached too quickly and very few more were sold. He had learned the lesson that some markets are short-lived.

When trying to sell licenses, Dyson experienced two American techniques: one was the equivalent of the 'good cop/bad cop' routine, the other was all 'bad cops'. In the first he was met in a hotel room by the president of a company and his entourage. Questions were fired at him, with the president's son seeming interested and keen, while the president himself remained hard and aloof. The deal collapsed, until the president's son telephoned a few days later to say that it was on again.

The other technique was for the corporation to field a team of specialists - production manager, finance director, lawyer etc, led by a vice-president of the company. They were all aware of their corporate strength and of Dyson's having to fend for himself. One would ask a question and before Dyson had finished his first sentence, another would intervene with the next question. The entire objective was to unsettle and intimidate the seller and exploit his need for cash. The lesson for Dyson is that a businessman must always assess clearly to himself the strengths and the weaknesses of his position, and become as expert as a poker player. More than once it seemed that a deal had collapsed only for the other side to telephone a few days later to agree it. Dyson's nerves were being strengthened all the time.

❖ ❖ ❖ ❖ ❖

Necessary though these other activities were, it is inventing and developing products that fires Dyson. The other aspects - sometimes exciting, often depressing, always a distraction - are necessary. But product design and development are what enthuses him.

He has a recurring theme when writing and talking about his work. It at first seems rather romantic and not at all practical.

The inventor "bonds with his invention". The inventor has an "intimate knowledge of a product that comes from dreaming it up and then designing it." Then you realise that this is precisely the factor that enabled a man like Dyson to spend three years in a workshop, created from an old coach house next to his home, designing his dual cyclone cleaner. There were two stages: the 'eureka' moment when he realised that a cyclone could collect debris and deposit it without suction having to go through a bag, and the long period of detailed work to translate the principle into a functional and saleable product.

The discovery of the cyclone and the thought that it could be used to make a bagless vacuum cleaner came to him when at a sawmill. The sawdust is sucked into a cone and, via ducting, into a bag, but without the suction having to work through the bag. It is a simple principle. Dyson could immediately see its application to the vacuum cleaner, not least because part of his family responsibilities at the time was to use a reconditioned upright cleaner for the household chores. The contrast between this cleaner, which became ever less efficient as the bag filled, and the continuously efficient extraction of sawdust from a large area was compelling. As important as his understanding was his persistence, even when confronted with the thought-stopping, "If there were a better kind of vacuum cleaner, Hoover or Electrolux would already have thought of it."

Conviction so strong as to enable a person to work away at an idea in solitude for two years is rare. To do so on the basis of putting your mortgaged home at risk is perhaps unwise. That is what Dyson did. Each morning, after domestic responsibilities were over, he crossed the yard to the converted coach house, returning for a half-hour lunch and then not returning home again until the evening. Day after day for two years he painstakingly modified his prototype. One of his maxims offered to young designers is that, when developing a product, only one feature must be modified at a time, so that it is possible to know which change has effected the improvement. For those two years, therefore, each day was spent making small alterations, testing, making further alterations, testing again and so on. It was the sort of activity for which large companies, including Dyson itself now, have teams of people in well-equipped research and development workshops. Dyson worked alone. It was not only the foundation of his most successful product, but the evolution of his approach to product design.

❖ ❖ ❖ ❖ ❖

The extraordinary determination shown by Dyson is the key to his current success. Its origins can be traced to his upbringing and particularly his education. He was both hurt and liberated by his schooling. The experience makes him particularly appreciative of recent developments in design and technological education in Britain.

Dyson's father was a classics teacher at Greshams, a public (that is, private) school in Norfolk. With the job went a share of a large house bordering the school's playing fields, the other occupants being another teacher and his family and the owner. Life was in many ways idyllic and Dyson still refers to the Norfolk countryside and coast with affection. He and the other children cycled to the village primary school, swam with seals off Blakeney Point, and had the empty buildings and grounds of Greshams as their playground during the school holidays. He was happy. Things changed when his father died from throat cancer. James had seen some signs, the coughing of blood, despite his father's efforts to keep it from his children, but he was only nine and had not understood their portent. When it happened, the shock was enormous.

There were two consequences. Dyson became more conscious of being younger and smaller than the other children and therefore of the need to fight his corner. He saw also, although perhaps not immediately, that his father was trapped in a conventional career rather than doing what he most wanted to do. Dyson senior had produced plays at Greshams and was about to join BBC television when he died in 1956.

Greshams was both kind and challenging, sometimes to the point of being hurtful. The kindness was principally to give Dyson and his elder brother places at the boarding school with half the fees waived when their father died. The challenge and occasional hurtfulness, ultimately productive in Dyson's personal development because of his reaction to it, arose from the conformity required, the unimaginative curriculum and the undervaluing of technical skills. It is possible to discern the development of Dyson's persistence, refusal to be intimidated and occasional arrogance from his perversity in confronting the prevalent values and curriculum at the school. He took up the bassoon, because it was an unusual instrument. He took up running and had that precious, confidence-boosting childhood experience of discovering something that he could do at least as well as others and better than most. He practised each morning and night over the sand dunes, and won most of his races. Gradually, whilst still suffering from the "ignominy of second-rate academic performance", he was finding success. He still runs. Next came swimming, the trick here being that few other boys wanted to plunge into the cold water of a Norfolk outdoor pool, so competition was reduced. Even that advantage did not bring success, however, and the swimming career was abandoned. Then on to acting, as Trinculo in *The Tempest*, and more importantly designing the sets for plays.

Academically Dyson did not shine. His elder brother was a classicist like their father and went on to read classics at Cambridge, where he later became a socialist and a comprehensive school teacher. Dyson's academic results were poor. The denigration of practical skills by academics then and now appals him. He cannot understand why they should take pride, as they sometimes do, in their ignorance of any aspect of human endeavour. He gained relief from this by going to stay during the summer holidays with a friend in Tonbridge, Kent. His friend shared a hobby with his father, that of making trains, boats and planes with small engines. In one way the experience undermined his confidence, because he was so unskilled by comparison with his friend and because he had no father of his own to teach him such skills. He did, however, have opportunities to develop some practical skills and, perhaps even more important, the value of the trial-and-error approach.

The one important subject that Dyson did value at Greshams was art. He was reluctant to approach the subject solely as an academic discipline, as required then by the public examination syllabuses. Again, the outcomes were to be important for the future. He consolidated his appreciation of the trial and error approach and also developed a personal and idiosyncratic style, if the brown blobs that were his speciality may be so called.

His art work was sufficiently interesting for him to gain a place at a not very reputable art school in London called the Byam Shaw Art School, Kensington. Like many specialist colleges at the time, one of its main functions was as a 'finishing' school for well-heeled young ladies. The principal, Maurice de Sausmarez, was better than the college. Dyson learned how to understand and draw form, not just sketch outlines. He was required to start with the middle of the object, not the profile. This activity took place not only in the college, but also, for example, at Queen's ice-rink in Bayswater. De Sausmarez took a wider view of the career options open to his students than did many traditional foundation art colleges, which looked forward only to fine art courses.

A stroke of good fortune took Dyson from here to the prestigious Royal College of Art, not far away from the Byam Shaw School, next to the Royal Albert Hall. The College had three places for students without the necessary qualifications, which included a university degree. This was the only way in which Dyson could have won a place. It was supposed to be an attempt by the College at anti-elitism, which rather came to grief when two of the three winners were from Eton (one later to inherit his peerage) and the third, Dyson, from Greshams. Dyson's own account of his admission to study furniture design shows how open it was. The tests were about the use of materials - plastic, glass etc - and about design projects. He completely failed to identify samples of wood. The importance of the RCA to his future development was crucial and he takes great pride now in being a member of its Council.

He did not last long on the furniture course, but transferred for most of his time to the interior design course, run by Sir Hugh Casson, Professor of Environmental Design and a future President of the Royal Academy. The course was not at all about designing room interiors, choosing curtains and such things. It was more about designing the interiors of cars, planes and boats. Casson had his feet firmly on the ground, having been a camouflage officer during the war and then a technical officer at the Ministry of Town and Country Planning as the war ended and post-war reconstruction began.

The work of the American, Buckminster Fuller, was recommended by Anthony Hunt, a structural engineer teaching at the College. Like Dyson, Fuller had not had great academic success or technical training. He was a thinker uninhibited by what was already accepted as knowledge. His greatest commercial success was with the geodesic dome, consisting of many equal triangles, now used widely for sports stadia, greenhouses and holiday complexes.

The greater part of Dyson's final year at the RCA was spent on the design of the Sea Truck, which constituted his graduation piece. He was awarded an upper second class degree, being a little disappointed, but having had some splendid learning and even greater opportunities to experience practical design work.

This experience of the British educational system has left Dyson with some firm views. He attacks the baleful effect of the prolonged emphasis on the classics - the subject of his father's and his elder brother's learning. It is indeed amazing that British education still had this emphasis almost two centuries after the cleric and wit, Sidney Smith, had denounced his own education at Winchester in the 1780s for precisely the same reason. As Smith eloquently put it, "Schoolmasters encouraged pupils to love not the luxury the difficulty encloses [by which he meant the literature] but the difficulty itself -not the filbert but the shell, not what may be read in Greek but Greek itself." Brought forward to our own times, substitute A-level mathematics and physics for design and technology, and you see how little has changed. Dyson derides the undervaluing of practical and technical skills. He finds early specialisation silly. He worries about the tramlines set for thinking by many academic studies.

Whilst his own education and that of his children was in private schools, he greatly admires the development of technology as a school subject which has been led mostly by state comprehensive schools and technology advisers and inspectors. Dyson has become the patron of the technology advisers and inspectors' association. School technology now puts into educational practice much of what Dyson values. It consists of identifying a problem, thinking about solutions and then testing those solutions practically, with an evaluation of what works and what further steps need to be taken. This could be a description of Dyson's months in his coach house-cum-workshop when he was developing the dual cyclone cleaner. The work of pupils is now often supported by engineers, put into schools by the Engineering Council's Neighbourhood Engineers Programme. It is also supported by the Engineering Education Scheme, created by one of Lord Sainsbury's family trusts. It is a major development in British education and Dyson is delighted.

He is now a frequent presence at school design and technology events. The Design Museum houses the Dyson Centre, three lecture rooms where teachers are trained, lectures given and school children welcomed. Dyson Education Boxes contain a vacuum cleaner, for school children to take to pieces and reassemble, with guidance notes and coursework ideas. In April 2001 Dyson took questions live on the Internet from pupils and teachers. The topics ranged widely from his own experience to fundamental design questions about the importance of prototypes and testing. Not many giants of industry share their ideas direct with school children. Dyson's aim with all these activities is not to produce the next batch of designers, but to "help in the creation of a design literate generation."

Dyson has commented that, "Schools are taking the biggest steps forward with regard to design of anyone in the country." There is only one disappointment. It is said that Margaret Thatcher, not one of Dyson's heroines as we shall see, was persuaded to make technology a compulsory school subject by the influence of Sir Terence Conran, another of its admirers. One of David Blunkett's decisions in 1999, based on the already outdated view that teachers found the National Curriculum too restrictive (a perfect example of conceding defeat after the victory has been won), was to make technology for 14-16-year olds optional again. Dyson's hostility to this misguided change was expressed forcefully. Still, this was only one step backwards after big strides forwards.

❖ ❖ ❖ ❖ ❖

It has already been seen how some people thwarted or deceived Dyson. More important are those who helped him. Two have already been mentioned. Jeremy Fry, managing director of Rotork, thought in similar ways and gave Dyson opportunities to develop the Sea Truck when he was still a student at the Royal College of Art. This relationship gave to Dyson not only the finance to develop ideas and test prototypes, but also an excellent subject for a final year assignment and the mentoring of an older man who had already taken steps along the path that Dyson was eventually to tread. Later he was Dyson's ideal collaborator on the development of the Dual Cyclone™ cleaner, by putting in money and leaving Dyson to get on with it.

The other person who has already been mentioned was his local bank manager, Mike Page. He delivered a loan when others had said no. The man holding the post usually associated with safe decisions was the one who delivered what was necessary to an obviously risky enterprise.

Many people helped at crucial stages. Indeed, as a student, Dyson had something of a charmed life. Before the Sea Truck opportunity came along, personal acquaintanceships and chance contacts had led to design tasks that were exceptional for a student. The RCA at the time was noted for students who made names whilst still there or very shortly afterwards - people such as David Hockney, Gerald Scarfe and Ossie Clarke had preceded Dyson. The opportunities were there for Dyson to design things that met a real need, like the present school pupils taking A-level design and technology, and in addition he was very fortunate in his work placements and his contacts.

Terence Conran had recently established his design group and one of Dyson's work placements with the group was to offer some ideas for the refurbishment of the Peter Dominic off-licence in Victoria Street. He also helped on the designs for the Conran facilities at Heathrow Airport.

In his second year at the RCA, at the age of 20, he had joined regular gatherings held at Clerkenwell pubs by Joan Littlewood, the idiosyncratic and pioneering impresario of the Theatre Royal, Stratford, in the East End of London. Littlewood had already had her greatest hit, *Oh What a Lovely War*, an ironical title for a piece that set the appalling statistics for casualties in the 1914-18 war against the popular songs of the time, and explained how innocent men were persuaded to volunteer for their own slaughter at the behest of callous generals and politicians. She was an 'alternative' theatre person, operating far from the West End in an old music hall, and unencumbered by the conventions of traditional drama. Dyson contributed to a community event that she organised, building a Pirelli-webbing wall with effigies of a barmaid, a hippo and Harold Wilson (then the Prime Minister) for the children to hit. It attracted the attention of the *Today* programme, generally required listening for prime ministers, so that Dyson's interview may have been heard at the highest level.

He also responded to a remark by Littlewood that she needed a new theatre, and so he designed one using a similar approach to Buckminster Fuller's domes. Littlewood accepted it and planning permission was obtained. Only the money was lacking and the scheme foundered. It was this particular opportunity, however, that brought Dyson into contact with Jeremy Fry who was to be such an influence on him and a help to him.

A paid commission was the first offer of help through Fry whose friend was developing the Roundhouse in Camden, London, formerly a railway shed with an engine turntable, for a performance of *Hamlet*. Fry's friend was Tony Richardson, already famous as a director at the Royal Court Theatre in Sloane Square, where he had directed the premiere of *Look Back In Anger* a decade earlier. He had moved into films and already had *Saturday Night And Sunday Morning*, *The Loneliness Of The Long Distance Runner* and *Tom Jones* to his credit. The Roundhouse, just a shell, needed an auditorium and seating, and Dyson designed these.

❖ ❖ ❖ ❖ ❖

Throughout the years of struggle Dyson was a family man. He had married his wife, Deirdre, whilst still at the RCA. They had met whilst at the Byam Shaw Art School. She was a Londoner, who had worked as a secretary and had gained a scholarship to the art school in return for providing secretarial services to the principal. She was emphatically not like many of the other students. She was not there to be 'finished', but to learn about art.

Deirdre later made her own career as an artist, selling her works in Bath, where the couple lived for many years, and in London and elsewhere. In addition, she contributed brochure designs to various Dyson products as the business developed. Perhaps more important than anything else, she supported decisions to take risks, including risks to their homes which were often used as collateral for loans when capital was needed. Dyson describes her as "the woman who would not only share my life, but make possible all the professional things that I did, and provide the strength to see me through the desperate years of struggle."

She had toughness and detachment when needed. At one point, the couple took a holiday in Provence in order to reflect on their future. Dyson was exhausted from spending so much time on trying to do deals, aware of the passing years and despondent at protracted litigation with an American corporation. He considered giving up this side of his recent activities, in order to concentrate on designing. She argued for holding out. A telephone call came through to Provence to inform them that the American corporation had decided to settle. When Dyson himself, quite out of character, had been on the point of conceding, it was Deirdre who advised that he should not be the first to blink. Dyson is amazed by her fortitude in supporting his risky career in the long years before a reliable income was assured.

His three children are very important to him. They were all born during his years of struggle and financial uncertainty. Emily, the oldest, is a fashion designer, Jacob a product designer. Before Dyson began his day's work in the coach house-cum-workshop, developing the Dual Cyclone™ cleaner, he took the two children to school. Sam, the youngest – now a musician - was born in 1978, when Dyson had the idea about the dual cyclone vacuum cleaner, and was 15 when the cleaner was first manufactured under the family name.

Dyson is a naturally gregarious man and it is not difficult to see why he liked having his family close to him. But he had other reasons for wanting them near as they grew up. He did not want them to be in boarding school, as he was himself. He has made a very sad analogy between negotiating as an individual against corporation teams and his being the smallest and youngest child in the large Victorian house at Greshams. In both cases, when he had made his point, others jumped in to put him down, trying to impress the boss/parents, whilst he was alone. The frustration of being right but being beaten by weight of numbers is still a part of him. It is not difficult to see why he wanted his children's lives to be different.

❖ ❖ ❖ ❖ ❖

Dyson is very much a man of the future as well as one with substantial achievement "against the odds" – the title of his autobiography - to his credit. He has very modern research and development facilities at Malmesbury. He has views on Britain's economic future and radical views on the ways in which companies should organise themselves. Politicians are listening. It remains to be seen whether they are understanding and will act.

His views on economic policy are very much coloured by his experience as an entrepreneur in the mid-1970s and the 1980s. Colourful epithets for those who have thwarted him, mistakenly or dishonestly, are plentiful in his writings and speaking. Few of the phrases used for these "blood-sniffing sharks" are as colourful as those saved for Margaret Thatcher. He was suffering at her hands whilst others elected her again and again throughout the 1980s and early 1990s. As he began his two years developing the dual cyclone, "Maggie was only just beginning to wreak her havoc", as he put it later. He then had to raise capital when her policies had driven the interest rate in Britain to 24 per cent. He was at the mercy of the money-men, "the monsters that the Thatcher revolution made into prime movers". The alternating policies of boom and bust were destroying, not renewing, so much of British industry. The British preference for finance and service industries over manufacture, cemented by the influence of the City and the Bank of England, is what Dyson sees as the enduring root of Britain's economic difficulties. He despises the "bean counters" whom he had for a time to court and who almost prevented his success.

His amazement at the time of Norman Lamont's financial debacle, when a single speculator, George Soros, forced Britain's withdrawal from the European Monetary Union, was not at the event itself. For Dyson this was foreseeable and, indeed, inevitable. His amazement was that, having made millions by speculating against the British currency and therefore against Britain itself, the perpetrator of this act should be feted as a kind of wizard to be admired.

By 1997, "with the vapid materialism of the Thatcher years petering out", he had a little more hope. It is still alive, but only just. As he sees it, although the Blair government is more understanding of the need to help new businesses - and Gordon Brown opened the new research and development centre at the Malmesbury premises - it is still preoccupied with the goal of low inflation which stifles new enterprises and manufacturing as a whole. He calls it "the thirty-year fetish of low inflation which has ruined industry with high interest rates." Eddie George, the Governor of the Bank of England, thinks that manufacturers are too complaining, pointing out that they create only twenty per cent of the national wealth. To which Dyson replies, "Yes, but it is the main driver of the economy," pointing in mid-2001 to Britain's huge trade deficit and the loss of more than half a million jobs in manufacturing in the previous year. Dyson's point is that sustained economic recovery has to be based on producing goods that people need, in large quantities and with a good mark-up that acknowledges the high cost of research and development. Government's role should be to nurture this achievement, in particular by joining the euro currency, maintaining low borrowing rates of interest and giving additional tax relief for research and development, the source of future wealth.

While he jibs at the word when put to him, Dyson's analysis of British industry at the end of the twentieth century is Marxist. His solutions, of course, are entirely different. He might agree with the comment in the *Wall Street Journal* that, "Marx was wrong about communism, but he was right about capitalism." What he has in common with Marx is his understanding that manufacturing companies, born of economic freedom and competition, once established become inescapably monopolistic. They use their freedom to destroy competitors. They contain the seeds of their own destruction because, with their rivals crushed, the virtues of the competition which created them no longer exist. They sit back, use advertising to keep their markets for a while, but eventually become senile and die. He does not name companies, but he does not need to. The phenomenon is easily recognised.

A pragmatic man whose ideas have been forged from experience not dogma, he prefers to explain this process as manufacturers having 'lost the plot'. They have forgotten how they created themselves and therefore what they need to do constantly to regenerate themselves. He has written that we live in "an age when the great monopolies have been able to dictate that progress has ended." This they did "when they were satisfied not with their product, but with their control of the market", underpinned by the advertising industry.

As a manufacturer, he has not been able to ignore the effects of economic globalisation. With Britain outside the euro and with a highly-valued pound, he has been forced to set up a factory in Malaysia to cover the large South-East Asian market and Australasia. Much to his regret, many of the components used in his factory in Britain have to be imported. He could not otherwise stay in business. The last straw in his decision to manufacture abroad came when a modest expansion of the Malmesbury factory, which had much local support, was thwarted. The factory had been built on three-quarters of a plot zoned for industry, but the original owner had kept the remaining quarter. That land became available, but Dyson needed a small additional piece that was not zoned. Permission to build on the extra bit was opposed by some local people, including, ironically, Roger Scruton, the right-wing, free enterprise philosopher opposed to state 'interference'. The decision was referred to the Secretary of State with the prospect of a two or three years delay, ridiculous for a manufacturing company with an urgent need. The plan was abandoned. Dyson remains a British, on-shore, private company, wholly owned by James and his family.

One of the richest men in the country, he has no particular regard for money-making. He dislikes the term 'business' precisely because it conjures up the image of the money-maker. It would be absurd, of course, to say that he does not enjoy the benefits of his relatively recent wealth. It enables him to have houses in the country and town, good cars and other features of a very comfortable style of living. His children were able to enjoy their student days without worries over money. Jacob's freedom to enjoy student London when his father had had to commit himself to hard work in the swinging sixties is a cause for the father's rejoicing, not envy. Most of all, Dyson enjoys the freedom to invest in his company and ideas which his wealth permits. Not being in hock to money-lenders is a freedom to be cherished. That thought gives him as much pleasure as the use of his wealth.

And the future of the company? He said a few years ago that he would never sell the company or float it on the stock exchange. It is still something that he does not countenance, but he can no longer say that it will never happen. One day, it might suit him and his family, but he does not sound happy at the possibility. Rather ruefully he comments that the stock exchange would not be interested in a company that ploughs most of its profits back into the development of new products. Still, there are constant improvements in the vacuum cleaners and a top-of-the range and innovative washing machine – the Contrarotator™ - that has already captured a significant share of its market.

Refreshingly and engagingly interested in many things, Dyson has avoided the main fault of the obsessive. Knowing how he had to struggle for so many years and commit himself to his then single idea, the temptation must have been strong, but it has been resisted. His interests are wide. Of course, what he does in his company is very important to him, but his conversation and interests range over many topics.

For Dyson the purpose of business is to design and manufacture new or significantly improved products that customers will buy at a premium and that can be made and sold in huge quantities. It is about imagination. It respects human values. The Prime Minister, Tony Blair, could learn much by spending a day at Malmesbury, seeing the factory and listening to Dyson. The fear must be that Dyson will continue to be one of very few voices telling us that the country's future lies in finding new, well-designed articles to mass-produce in excellent working conditions that respect and develop people's talents. Might Dyson go the way of Robert Owen and his New Lanark Mills, near Glasgow, once a model for the way forward by a business man with an understanding of the human perspective as well as profits, now a splendid museum? Might he be the pioneer who succeeded personally, but who did not change a nation's ways? That would be a terrible waste.

PAT, WAYNE and GARY YOUNGE

EXTRAORDINARY PEOPLE

Patrick, Wayne and Gary Younge are a remarkable trio, making their marks in different ways and reflecting both the qualities that were instilled by their clear-minded and committed mother, who raised them single-handed for most of their lives, and their own intellectual toughness. Now all in their thirties, Pat is Head of Programmes and Planning at BBC Sport, responsible for *Grandstand*, rugby and finding new talent, Wayne lectures on radiography at the City University in London and Gary is a writer and a featured columnist in *The Guardian*. Born to Caribbean parents, they were brought up in a new town, educated at state comprehensive schools and universities that are 'redbrick' or 'new', and lived for much of their childhood years on the verge of poverty.

Their parents Reba and Patrick senior came from Barbados in response to the recruitment carried out there in the 1950s and 1960s by the British government. There was a chronic shortage of labour in Britain and other European countries at the time. Germany, lacking an imperial history that provided links to countries with skilled but low-waged workers, responded by huge capital investment in labour-saving machines and vocational education programmes. Britain imported workers.

Reba and Patrick, who were already going out together in Barbados, came to Britain initially with the intention of making some money and returning home with their savings. Patrick came first and obtained work in the International Wine Co-operative Society in London. Reba was a primary school teacher in Barbados, but responded to the recruitment drive from the British ministry of health, headed at the time by Enoch Powell. She was sent on arrival to train as a nurse in Derby. They married a few years later in London, where Patrick junior and Wayne were born. When the wine co-operative moved to Stevenage, the first of the post-war new towns, the Younges moved with it.

Stevenage in the 1960s and 1970s was a good place to bring up children. The two most important conditions for a reasonable life were guaranteed. Once you had accepted a job, you were invited to the town, given the keys of three properties, and invited to choose one of them. The choice for Reba and Patrick was made easier by the response of a Mrs Stilling. Black people were a rarity in Stevenage. Mrs Stilling lived next door to one of the houses on offer. She was a kind and welcoming person who, as soon as she saw the baby Wayne, greeted the Younges and offered to warm his milk. She remained a good neighbour until her death only a few years ago. Wayne still lives in the same house.

The family settled in at the start of a promising life in Stevenage. Pat, the eldest, is of course the one with the most vivid memories of this time. He recalls visits to other West Indian families in Welwyn Garden City, Hitchin and other nearby towns, "eating Caribbean dishes, using chickens and rabbits reared in back gardens just as they would have been back home." A short while later, the third of the boys, Gary, was born. All was going well for the family.

Then it all fell apart. Pat had been aware of the arguments raging between his parents and had noticed that father sometimes did not come home at night. The morning after one more night's absence there was a furious row, father walked out never to return and Reba threatened suicide, using some tablets that she had for epilepsy. Patrick rushed next door to Mrs Stilling who calmed everything down. Life continued but now there was a single, working mother and three boys, the youngest being only fifteen months old.

The Younge brothers have vivid memories of life on the edge of financial disaster. Apart from a trip to Barbados, their only holiday was with the Elim Pentecostal Church to the Isle of Wight for camping and church services. They were often allowed to sleep together downstairs in the living room, not understanding until later that the real reason for the treat was that there was no money for heating bedrooms. They began to understand that their mother was having to use tricks, such as switching the cheques for gas and electricity between envelopes, so that the suppliers would have to return the cheques, thus giving her a few more days to find the money to meet her bills.

Wayne remembers innocently querying his mother's suggestion that the £2.50 being paid for each boy by their absent father was insufficient even to feed them. Reba rose characteristically to the challenge, giving him the £2.50 to feed himself for the week. He soon realised that the milk from the fridge was not 'his' because he had not paid for it. Eating well for two days, he was left with only apples for the rest of the week. A lesson was learned for life. Teachers were often helpful and tactful, allowing the boys to go on school trips 'on tick', giving Reba more time to find the money. Gary has called his childhood "the reign of Reba." She was a formidable woman who had to cut corners to see them through to independence.

Reba taught the boys other lessons. A tenacious believer in the value of education, she saw it as the means of rising above disadvantage and of achieving the most important freedom of all in a mostly free society, the economic freedom to control your own life. She committed the boys to their schooling. Gradually they committed themselves too. They cannot recall not having been able to read. They could do it before going to school. It was also assumed by their mother, and quickly became their assumption also, that they would stay at school until 18 and then go to university. One of Reba's oft-repeated pieces of advice was that, "If you go for a job and an Englishman goes for a job, and he's got eight O-levels, you are going to have to have nine or you're not going to get the job." The motivation was the same as that of grammar and then comprehensive school pupils competing against public schoolboys, and of women competing against men.

She also taught them to take responsibility for their actions. One of her warnings was that if one of them ever got a girl pregnant, she, Reba, would take the girl in and turn her son out.

She had a social conscience and a practical view of life rather than a religious faith. Gary describes it as "residual, unformed Christian views from her childhood, little more than you would find in a fortune cookie." She had seen too much religious hypocrisy, people professing but not acting Christianity, to become a devotee.

At the time of the parents' split, Reba was working as a civil servant at the land registry. Before starting work she would take the three boys, with Gary in his push-chair and the two other boys clinging on, to Auntie Val who had two children of her own. School holidays were a big problem. When Reba looked for a job that would allow her to be at home when schools were closed, teaching was the obvious choice. She had taken A-levels in Barbados, thus having the necessary qualifications for teacher training, and she enrolled at the nearest training college, out in the country between Hitchin and Luton.

The boys' routine changed. Just before 8 o'clock each morning the whole family would walk to a nearby bus stop. Reba would catch her bus, then Pat would push Gary in the push-chair (with Wayne holding on to the side) along a quarter of a mile stretch of uninterrupted pavement to the child-minder. Pat and Wayne would then walk to school. Understanding the unsatisfactory nature of this arrangement, but seeing no alternative, Reba was shocked one day to receive a visit from a social worker. An anonymous complaint had been received. With characteristic verve, Reba's response was, "Take them. Boys, go and get your things, you're going with this lady." Bluff called. Unsatisfactory it may have been, but it was the best she could do and better than anything that could be done by anybody else. The situation was eased once Reba started her teaching practices in schools, for those were in Stevenage.

Financial problems persisted. One solution was to take in lodgers. For a time two Irish girls took a room, so that the three boys had to share one bedroom. The house was very cramped, but the boys did not know any different. It was at the height of IRA activities and the girls were often questioned by the police, an early example to the boys of all people from another country being seen as 'the same'.

Working hard to keep her family afloat, whilst living on a training grant and the small amounts received from the boys' father, Reba now took on weekend work. Her old nursing qualifications proved useful as she took the weekend night shift at a psychiatric hospital. On a Friday night, Reba would return from training college or teaching practice, make the tea and then leave for the night shift, locking the boys in the house. At about ten o'clock she would telephone to check that they were all right, had gone to bed and had turned off the light to save on the electricity bill. Returning in the morning, Reba would then sleep for most of Saturday and the same routine would be repeated that night. It only worked at all because the boys had good friends and neighbours, with whom they would play in the gardens during their mother's day-time sleeping. The boys were learning early in life to be resourceful and outgoing.

When Reba had qualified, she was engaged to teach mathematics at Bedwell School, one of the twelve comprehensive schools in the town at that time. There was a clash of cultures but race was not a major component. A few parents wanted their children only to be happy. To Reba, a mostly jolly person, happiness was an outcome of achievement, not a goal in itself. Most parents of her pupils shared Reba's view that education was the way up the social ladder towards greater independence. For those white parents, consciously or unconsciously, it was a matter of class not race. Reba got on well with most of her pupils, who understood that she wanted them to succeed at school even if some of them did not share her enthusiasm.

The boys did, however, encounter occasional racism as well as the friendship of many white people. One family of neighbours, the Norrises, were a nuisance. A National Front election candidate called canvassing one day, not knowing when he knocked on the door that he was about to meet a black family. Reba invited him in and kept him in conversation for more than an hour. She wanted to know from him how much he would pay her to return to Barbados, since funding the 'repatriation' of immigrants was the NF policy at the time. When he told her, she revealed that, of course, her three sons would stay behind as they had been born in Britain. She was also pleased to have "kept the NF man off the streets" for an hour, preventing him from doing more damage.

Gary has described in his book, *No Place Like Home*, the varied responses of white people to the few black people in the town at the time, classifying them as welcomers (Mrs Stilling next door, Alan and Sue three doors away), toleraters (the vast majority) and racists. There was racial prejudice but it was rarely overt and mostly irritating rather then frightening. Gary has also described the terrifying experience of being in an all-black coach party from London that was attacked by skinheads on the Brighton sea-front. By and large, though, the family had only occasional problems in Stevenage.

The boys were brought up to understand their cultural origins as Babadians. The small black community of Stevenage met together socially and through the cricket club. The Younge boys were taught to be proud not only that they were black but that they were Barbadians and had their own cultural heritage. Reba's simple rule was that the boys were British until they entered their house, when they became Barbadians. This surrogate experience of what it was like to be a Barbadian, however, gave the boys no hint of the real thing.

A trip for the entire family to Barbados forced the boys to confront the reality of life in what their mother had taught them was their spiritual homeland. This was not to be just a Christmas break in the Caribbean. Reba had arranged for the boys to attend St Martin's primary school. They did not realise it at the time, but saw later that Reba was testing them to see whether she could leave them in Barbados to be educated.

The first day at school is described now by Pat, then aged nine, as though he is still experiencing it. "We were all lined up. The teacher lifted our hair with a pencil to check that we had combed it. Our fingernails were inspected. If we passed, we went straight to the lesson. If we failed, we got three lashes. The lessons were taught in a large hall, with six classes divided by blackboards. They were always the same, starting with the oath of national (Barbadian) allegiance followed by tables and spellings. If any boy got less than three out of ten, he had to remove his belt so that he could be lashed across the shoulders with it." Gary, who was only just approaching school age, found it terrifying. He recalls the pupils having to sit with their eyes shut, knowing that the teacher at the front was brandishing a cane ready for use. He was so frightened that he ran away almost daily to his mother who was helping out in the school next door. This may well have been the spur for Gary's continuing quest for his roots described in *No Place Like Home*. It was not quite what the boys had expected.

Reba realised that Gary, and probably the other two as well, could not stand the harsh discipline. They were not 'tough' enough and she brought them back to England. The toughness that they were acquiring in England was of a different kind.

A tireless and clear-sighted mother to the three boys, Reba also saw the need to raise the aspirations of black children living in cities and she took a post at what is now known as the Robert Hart Supplementary School, set up by the Caribbean Teachers' Association in Peckham, south London. But the daily travel to London became too burdensome and she finished her life teaching at Heathcote School, another comprehensive school in Stevenage.

She was a large lady who sporadically got some of her school colleagues to join her in weight-watching regimes. Jolly, energetic and thoughtful, she provided a loving, demanding, chaotic and in many ways cultured home for her sons. Although there was a hiccough in Wayne's progress through the system and Gary's secondary education was far from conventional, all three boys did well academically, between them achieving 31 O-levels and 12 A-levels whilst also learning musical instruments, playing rugby, football and cricket, and enjoying life. Sound education in a secure environment (home and school) delivered the goods.

In May 1988 Reba died. There was no warning. It was the bank holiday weekend and none of the boys, all now living away from home, could be contacted easily. Pat was in Wales for the weekend on National Union of Students business followed by a friend's wedding. A friend took the call during the wedding reception and broke it to Pat , who had to contact Wayne in Northern Ireland by telephone before friends drove him, heart-broken, to Stevenage. Wayne caught the first available plane. Gary was at university in Edinburgh, but out for the day. When he returned in the evening, friends told him to see his tutor, who broke the news, and he too was driven by friends to Stevenage.

On his arrival in Stevenage Pat was, in truth, pleased to greet the father of whom he had seen little for some time, but unhappy to see his father's second wife in Reba's home. The boys had different relationships with their father, as determined by their own judgements. Reba had always told them, "He's not a bad man. You must make your own relationship with him. It's for you to decide."

A big memorial service was conducted by the Bishop of Croydon, Wilfred Wood, himself from Barbados. His wife, the daughter of a Barbadian MP, was an old friend of Reba's from their school days. Friends, teaching colleagues, students, neighbours and members of the Stevenage West Indies Sports and Social Club packed the church. The father of the Norrises, the family's old tormentors, was spotted amongst the mourners. The headteacher of the school where Reba had last worked read

Martin Luther King's "I have a dream" speech. Wayne spoke about his mother. Her work was done. Reba's last journey was with her three sons back to Barbados, the warmth of which she had missed so much and where she wanted to be buried.

The three boys met their relatives again, including their grandmother, who was bent and muscular from years of working in the fields but spirited. A shock for Gary was a quarrel with the priest who was to conduct Reba's funeral service. Wearing hair in plaits, as Gary did, was not acceptable in church. It was an example of Caribbean class, for plaits were worn by roughnecks, not respectable Barbadians. Gary was unprepared for the confrontation. There was no point in arguing, since the priest was unbending on the matter, so Gary had to remove his plaits and brush them out, appearing in the photographs with an outrageous Afro head of hair as the price for attending his own mother's funeral.

❖ ❖ ❖ ❖ ❖

Pat, born in 1964 and the eldest of the three boys, had to take responsibility early in life, but did not feel burdened. Sitting in his office at the futuristic Norman Foster Channel 4 Television building, where at the time he was a commissioning editor, he recalls a happy childhood despite the ups and downs. "I had a great time as a kid." Whether naturally gregarious or becoming so as a result of circumstances, he enjoyed a full social life from his earliest memories. There were always other families or friends around.

"I was leaner then and sport was a major part of my life", he recalls. He was good at it. At the age of seven he joined the Gonville Rovers, a Stevenage boys' team renowned for losing all their matches. Their most memorable defeat was by ten goals to one, but it was Pat who scored the one. With his two great footballing friends, Colin Hull and Jimmy Gilligan, he then joined

Longmeadow Athletic. The two other boys, both white, were outstanding footballers for their age and later joined Watford as schoolboys. Their parents were a great help to Pat, always taking him in their cars to matches, realising how tight money was in the Younge household. Another great friend was Roger Frith and the two boys often camped together in Roger's garden. Roger and another friend, Jean Terry, were a bit older than Pat and in effect 'baby-sat' him, without cost to his mother, by playing with him.

Pat went to Nobel School, next to the school where Reba was teaching so that she could keep an eye on his progress. Pat was well prepared. When aged 11 or 12 and only himself in his early years at secondary school, he and Wayne helped their mother on Sunday evenings to mark the work of her pupils who were much older than they were.

His teenage memories bring pleasure. "I had a great time at school and at sport." At school he played for most teams, particularly rugby and cricket. There were only two other black boys in his year and not many more in the whole school. The three of them were good at sports and often played together in the same teams. They attracted the name 'the three degrees'. "We liked that", Pat says. He was well regarded by other pupils because he was good both academically and at sport. One pupil did try to pick quarrels, to which Pat responded despite his mother's advice to keep away from trouble. They had three fights that Pat won. As Pat now says, "All three of us are pretty good at looking after ourselves in that way."

When he was 13, Pat joined the Stevenage West Indies Sports and Social Club to play cricket and it was there that he met his father again, for Patrick senior also played cricket. It was not easy for the young Pat, for his father had taken up with a woman who would appear outside the court, when Reba was making another appearance to try to get reasonable maintenance for the three boys, and abuse her in the street. Reba was well known in the town and a woman of some standing. The public ranting of this woman was hurtful.

Like most teenagers, Pat went through crazes. Soon after the death of Elvis Presley, he donned the gear and got heavily into rock and roll, being dubbed by his friends "the only black Teddy boy in Hertfordshire." The only problem was that, instead or crepes or blue suedes, he had to bop away in the sensible polyveldt shoes which his mother had bought for their durability.

His greatest ambition as a teenager was to become a professional footballer. At the age of 14 he was invited to train at Watford, joining his two friends who had been signed as schoolboy players. After six months he was turned down and was devastated by the rejection. His dream shattered, he did not give in but immediately wrote off to other clubs. A trial at Colchester brought further disappointment. He was then invited to Luton for a trial. His hopes rose when a man from the Luton club called at the house with papers for him to sign, only to be dashed when Reba refused to countersign. Pat had prepared Reba, or so he thought, by telling her about a Manchester United player, Steve Coppell, and Liverpool winger, Steve Heighway, who had degrees, but this argument now rebounded on Pat as Reba said that he could get his degree first and become a footballer later. On the threshold of realising his dream, Pat was now even more devastated than earlier. The "reign of Reba" was sometimes harsh and not easily understood by teenage boys.

Another sporting disappointment had to be endured. From the age of 14, as the first team wicket-keeper for Stevenage Cricket Club, Pat went for trials three times with the Hertfordshire Schools cricket team. Each time he failed, even though he was the only first team wicket-keeper being considered. Racial prejudice crossed his mind, but he realised that there was another kind of prejudice - class. Although called the Hertfordshire Schools team, there was only one boy in the team who was not from a public school. British Aerospace was the biggest employer in Stevenage at the time, with a sports ground not far from the

Younges' home. It showed no prejudice of race, class or age. Despite Pat's having no connection at all with the company, he was a regular member of their rugby first XV.

In Pat's own estimation and that of his teachers, nine O-levels was a good outcome for his five years of study. Not good enough for Reba. Gary remembers sitting with his mother and Wayne at the foot of the stairs, waiting for the news. When Pat telephoned her from school with what he thought was good news, Reba went mad at his failure in one subject.

The teacher of German, his failed subject, was Angus McEwan, an eccentric Scot noted for his captivating school assemblies, such as the one he gave for Burns's birthday dressed in a kilt. Another of his assemblies had a profound effect on Pat. McEwan had been at the weekend to Cardiff Arms Park to see Wales play rugby, which gave him the material for an electrifying assembly with a strong message. The Welsh singing that reverberated around the stands had overwhelmed him, and the lesson of the assembly was that in sport everybody should "support the country where the sport is the game of the masses, the game of the working people." Coming from a Scot, this was a powerful message. Pat was hooked.

After A-levels, Pat planned to go to Loughborough University, then as now a leader in sport and physical education. Reba was alarmed. Pat might finish up as a PE teacher, not at all her hope for him. His thoughts then turned first to geography and in the end to mining geology. Much more to Reba's liking. The prospect of a good job. He was offered places at three universities, one of which was the University of Wales at Cardiff. Rugby decided it, and he went to Cardiff in 1982.

The Mineral Exploitation department was an uneasy mixture of public school boys, who wanted to go to South Africa and Australia to manage mines, and the sons of Welsh miners who wanted their boys, all valley lads, to become managers of Welsh pits rather than have to spend their lives underground in hard labour. Aspiration was common to both groups. The entire college was male dominated, but particularly so in Pat's department, with freshmen who paid their £5 membership fee being welcomed with beer, sandwiches and a porn film.

Two criticisms were made about his academic work during his early years, one of which he rejected and the other he accepted. In his first year he was given a warning by his head of department to restrict himself to geology when writing essays - rather difficult when the subject was low productivity in South African mines. Pat had covered the necessary technical aspect, that seams were narrow in South African mines, but had then gone on to tackle the economic factor, explaining that there was no need for high productivity when there was plenty of cheap labour under the apartheid system. A comment too far for a tutor in the 1980s.

In his second year he ate humble pie and was rewarded with understanding and wise counsel. Rugby was played on Wednesday afternoons and followed by heavy drinking sessions, with 9 o'clock lectures the following morning. Pat attended very few of these lectures. He received a written warning, went to see his tutor and confessed. The tutor explained in a fatherly way, "The thing about mining geologists, Pat, is that, however much they drink the night before, they are always up and ready for work on time the next day." The point was taken.

Pat's was a prolonged undergraduateship, lasting from 1982 until 1987, all for the one degree, for he had two sabbatical years of office in the students' union. Those were the days. 1984-5 was Pat's first sabbatical year, the reward for being elected President of the Athletics Union.

But he continued to upset his tutors, this time by making a speech, supporting sanctions and boycotts against apartheid South Africa, that was unwelcome to a department with close South African links. "It was a great year", as he recalls. The Athletics Union hosted the Australian rugby team, including

Michael Lynagh and Nick Farr-Jones, who went on to play for the Wallabies. Pat's office gave him a seat on the university Senate, where he learned much about how things are done. This was also the year of the miners' strike and the battle of wills between Arthur Scargill and Margaret Thatcher, an event of particular significance to a mining department in south Wales.

The following year Pat was elected as the first black President of the Students' Union, standing as an independent Labour candidate. It was a politicising year, with a rent strike and a catering boycott in protest against increased charges. But there was an even bigger political battle going on, for the independence of the college itself, and Pat and the Students' Union knew clearly where they stood on that question. The Principal of Pat's college had so mismanaged the finances that the government threatened to withhold grants unless it did as it was told to resolve the problem. The contest hit the national headlines over several months. The Students' Union, led by Pat, was much involved in campaigning to save the college, but the dice were heavily stacked against them and in the end they lost when their college, though theoretically amalgamated with the other college of the University of Wales in Cardiff, was actually taken over by it. But Pat's experience of management, politics, campaigning and negotiation was vastly greater at the end of it all.

He also found time to keep up his sporting activities, and for two years was selected to keep wicket for the Welsh Universities. In 1986 he was selected to play for the British Universities team against Essex CCC second XI. His side lost, but he nabbed four victims including one N Hussein, who went on to captain the England team.

In his final year at Cardiff he needed to concentrate on getting a degree, but not exclusively so. Success in elections for the National Union of Students as Vice President, Education got him on to the national executive and took him to the heart of student politics, and he also became active in the Black Students Alliance, trying to get the NUS to take race questions seriously. He got a degree, not one that would necessarily bring joy to the demanding Reba, but good enough. He reckons that he was lucky to do so, believing now that, once the examiner at his *viva* was convinced that Pat would never go down a mine, he visibly relaxed and let him through. It was not yet time to start a job.

Being the NUS's Education Officer and on its national executive for the two years after leaving Cardiff was a job of sorts. He had an office, paid staff and full-time work, but not a wage. NUS executive members at that time were given full maintenance grants. Those were indeed the days. Fellow NUS executive members of that period included Phil Woolas, Stephen Twigg and Lorna Fitzsimons – who all became Labour MPs in 1997. Several others became advisers (paid civil servants) to Labour ministers.

These were in effect two more sabbatical years, making four in all, when Pat had lived on a student grant to carry out student activities rather than study for a qualification. When some NUS members now approached him to stand for the presidency, he decided that a fifth year could not be countenanced. He had become a student in 1982 and it was now 1989. Time to work, but as what?

Having done some writing whilst at university, Pat applied for the BBC fast track training scheme to be a reporter but failed because he had no experience of writing concisely at speed to a deadline. Instead, he went to Ealing Borough Council as a paid adviser to the Chair of the Education Committee, Hilary Benn, Tony's son. Although this was 1989 and both Harold Wilson and Margaret Thatcher had appointed many such policy advisers as civil servants, Ealing was breaking new ground in doing so in local government. Pat's role at Ealing was to progress chase the decisions of the Education Committee and its Chair through the council corridors.

In the 1990 local elections Labour made big gains everywhere. Pat was himself a candidate in North Kensington and was elected, becoming Deputy Leader of the opposition Labour Group. But there was one place that went against the tide: Ealing. All eyes were on the London borough, not only because it had regularly hit the national headlines in recent months (radical policies and Tony Benn's son were sufficient to guarantee that) but it was also the place where Neil Kinnock, leader of the Labour Party, lived.

It was a curious situation. There were complex racist elements in the contest. The council's decision to give planning permission for a mosque attracted political attacks. On the other hand, there was agreement between the parties on a new religious education syllabus, condemned by others for not giving a unique place to Christianity, but defended in the courts by the Conservative group that came to power after the election.

The appointment of the large number of advisers, some of whom were what would now be called language support teachers and entirely uncontroversial, was the nub of the matter. The Conservatives were pledged to their abolition and acted swiftly once they had a mandate. For Pat this was financial disaster. On the basis of his salary he had taken out a huge mortgage. The day after the election, Hilary Benn telephoned Pat with his apologies, realising that unemployment was his fate. There was a brief, tactical stay of execution in the form of a transfer to a menial post in the homeless persons' unit, which involved telephoning hotels and hostels each day to confirm the number of residents overnight. But it was only a stay and perhaps even intended as a humiliation. At its first meeting the new council axed seventy-eight jobs. In the view of *The Times* the cuts were made to cancel "the interests of homosexuals, lesbians, blacks and women… as part of a return to Victorian thrift." *The Sunday Times* ran a story under the headline, "Red Flag comes down in Ealing's Kremlin."

Pat was also caught up in the hostile press that all things Benn attracted at the time. Days after the election Tony Benn helped Hilary pack up all of his papers into boxes. Hilary's mother, Caroline, collected the boxes the following day and Pat helped her to load the car. *The Daily Mail* ran a story about Labour's secret papers being whisked away. A further lesson in the wily ways of the press was coupled with the abrupt termination of his first paid job and a financial problem with his mortgage. A career crisis.

The life of a freelance writer was Pat's answer, hazardous enough as a route for established, professional journalists but doubly so for one with only a student's experience of writing. His pieces were published in *The Voice*, and occasionally in *The Times* and *The Guardian*, while he worked part-time running *The Black Parliamentarian* magazine for Labour MP, Bernie Grant.

Grant, the MP for Tottenham, invited him on a visit to Nigeria, for which his two trips to Barbados did not prepare him in any way. "I had never seen so many black faces before." The politics of the trip were fascinating at the time and appalling in retrospect, for he met Chief Abiola, the chairman of a newspaper group who was demanding compensation from ex-colonial countries, similar to that being awarded to Jews by Austria and Germany for the holocaust. Abiola was later elected President of Nigeria, deposed in a military coup and died in custody.

On his return from Nigeria in 1990, Pat was urged by Trevor Phillips to apply for work with London Weekend Television. Phillips had been elected NUS President in the late 1970's and was by this time editor of LWT's *London Programme*. Pat got the job.

His first big task was on a programme, *Return to Brixton*, to assess progress since the Scarman Report on its tenth anniversary. Pat persuaded Lord Scarman to go there to meet the young black people and businessmen. The former were bowled over by Scarman's being able to say that he had been at college with a young man called Ras Tafari who went on to govern Ethiopia as Haile Selassie, whilst the presence of the businessmen indicated the achievement of one of Scarman's objectives, the creation of a black middle class.

The LWT experience was invaluable training in television research, journalism and production. Pat had triumphs, including the journalistic coup of interviewing two Jamaicans on death row. A two-year contract as a community affairs correspondent in the south-east for the BBC followed and included covering the death of Joy Gardner during an attempt to arrest and expel her from Britain. During this time Pat met and married Jill, a regional political correspondent for the BBC. In October 1995 they had their first child, Rebecca .

Pat stayed with the BBC until 1999, moving first to BBC2 where he created and produced the award winning *Black Britain* series that was aimed at a mainstream audience. With that experience in 1997, he moved to BBC1 in the same role for *Here and Now*. This was the big break. *Here and Now* was a live, prime time programme that required him to manage thirty staff and control a production budget of £120,000 an hour. It was professionally a very good experience for Pat, but there were problems. The new job required Pat and Jill to move to Manchester where their second child, Alexander, was born. They planned to settle in the area, which was much closer to Jill's parents in Newcastle. But on maternity leave Jill found insufferable the material ambitions of most of the other young women with whom she was perforce spending much of her time. Also unable to secure a suitable BBC job in Manchester at the end of her maternity leave, Jill returned to London with the children to resume her career. Pat followed a month later.

Back in London, Pat was appointed an executive producer with BBC Current Affairs and Jill restarted her career part-time. Pat's most important work was to produce the Charles Wheeler programme, *Why Stephen?*, on the murder of Stephen Lawrence, which won a Royal Television Society award. The problem was that current affairs generally were being squeezed out in the BBC's bid to maintain ratings. There was no clear plan, no obvious way forward for a career in current affairs.

Pat had previously been approached by Channel 4, but had not immediately responded. Now he did, and was appointed initially Deputy Commissioning Editor and then the Commissioning Editor for multicultural programmes. This put him in joint control of a budget of £4 million.

The new post suited his domestic requirements much better than being 'on the road' or under the daily pressure of producing programmes. It gave him much scope for thinking, imagining, and exercising judgement, and he could usually return to the family home in Ealing to be with the children before bedtime. It also gave Jill more scope for her own career. In the autumn of 2001 he returned to the BBC and to his first love of sport, when he was appointed Head of Programmes and Planning at BBC Sport.

❖ ❖ ❖ ❖ ❖

Wayne, born in 1965 and the middle of the three brothers, has had the least orthodox career, directed in its early stages more by chance and mischance than by ambition and planning. He followed his elder brother through primary school to Nobel School. All went well until the Sixth Form, then everything went wrong. Then, choosing sciences for A-levels because of the assumed better career prospects, he abandoned the modern languages and English literature in which he had had greater success. Embarked on the wrong course, he failed to get the highest grades but recovered by retaking his subjects at the local further education college, achieving well enough to begin a modular science degree course at the University of Ulster, Coleraine.

The mistake over A-levels was not so easily shrugged off, for after two years Wayne was clear that the course was not the right one for him. As a modular course, it was not sufficiently profound to engage him and he dropped out. Coleraine was now his home. It was where he had a flat and the company of friends, played rugby and could fish. Aged 21 and unemployed in the province with the highest unemployment in Europe, he survived on state benefit and his own resources. Jobs were not sought in Ulster at that time, they were allocated. Wayne's disadvantage was not his blackness but his lack of Protestant credentials. He was outside the tribe. It was better to stay in Coleraine, with university friends who were apart from the sectarianism that pervaded Northern Ireland, than move to Belfast. Odd jobs and seasonal work, mainly a job with a lumber company where his strong physique was of use, saw him through, but by the end of 1987, aged 22, he faced the fact that he was going nowhere.

This time his return to the job centre was more productive, for the woman there took some trouble to advise him on how to re-assess his career. It was she who suggested that, with his science background, training in radiography might be the answer. It would use his science, engage his mind and give him a qualification. Wayne had little idea of what it would entail, but it was the best offer he had had to date.

So it was that he applied for a three-year paid training at Belvoir Park Hospital in Belfast and began three good years. Older than most of the other trainees and with an ability to apply himself to study, he did not find the course intellectually very demanding, but the work was rewarding. It had purpose. He and his colleagues were doing good. Patients and colleagues were pleasant people. His social life remained at Coleraine, to which he returned most weekends. At the end he had a diploma and was qualified to practise clinically anywhere in the UK.

The one drawback was that there were no vacancies in Northern Ireland, but the south came to the rescue in an extraordinary way. Wayne telephoned St Luke's, a Dublin hospital, to enquire about vacancies. "When can you start?" "Monday." "Leave it 'til Tuesday to give us time to sort out the paperwork." Sorting out the paperwork was never done. There was no application, no interview, no references – and no contract. But there was valuable work to be done and an income. And there was Fiona, another radiographer, who had worked in Australia and Canada before returning to her native Eire.

St Luke's was good for its patients but financially chaotic. It had become reliant on radiographers doing much overtime, paying them £26 a patient for all work after 5.30 pm, an arrangement very welcome to young radiographers trying to make ends meet. At the same time as the hospital came prematurely to the end of its entire budget for the year, the only other radiotherapy unit in Eire, at Cork, broke down and St Luke's had to meet the needs of both sets of patients. As is usual in organisations providing essential services, when the government does not have the money or is unwilling to spend the money, the management's problem was transferred to the staff. In a spectacular mishandling of the crisis, the authorities announced that all overtime payments were postponed until the authority could afford to pay them. They expected the needs of the increased number of patients to be met by staff working however many hours were necessary. The dilemma for the staff was acute. Led by Wayne and others, a few tried to negotiate with the management, but the local staff, who had contracts, were mostly compliant. The locums, such as Pat and Fiona, did not have contracts, a weak basis for any negotiation, and the management had its way. It was time to go. Wayne and Fiona left for England and Wayne's former family home in Stevenage.

The move was a good one, for both Wayne and Fiona obtained senior radiographer posts at London teaching hospitals, Wayne at Charing Cross and Fiona at Barts. Still paying the price for that A-level mistake by having to climb the academic ladder the hard way, he returned from London at midday once a week and studied in the afternoon and evening for his MSc. In his second year he was appointed to lecture in radiography at the City University. During his final year of his studies for the MSc he also did a part-time teachers' training course at his local college of further education. For one year his week embraced a full-time lecturing post at the City, a part-time higher degree course at Hatfield and a part-time teachers' training course in Hitchin. It was during these years of combined work and study that Wayne and Fiona's two children, Eleanor and Louis were born.

Wayne's final dissertation for his master's degree was on the work that he had done as a clinical radiographer to prepare patients and their families for their treatment, by enabling them to see that it was not invasive or painful. His work on this led to the presentation of papers at academic conferences in Ireland, Scotland and finally to the conference of the International Society of Radiographers at Lisbon.

An important part of Wayne's recent work has been his chairing of the minority ethnic section of his professional society. His brief experience of union work in Dublin has been helpful in this. The aim is to ensure that radiographers from ethnic minorities make proper progress in their careers. In London, black and Asian trainee radiographers are probably over-represented, despite many Asian families not regarding the work as having a sufficiently high status. But there is still a need to monitor progress in careers. Initial evidence suggests that this may be a career where fairness and equality are being achieved. It can only help to have a black lecturer, particularly one who had Reba's guidance when young and who still expects male applicants for the course to turn up in a jacket and wearing a tie.

❖ ❖ ❖ ❖ ❖

Gary, the youngest of the Younge brothers, was born in 1969 and lives with his American wife Tara Mack, herself a journalist, in Hackney. He is a regular columnist in *The Guardian*, covering a wide range of topics, travelling the world, and altogether jollier than he looks in the scowling picture that heads his column. He laughs frequently.

Thanks to a wise psychologist he started school early. Returning from the family trip to Barbados over Christmas when he was four, he developed such bad eczema on his head that it bled. The diagnosis was that he was bored and needed to start school. Despite some mutterings about preferential treatment from the mother of a white child with a similar birthday, he was admitted early. When the time came for secondary school, Reba was beginning to relax and no longer felt the need to be at the school next door so that she could keep an eye on him, so Gary went to Heathcote School, another comprehensive but closer to home.

He was an ardent student who had an unconventional schooling. He started going to evening classes in French at the local further education college and took his O-level when he was 14, doing A-level at 16. The further education attitude of his lecturer, Pierre, would not have worked with most students, but for Gary is was liberating. "Anything you do, I will mark. Anything you don't do, I don't care about." He did A-level German at a neighbouring school, and only English and economics at his own school. Even the economics tuition played to his strength, for the teacher was in school only once a week, going over difficult topics, checking on progress and setting work for the next lesson. Gary sought and found opportunities for independent learning, which suited him at an age when most would not have coped.

Underpinning his attitude to study was a single-minded determination. "I had to get to university. It was a massive task that just had to be undertaken." It was Gary's response to Reba's teaching. "It was your destiny, so you just did it," is how Gary now remembers it. One of Reba's homespun but profound dicta put it like this, "You can lose your house, your money and your wife, but nobody can take away your education." With that drive, the distracting influence of friends was not a problem. The Younge boys were so different from their friends in all other ways that being different from most of them in this regard did not seem unusual. They had learned to swim against the tide

Gary was good at other things. He played football for the district, and the tuba well enough to be in the county wind band. His political virginity was lost as a result of his flirtation, "between his first kiss and A-levels", as he recalls, with so-called Trotskyites. It was 1984, the year that saw the miners' strike and the IRA Brighton bomb at the Conservative Party conference. As a "self-important teenage vegetarian", his self-description, and having spent a day demonstrating against a visit to Britain of P W Botha, the South African President, Gary got caught up with groups of the sectarian left – "57 varieties of hard-left parties, some with less than 57 members", as he described them. Their paranoia and their fantasising that they could bring down capitalism were proof enough to Gary that there had to be more effective ways than theirs of achieving a better world. But their greatest weakness was the challenge that they posed to Reba's rules. Party discipline was harsh. When Gary was not allowed to leave a meeting in time to meet Reba's deadline to be home, Gary knew where true power lay and left the party.

Before university he spent a gap year teaching in a Sudan refugee school, a rewarding and politicising experience. University was Heriott-Watt in Edinburgh. The choice was not difficult. Reba's emphasis on education was, Gary says, "not part of a higher cause". It was about employability. She would have preferred science, more obviously vocational than modern languages, but Gary benefited from the parental relaxation available to younger siblings, which was beginning to affect even Reba. The merit of a vocational course was now ingrained in

Gary's own thinking, so he began his training as a modern languages interpreter.

It was a demanding course with good tutors, but too narrowly focused for a young man with widening horizons. Gary was aware of the broadening experience that his friends on other courses were enjoying. Thoughts were germinating about a move to another university when Reba died, and it seemed easier to stay put. So he broadened his own horizons at Heriott-Watt by becoming even more involved in student politics generally and the Anti-Apartheid movement in particular. In his third year he was given a sabbatical, having been elected as Vice-President of the Students' Union with responsibility for student welfare.

He had also been elected as Communications Officer of the National Organisation of Labour Students, a group operating mainly within the National Union of Students. This was a depressing experience that taught him as much about the evils of sectarian in-fighting as had his teenage dabbling. The executive of NOLS was quite small, about six in number, and he was the candidate of what was called the hard left. The others were all denizens of what was to become known as New Labour – people like Stephen Twigg and Lorna Fitzsimons, in successive years presidents of the NUS, and loyalist New Labour almost before it was invented. They both became MPs in 1997, Twigg as the young man who kept viewers up late watching the election results when he unseated Michael Portillo.

Their hostility to Gary, the sole representative of the left and therefore an intrusion, was unbounded. By far the worst was Derek Draper, who did not become an MP, but for a time was far more influential as a lobbyist with access to New Labour ministers. Tricks were played, like inviting Gary to meetings in London that were either non-existent or were cancelled without telling him, so that he had wasted journeys from Edinburgh. Sometimes they would change the venue and not let him know. As he wrote in 1998, when Derek Draper fell from New Labour grace, "Their rosettes said Labour, but theirs was the politics of ambition." Fed up with such malign silliness, Gary eventually made an issue of it, getting the Black Section and his brother Pat involved.

His work on student welfare in Edinburgh was challenging. The students were generally very right wing in their political outlook and refused twice to affiliate to the National Union of Students. Persistence brought its reward at Gary's third attempt. Gary also succeeded in keeping student rents down, again not initially when the rent strike that he led failed, but the authorities took the point when fixing rents the following year.

A year abroad was, of course, part of the modern languages course. Gary's languages were French and Russian, giving him six months each in Paris and Leningrad, as it then was. Paris was not to his taste. He met much arrogance and racism, and the police were particularly hostile to anybody not obviously of French blood, on one occasion beating him up and thereby adding to his growing conviction that journalism to expose iniquities could be the basis of a worthwhile career.

Paris became tolerable when he met a French journalist in a very odd way. Desperate to find accommodation, he started to leave cards in the most unlikely of places, including the English church. One of these was picked up by an old Etonian who considered that God had spoken to him and that he had to answer His call and find Gary accommodation. The result was a room in the flat of a journalist working for Radio France who had got her job partly through a lie. She needed rapidly to acquire the proficiency in English that she had claimed at interview. So Gary had free accommodation in return for daily English lessons. He never rated her English very highly, despite his tuition, but he learned much because she came to the lessons in the evening having covered events in eastern Europe, on one occasion having just interviewed Mikhail Gorbachev. He spent most of his other time seeing films, usually one a day, sometimes two.

Leningrad was, by contrast, wonderful. He lived with a family, friends of his Heriott-Watt tutor, Ilena Crosbie, and attended lectures at the Leningrad Philological Institute. This was during Gorbachev's reforms, heady times for Russia, with the coup that toppled him occurring soon after Gary's return to Edinburgh. After his initial dissatisfaction, Gary reckoned by the end of his time at Heriott-Watt that he had "had a ball."

Although he had a degree that qualified him to interpret French and German, he did not consider himself committed to such a career. Teaching abroad was something that he considered. Going into the corporate business world was something that he ruled out. He had done occasional pieces of journalism whilst at Heriott-Watt, for example on the students' rent strike, at the suggestion of Don Macleod, at that time at *The Scotsman*, now at *The Guardian*. What is more, he had been paid for something that he had enjoyed doing.

He now spotted two bursaries, one offered by *The Guardian* and the other by *The Independent*. He applied for both. Silence from *The Independent*. As *The Guardian*'s advertisement included an equal opportunities undertaking, there was more hope and Gary succeeded when interviewed by a panel that included the present Editor, Alan Rusbridger. The bursary paid minimum living expenses and the fees for the one-year newspaper journalism course at City University – a year providing a coveted qualification although not a very good course, in Gary's view, for it took nine months to cover what could have been covered in three. That qualification, with his French and Russian, certainly got Gary his first job, working at the lowest level on *The World This Week*, the Yorkshire TV international affairs programme, presented by Sheena MacDonald. This led to three months as an 'intern' and shifts as a translator of foreign newspaper items for the *Guardian European*.

The big break came in 1994 with the first post-apartheid

election in South Africa. By this time Alan Rusbridger had reached the post of Deputy Editor at *The Guardian.* He had sent Gary, as an educated black Briton, to live in the townships near Johannesburg for two weeks where by chance he had met Nelson Mandela. Gary became an obvious choice to join the newspaper's team going out to cover the election that would see Mandela elected as the first black President. His piece on the making of the President, headlined 'The Black Knight', effectively got him a staff job at *The Guardian*, with the grand title of Assistant Foreign Editor, although he says that in reality he was a news editor and the most junior of the four staff

The piece itself had the qualities that were to become apparent in all of Gary's writing – carefully based on the evidence, honest (as scathing about warm-ups to Mandela's rallies as he would later be about those in British elections), revealing (for example about Mandela's royal lineage, going back five centuries), candid (noting that Mandela is not a great orator), but most of all giving the reader an understanding of the election that could be got nowhere else.

1996 was one of those years in people's lives that become turning points. Success in winning a Lawrence Stern Fellowship gave him a five-month secondment to the prestigious *Washington Post*, putting him in touch with American politics at its epicentre and with Tara Mack, a young Afro-American from Chicago on work experience.

A rather unhappy time on his return to *The Guardian* in London was short-lived, for the quality of his writing catapulted him on to the next stage in his career. When a piece called 'Black Bloke' that he had written for the *Washington Post* was reprinted in *The Guardian*, he was approached by several publishers. His experience of being black and British in America led to the idea of testing the state of black-white relations in the American South, after years of campaigning for equality. Gary would go amongst people, attending services for example in white churches, where worshippers would assume that he was an American black. In this way he might understand what it felt like to be black in the deep South, and see the reaction when people realised from his accent that he was not local and therefore not part of the established ethnic relationships. He would be able to compare the relationship of black and white people in America and Britain.

It was also about routes and roots. He would follow the journey, for example, taken by black Freedom Riders in 1961 to challenge the segregation imposed at that time in some southern states contrary to a Supreme Court judgement that travellers between states should experience no segregation at stopping points. At a deeper, personal level, it was also about Gary's own racial identity. His mother Reba had brought up her sons to feel Barbadian, yet even by their thirties they had visited the island only twice, neither visit having happy connotations. She had also instilled a sort of anti-Englishness that, wittingly or not, led to their going to universities in Wales, Northern Ireland and Scotland, but not England. As a boy Gary had reacted by identifying with black Americans, or rather the glamorous musicians, sports stars and politicians who were unrepresentative of the whole. Perhaps he would discover something about himself in this quest. He would certainly be able to see Tara again.

Finding himself in demand by several publishers, he accepted Picador's offer of an advance that would finance the trip. Alan Rusbridger, by now the Editor of *The Guardian*, agreed to six months unpaid leave. The result was *No Place Like Home*, the vivid account of his experience, which gave him a new confidence and the strength to confront indignities, such as those of passport control at Heathrow Airport, unknown to those of us who like him were born in Britain but with white faces.

With the book published, Gary was offered a staff post as a features writer on *The Guardian*, which also serialised the book.

In 1999 he became a columnist for the paper, with his opinions appearing regularly. Frequently he contributes pieces that are topical, for example on the travails of the London Underground, or part of wider series, such as his item about the Finnish prison system. His recurrent personal themes are about politics, America and race.

All of his writing is lucid and compelling. It is often passionate, for example when rejecting any notion that black people win gold medals at the Olympics because they have racially-based different physiques. Sometimes it is iconoclastic, as when he defends Ralph Nader's candidacy in the 2000 US presidential election against the argument that, but for his splitting the Democratic vote, Gore would have won and the world would be a better place. It is never self-indulgent. The argument is logical and the evidence solid. Unlike some of his fellow-columnists, he does not rant nor does he achieve the necessary wordage by telling us about his responses to the ephemera of his week. He engages and entertains the reader by the use of his intellect, respecting theirs.

❖ ❖ ❖ ❖ ❖

'Lifting as we climb' was the title of the 14th annual Martin Luther King Memorial Lecture, which was given in London in January 2001 by Gary Younge. Pat and Wayne were in the audience, welcomed by Bishop Sir Wilfred Wood, providing a link to their mother, Reba, at whose own memorial service he had officiated. The lives of the Younge brothers exemplify the lecture's message.

In his lecture, Gary analyses the role of minorities who join the establishment. It is, of course, about race, but could equally be about gender or class. Taking Colin Powell as an example, he notes that the ex-general's rise through the army was possible only because of action by the head of the Brotherhood of Sleeping Car Porters to achieve desegregation in the army in

1948. Without that, Powell's undoubted ability would not have got him anywhere in the army, as it would not have got him anywhere in other fields where segregation and prejudice continued to flourish. The question therefore now to be asked is what will Powell, as a member of the most ethnically diverse administration in American history (more so than would have been the case if Gore had won) do about the promotion of civil and trade union rights? Having himself benefited from the fruits of earlier campaigners for such rights, what will he do to lift up others? What will others (women, working class or black), who are where they are because of what others before them have done in the cause of equality, themselves do to advance that cause?

"True, King wanted a seat at the table. But he wanted to see the menu. Having led the battle to ensure that black people could eat in a restaurant of their choice, he knew that this important victory would remain academic if they didn't have the money to pay for the meal. His targets were moving from race to class, which is how it came to be that he was killed while in Memphis supporting a strike by dustmen over pay, conditions and union recognition."

If Reba were still alive her stout heart would be swelling. As it is, all we can say – but say it with certainty – is that she would have been proud of her three boys, their achievements and their values.

WILLARD WHITE

Willard White is a big man with a big voice. In conversation the voice is both soft and commanding. It is low, warm and resonant, coming as much from the diaphragm when speaking face-to-face as it does when at full volume accompanied by an orchestra in the opera house. At lunch in a Westminster restaurant, dressed casually and comfortably, having removed his fedora, it is he who is at ease, making the rest of the lunchtime clientele - politicians and businessmen - seem ordinary.

In an odd combination of openness, that can sometimes startle, and occasional reserve, which betokens past uncomfortable experiences with strangers, he talks about his approaches to singing, the art that now defines his life, and his personal philosophy. If you did not realise that his initial wariness of strangers comes from his experience of life, you might think on first meeting him that he had come direct from an assertiveness class. The guardedness is gradually relaxed as his confidence in you grows. This is a mature man, who is conscious of his past, happy to be doing what he knows he does well, and confident to take whatever the future brings.

Seeing no particular pattern in his career and denying equally both careful planning on his part and the role of mere chance, he has taken what has come his way. Currently, his singing is diversifying and, in this regard, there is a conscious element. Although classically trained and having spent most of his career singing the traditional repertoire in opera houses and concert halls - still the bulk of his work - his recent and forthcoming performances cover a very broad range. An admiration for Paul Robeson and an affinity with much of his outlook have led White to create a tribute programme. Branching out into jazz is another strand of his current work, this time with the saxophonist, John Harle. They have now done several concerts together, with special arrangements of some well-known songs such as 'I get a kick out of you' and Duke Ellington's 'Mood Indigo' and a suite of pieces from *Porgy and Bess.*

Operatic and other classical singing remain, nonetheless, the basis of White's singing, but here too he is an innovator. He has recently been the creator of two roles in new operatic works. *Le Grand Macabre*, in a revision by the composer Ligeti, was first heard in Salzburg in 1997, then recorded and repeated in Paris in 1998. It was to have been part of the re-opening season at Covent Garden after the reconstruction but was sacrificed when problems with new stage machinery caused several disastrous and delayed performances of staple operatic fare and more rehearsal time was needed for the machinery. At the end of 2000 White created the roles of Joseph and others in *El Niño*, a new slant on the nativity story written by John Adams, already celebrated for his *Nixon in China*. This was at Le Chatelet Theatre in Paris, followed by performances in Salzburg, with more to follow at the Barbican in London (in 2003) and in Berlin.

White's 2001 programme was typical of his recent work: *Turandot*, *Parsifal* and *Bluebeard's Castle* at Covent Garden, a new *War and Peace* for the English National Opera, the company that brought him to Britain, and *Rigoletto* in Paris. His summer was spent in Provence, at the Aix-en-Provence Festival, where he sang his first *Falstaff*, and at the conveniently close Orange Festival, singing *Don Carlos*, as part of his big Verdi programme to mark the centenary of the great Italian composer's death.

❖ ❖ ❖ ❖ ❖

Singing came naturally to White as a child and gave him a sense of power when he most needed it. Born in Jamaica in 1946, just a year after the end of the war in which Jamaicans had fought for the British Empire, he was only a young boy when his parents separated. Gertrude, his mother, was illiterate, which initially embarrassed him, although he came to understand it. She was loving in a way that did not need to be declared. They had a good relationship. Many years later when her son returned to Jamaica as the celebrated singer, she did not wish to dress up and go to see him perform. She never heard him sing in opera. At the age of five he was separated from her when he was sent to school in Kingston, the capital, where his father, Egbert, worked. He lived there with his father, resenting the new woman with whom his father lived and whom he had to regard as his stepmother.

White's recall of the moment when he first realised his gift is still vivid. As often happened, he and his stepmother were at odds. "She was causing me pain", as he puts it. He resented her displacement of his true mother, although he also felt that she was hostile to him. Maybe she was struggling like many parents with a child going through a difficult period. Certainly, White longed for his real mother. After one collision, the young White took himself to the bottom of the garden to get away from her and to dwell on his pain. He began to sing. It became an answer to the misery that he was feeling, not for its impact on others, but for its use to himself. Believing, in his childhood way, that the perpetrator of his pain was feeling no pain herself, he began to sing more loudly. How could he change the relationship? How could he keep his end up? The timbre and tempo as well as the volume of his singing began to change. His confidence was growing. He went back up the garden to his stepmother, singing very loudly, not looking at her for that would have seemed insolent, but proclaiming his confidence. She was no longer hurting him.

Most people can think of small events when they saw that they could change things and take greater control of their lives. It is an aspect of growing up, of gaining confidence. For White this one event was bigger than all the others. It was a turning point. He glimpsed the possibility of becoming confident and independent through singing. Abandoned was his own ambition to become an economist and his father's that he should become a dentist. Singing was now to be the career. As for his stepmother, she was from now on regularly subjected to his loud rendering of Nat King Cole's, 'Smile though your heart is breaking.'

In the halls of Excelsior High School in Kingston, White's voice could now be heard with increasing regularity. It always commanded attention. He dabbled with Elvis Presley songs and those of various crooners. The school turned him towards the classical repertoire. He and the other pupils were, he says, "force fed the classics". It was during a lesson, when he was singing very loudly behind another boy, that a teacher noticed his skill as well as his volume. Mrs Fitchett was Hungarian, in Kingston as the wife of a high-ranking British official. She told White that she wanted to see him after school. Fearing a detention, he appeared as required, full of foreboding. Instead she told him that he had a fine voice and must enter a singing competition, one of the small-scale competitions in piano and singing that were common throughout the British Isles and the Commonwealth at that time, mostly run from the schools of music in London. White sang Valentine's aria from Gounod's *Faust*, prophetically a baritone piece, and the familiar setting of Shakespeare's *Who is Sylvia?* He won. Another turning point.

White now took his talent more seriously and his father encouraged him. Whilst still at Excelsior he started attending evening classes at the Jamaican School of Music, being taught by Marian Navaakowski, a Polish singer who had performed at Covent Garden and on the BBC.

Sir John Barbirolli and the Halle Orchestra were on a tour that included Kingston. Barbirolli had been Toscanini's successor in charge of the New York Philharmonic until mid-way through the war and was now well established as the conductor of the Manchester orchestra. White had a friend, Ross Murray, who worked at the Ministry of Education and he suggested that Sir John should hear White sing.

At the appointed hour White went to the hotel, only to be told that Sir John was resting. Barbirolli was a formidable man, not one to be disturbed. Amongst his many acerbic comments was his description of all 'modern music' as "three farts and a raspberry, orchestrated". Lady Barbirolli, herself a noted musician, agreed to substitute. White was by now twenty with growing confidence, but it was still an ordeal and a very odd event. The 'lady' from Britain seemed not to respond to his voice, giving no inkling of her judgement, but at the end went to a writing desk and penned an open letter, 'To whom it may concern'. Her judgement was that the young man had talent, that it was already very late and possibly too late, but that he should be given training at once. She suggested London or New York. For White this was "a very important notch on the stream of encouragement."

Discussion between father and son decided in favour of New York. It was closer and the fare was cheaper. White wrote to the Juilliard, the famous school of music sharing the Lincoln Centre campus at the top of Broadway with the Metropolitan and New York City Operas and the Avery Fisher concert hall. He was offered an audition.

The experience of an audition in New York was unimaginably demanding for a young man who had not previously set foot outside the island of Jamaica. Not just a big city, but New York. The people were courteous and pleasant. Nobody had ever called this twenty-one-year-old 'Mr White' before. Reading *The Power of Positive Thinking* helped. Singing an aria from Verdi's *Don Carlos* won him the second highest-valued scholarship on offer. He was in.

Studying at the Juilliard was as daunting an experience as being auditioned. He was never so aware of his poverty. And all the other students had such high standards and spoke the European languages of opera. White had no Italian, which made studying opera particularly difficult. What he did have was a keen ear and that has enabled him to learn languages quickly. Nowadays working frequently in France, he denies fluency in the French language before recounting in perfect transactional French the tale of a brush with a rude Parisian. He had never sung with an orchestra. The weather too was entirely outside his experience. He had known cold in Jamaica only as an occasional sensation when opening the fridge door, and was entirely unprepared for a New York winter with its snow falls and sustained sub-zero temperatures.

Abandoning his studies and returning home was something that recurred in his thinking during the first six months in New York, but in truth he could not do so and he knew it. He had little choice but to succeed, for his father had provided him with a one-way ticket. "What will I say to them? How could I face myself? I must try harder to make this work."

The biggest problem of all was that he did not have enough money. His father had given him $100 but that was soon used up. The Juilliard scholarship was $300 short of the fees that had to be paid on registration before he could begin the course. With foresight, his friend Ross Murray back in Jamaica had been working to win him a grant of $330 a month. The first instalment arrived just in time for him to register, leaving $30 to live on for the first month. Dinner for that month, and quite a few more, was a slice of pizza costing 25 cents from the corner of 72nd Street and Broadway. He had arrived in New York very slim and remained that way.

Juilliard was good for White and he got his first paid professional work whilst still a student there, touring with a gospel group to the south-eastern states, playing Father Truelove in Stravinsky's *Rake's Progress*, and performing in Strauss's *Salome* in Washington. It had been a long journey in a very short time from the moment when he had sung for Lady Barbirolli in a Kingston hotel.

His formal professional debut was as Colline, the philosopher in *La Bohème* for New York City Opera, on the same Lincoln Centre campus as the Juilliard. This engagement alerted him early to the ways in which performers could be exploited at that time. He spent his first year with few scheduled performances but was frequently asked to step in on the day when someone else could not perform. The management saved performing fees unless he was needed. He was at their beck and call. When the contract offered for his second year included only two scheduled performances of *La Bohème* with the same stand-by arrangements, he walked out. A brave thing to do but he fell on his feet.

Tom Graham wrote to him from London. Lord Harewood, chairman of English National Opera, had heard White sing at the Juilliard in Dvorak's *Rusalka* and Bellini's last opera, *I Puritani*, set in the English Civil War. Would he come to London? By that time White was married to an English girl and the couple had a six-month old baby. He needed an income. The couple set out for England, where White met his wife's parents for the first time and launched his ENO career. A quarter of a century later he is still singing regularly at the Coliseum.

❖ ❖ ❖ ❖ ❖

Besides singing many operatic roles every year, White is a frequent singer in concert halls and a great favourite at the BBC Proms in the Royal Albert Hall. Apart from leading the last night revelries in 1999 and then moving to the outdoor Hyde Park extension of the last night in 2000 to do some of his 'songs from the shows' repertoire, he has regularly performed in Proms, often in the most prestigious of the concerts.

In 1991 he sang in the opening night concert, Elgar's *Dream of Gerontius*, electrifying in the baritone's dramatic first entry of 'Proficiscere, Go forth'. A year later he was in the penultimate night's great choral work, Tippet's *A Child of Our Time*. In 1993 he was in the opening night's concert version of Strauss's *Elektra*. 1996 saw him in Handel's *Semele*, with William Christie and *Les arts florissants*, an outcome of White's connection with the Aix-en-Provence Festival. In 1998 he led a re-creation of the famous Glyndebourne cast in Gershwin's *Porgy and Bess*, this time conducted by Wayne Marshall. White made his second appearance a fortnight later in the same season in Beethoven's *Ninth Symphony*, conducted by Simon Rattle with whom he has often worked. In these seven appearances at Proms in the last decade of the twentieth century, White sang big parts in big works. The range of works was also impressive, requiring singing of very different kinds.

White's stature and dignity, as well as his voice, make him a natural for big celebratory occasions. One of his several *Messiahs* was in Westminster Abbey to celebrate the 85th birthday of Lord Tonypandy, the former George Thomas MP and Speaker of the House of Commons. He has performed to celebrate the lives of other people, ranging from the retirement of his Zimbabwe-born friend Michael Hussey, from a career in teaching and school inspection, to reading Shakespeare at the Westminster Abbey memorial service for Dame Peggy Ashcroft.

Of course, not all potentially prestigious events turn out as planned. The British celebration of the new millennium at the Dome in Greenwich was a fiasco in every way, including the musical, but not because of the musicians. With Paul Daniels of English National Opera in charge and Willard White singing, along with pop groups such as The Corrs, all was set fair for a musical treat, but the staging was all wrong. The musicians could have set the Albert Hall aglow, but not the Dome. But still, White was at the centre of things as the third millennium dawned, singing to a distinguished, if disgruntled, audience.

There was also something unsatisfactory about his role in the London Philharmonic's event to welcome its new principal conductor, Kurt Masur, to London in 2000. The entire event was rather out of kilter with Masur's strengths. Accompanying White in Gershwin might have seemed a good idea, possibly linked to

Masur's arrival from his tenure in New York, but it was not a natural choice for the distinguished conductor.

White's charity performances have raised money for a wide variety of causes, as diverse as Sir Malcolm Sargent's cancer fund, when he sang at the Albert Hall with that fund's special choir, and AIDS charities for which he performed extracts from *Porgy and Bess*. He sings on behalf of music charities. In 1997, in a concert to celebrate the record company, EMI's one hundred years, White's performance of the Robeson classic, 'Ol' Man River', was a show-stopper. The gala was to raise money for the Music Sound Foundation, which aims to widen the audience for classical music. He was the "terrific baritone" who sang for Prince Charles and his 250 guests at St James's Palace in 1995 to raise funds for the Royal College of Music.

❖ ❖ ❖ ❖ ❖

Porgy and Bess is a work that has been particularly associated with White, ever since he led the cast in a celebrated production at Glyndebourne, conducted by Simon Rattle and produced by Trevor Nunn. It was the operatic production of the 1986 season, breaking the barrier of stuffiness in British opera houses and getting the quality of production and performance that it deserved for the first time in Britain. White's voice was ideal for the part of Porgy and the acting of the cast, not least White's, was superb. The painful duets - sung conversations between Porgy and Bess - were distressing to watch. White's Porgy was the wounded lion, the man with the big heart in the crippled body, beaten but noble, and at the end still retaining some hope. It ended with a theatrical coup as White/Porgy cast aside his crutches and walked off into the light. Glyndebourne audiences let their hair down and cheered.

This was one of those rare, sensational productions that seem to go on and on, reaching an ever-widening audience. The production was recorded and put on general release. In 1992 it arrived almost intact at Covent Garden, receiving its first ever performance there almost sixty years after it had been written. Although without Rattle, who could not be freed from other engagements, it was the hit that the Royal Opera House badly needed. In great financial difficulties and not yet having secured sufficient money to re-build itself, the ROH arranged extra performances after the opening night's success. Asked for a comment by the press, White could not resist revealing his pleasure: "The management says this will assist them immensely to recoup some of the losses they have made on various other operas. I find it particularly gratifying that this opera should come to the assistance of an international house." An opera, written by the Gershwins in the 1930s that showed wealthy America how blacks had to lead their lives and failed commercially as a consequence at its opening, was coming to Covent Garden's financial rescue in the 1990s.

A concert performance in the vast National Exhibition Centre in Birmingham followed. Then the BBC, Rattle and Nunn assembled almost the entire original cast, no mean feat after seven years, to film the Glyndebourne production at Shepperton studios. The film featured in the BBC's Christmas ratings battle against ITV alongside *Only Fools and Horses* and *One Foot in the Grave* in 1993. Two years later Rattle and White based a charity concert on *Porgy and Bess.* In 1998 most of the Glyndebourne cast was again reassembled, now twelve years since the first performance, for a Proms concert performance in the Albert Hall, this time directed by Wayne Marshall, the young black conductor. The songs from *Porgy and Bess* have been part of White's concert repertoire ever since.

The work has been a major part of White's career. He brings special insights to the tortured, humiliated but still hopeful character of Porgy.

❖ ❖ ❖ ❖ ❖

To be a success, an opera singer must be a great actor as well as a voice. White had heard a talk by Maria Callas, one of the greatest actors on the operatic stage, whilst at the Juilliard. She was an inspiration. Finding himself in a lift with her afterwards was for the trainee singer a memorable experience. She exuded power and was so beautiful. There are other singers who, statue-like (or, in the case of some ageing stars, seated), can impress with their voices, but opera is music drama and there is something vital missing from their performances. You might as well close your eyes or stay at home and listen to a recording. To sing without conveying the character is like an actor just mouthing the words.

White is a great actor in opera, portraying a vast range. He prepares carefully, for example observing a cripple in Jamaica before playing Porgy. At one end of the chronological range, he has sung Mozart, Handel, including a memorable recording of *Acis and Galatea* with John Eliot Gardiner in 1982, and Gluck's *Alceste* in Amsterdam in 1999. At the other, he has sung in operas by Debussy, Schoenberg, Janacek, Stravinsky, Shostakovich, Britten and John Adams. In between he routinely sings, of course, the bass-baritone parts of Puccini, Verdi, Wagner and the other nineteenth century composers. The range of acting as well as vocal styles required is enormous and White has versatility as well as a great stage presence. His physique is part of it, of course, but stature and presence are more than that.

In 1989 White, who had never before played in spoken drama, went straight to playing Othello for the Royal Shakespeare Company at Stratford. White's Iago was Ian McKellen. The casting was typical of the insight that the director Trevor Nunn has for dramatic possibilities and his willingness to take risks. He had directed White in the Glyndebourne *Porgy and Bess* and knew his talents, but putting an opera singer with no experience of spoken drama, let alone Shakespeare's verse, into such a role, alongside one of the country's greatest actors, was a risk.

Perhaps because of the uncertainties about what would

happen, the performances were given in the smallest of the RSC theatres at Stratford, The Other Place, then still little more than a tin shack. Thousands were turned away and further performances were then put on at the Young Vic in London. It was the unrivalled success of the 1989 Stratford season, with Imogen Stubbs and Zoe Wannamaker in the female roles, and was then filmed for BBC television in 1990.

The role of Iago is as important as that of Othello and getting the balance right is crucial. White and McKellan got it right. The intimacy of the theatre and the even greater intimacy of the television screen were part of the success. It was a close-up performance, with no need for grand gesture, just words, facial expression and movement. This too was something new for White, more used to projecting his voice and characterisation across a large orchestra to several tiers of people.

Initial enthusiasm for his adventure quickly turned to fear. At first White thought, "Good. I shall be free. No need to keep to a beat, to count, watch the conductor's baton, or worry about pitch." Then he felt imprisoned by the relentless need for pitch and modulation of the voice whilst keeping to the discipline of Shakespeare's pentameters. The last held him up for some time, until another actor revealed a simple trick, telling him that Ralph Richardson had always underscored the last word of every line to ensure that the emphasis fell there. White's initial thought was that this sounded daft and would never work, but he tried it and it did.

The other startling thing for him was the quietness of the whole thing. With an orchestra and sometimes several voices ringing out at the same time, silence is rare in opera. On the theatre stage there is usually only just one voice to be heard, and White was at first disturbed by the silence around him. "It was so quiet," he recalls, "unnerving. Was I connecting with the audience? Was anybody there?" He got used to it and played Othello with poetic simplicity, winning praise from all sides. The production was hailed as the best thing to come out of the RSC for five years. As a beginner he had entered the lions' den at Stratford and emerged victorious.

Perhaps because the baritone in the opera version of *Othello* plays the part of Iago, the white believer in evil set to destroy the self-doubting Moor Othello, White has not sung in Verdi's work. It is often said that Shakespeare gains in intensity in Verdi's treatment, because music adds another dimension to what is already a powerful drama. The Covent Garden programme for Placido Domingo's portrayal of Verdi's *Otello* in 1990 repeated this cliché. In reality, whilst Domingo was vocally impressive, he lacked the powerful acting that the singer, White, had brought to the part as an actor the year before. Perhaps because he is such a good actor in opera, the intensity of White's performance in the play outdid that of Domingo in the opera.

❖ ❖ ❖ ❖ ❖

White was the second black bass-baritone to play Othello at Stratford. Paul Robeson had done it many years before. Hearing a record of Paul Robeson singing *Trees* is an early memory of White's. He had long wanted to add spirituals to his repertoire and in 1995 began singing arrangements written by Melanie Marshall, the singer sister of Wayne, the organist, pianist and conductor. Someone then suggested a programme rather like Robeson's broadcasts from the USA to Britain. This was followed by more research into Robeson's performances and writing, and an expansion of the programme, until the idea grew into a full concert.

The initial performance, given in a packed Salisbury Cathedral, was a huge success. It was more than a concert – it was a tribute to Robeson. Trevor Phillips, the television presenter and London politician, narrated the story of Robeson's life, using mostly extracts from the singer's own writing. White told the audience that a record of Robeson had inspired him to pursue singing as a career. He sang, with the Matrix ensemble, not only spirituals and other songs from the deep South, such as 'Ol' Man River', but also Russian songs as a reminder of Robeson's interest in the Soviet Union that led to his persecution by the American authorities. Further performances were given in the Queen Elizabeth Hall as part of the London Jazz Festival and at Queens University as part of the Belfast Festival, the latter a particularly poignant venue for a programme about the struggle for equality.

White is beginning, as result, to see what both Robeson and he stand for. White sees in Robeson a life devoted to upholding the truth of equality, "a truth that did not need to be proved, its rightness being self-evident, but a truth that, nonetheless had to be won." When White speaks and sings Robeson's words it means much to him and to the people who hear him.

❖ ❖ ❖ ❖ ❖

Good and evil, comedy and tragedy, and the closeness of these opposites crop up frequently in conversation with White. He has played Britten's villain, Claggart, in *Billy Budd*, but sees him as a complex character, not as a simple embodiment of evil. When Peter Sellars directed him as Golaud in Debussy's *Pelléas et Mélisande* and wanted him to kick the pregnant Melisande during the scene in which he drags her by the hair, White said that he could not do it. Sellars said, "OK" and did not press him, but then White said, "Well, give me some time to think about it." He analysed his difficulty in doing something that was, after all, not him but Golaud. Could he or anyone be certain that, in extreme circumstances, there was anything that they could not do? Was his objection that it was something evil and some people would associate it with blackness? Whilst he could not do it in life, could he deny that such evil does exist and should he not therefore be prepared to portray it? He did.

Later, when talking about his preparation for *Falstaff* at the Aix-en-Provence Festival in the summer of 2001, he responds quickly to the observation that he has not played many comic parts. "Is it a comedy? Is Falstaff funny? If you find him funny then he is." His point is that comedy is often about human failings and may be funny to watch but it is not funny to be the victim. It was as though he felt deeply the humiliation of the character that he was about to play for the first time.

There is also much talk about positive and negative, and the reaction between the two, in the conversation of this thoughtful and reflective man. It is almost Hegelian. When his thoughts are compared to a tennis match where you use the force of an incoming powerful volley to return the ball, he replies, "In tennis the aim is to win. In life, you can afford to lose the point." He develops the argument by asking, "When we ball somebody out and slam the door on them, why is it we who feel bad?"

The conversation then turns to his older children by his first marriage, who went to private schools. Why? He saw that the teachers in their local school arrived each morning with an attitude, justified by their circumstances, that the day ahead would be hard. The day's struggle had begun. There was no opportunity for them to liberate, enthuse, enlighten the children. Instruction was the only possibility.

Brought up a Christian, White does not now have a specific faith. He has seen too much religious hypocrisy, and has himself felt the tension between his professed beliefs and his actions at difficult periods in his life, to find the tenets of any denomination valid. He has faith in his own work and an evident spirituality about him. It is self-awareness beyond the ordinary, combined with the intellectual and emotional experience derived from understanding all the diverse characters that he has sung in opera and all the feelings that he has experienced in music. Arriving by underground for an interview in mid-morning having been in *Turandot* at Covent Garden the night before, he has none of the trappings that some attach to the operatic star's life-style. In that sense he is down-to-earth. But he carries the accumulated experiences of his performances. Through them, as well as all the experiences of his life, he has grown.

It is perhaps inevitable, given the importance of religious music in the choral repertoire, that he has often sung in Christian or at least spiritual works. In addition to *Gerontius*, he sang in Berlioz's *L'Enfance du Christ*, two days before Christmas in London in 1992, in the traditional *St Matthew Passion* with the Bach Choir and Sir David Willcocks on Good Friday in 1994, and in Adams's *El Niño/La Nativité* in the week before Christmas in Paris in 2000. In 1996 he opened ITV's Christmas Eve programme by singing 'Oh come, Oh Come, Emmanuel' from the pulpit of a London church. Some of the works that he sings, such as Tippet's *Child of Our Time* and Britten's *War Requiem*, are more spiritual than religious, in these cases also with a message about war and the harm that people are capable of doing to each other. It was perhaps his recall of his early Biblical training that led him, during preparation for Schoenburg's *Moses and Aaron*, to burst out with indignation at the opera's particular slant, "Who does this guy Schoenberg think he is?"

❖ ❖ ❖ ❖ ❖

The question of race hovers in conversation with White. He says, more than once, "Some people don't want me" or "Some people don't like what I do." He follows these with, "That's all right", quietly said and indicating that it is they who have a problem. He does not volunteer but confirms when pressed that this is in part a reference to race. Whilst a boy in Jamaica, friends had warned him against trying for a career as a professional, classical musician, as "black people don't do that sort of music." At the Juilliard a girlfriend said that he had got in because he was black, a view with which White strongly disagreed. He was already confident about his ability, even if he had some catching up to do.

Most of his professional experiences involving race are now more often thoughtless than hostile. It can be imagined that the journalist who wrote an interesting and thoughtful piece on White's singing for *The Scotsman* in 1999 was not pleased when a crass sub-editor gave it the headline, "A little White magic." White no longer has much concern about race in his professional life. When he appeared at the last night of the Proms in 1999, where the requirement was, as always, to lead the singing of *Rule Britannia* to a sea of union jacks (but also an increasing number of European, European Union and Australian flags), White hit on a neat compromise. Dressed in a black shirt and trousers, he wore a cummerbund and a bandanna, proclaiming his dual nationalities with a Jamaican waist and British head. It was not only self-respectful, but also represented some kind of final triumph. Here was the boy who started life in the colonies leading a packed Royal Albert Hall of overwhelmingly white people in the singing of a song from the days of Britain's imperial past. It was a party. That nobody saw anything odd about it shows how far both White and Britain had come.

It was not always so. In 1984 a crisis arose at the English National Opera, where White had started his British career. Expecting to sing in *Rigoletto*, White came up against what was explained as an artistic objection by the director, Jonathan Miller, who was quoted as saying that he did not believe a black Count Monterone or Sparafulcile, the bandit, was "feasible in our Rigoletto." The agent who had brought White to Britain and is his agent to this day, Tom Graham, saw this as racist, commenting that opera had been colour blind for the last forty years. After all, Europeans routinely played Japanese and Chinese characters.

The ENO's ham-fisted attempt to justify its decision on musical and artistic grounds was matched by its political ineptitude. The previous few years had seen ENO staggering from one crisis to the next. It was financially precarious, had faced strikes by its musicians with cancelled performances, had had to hold fund-raising events such as a fifty-hour music marathon and had spent much energy seeking a new home, bidding unsuccessfully for the Old Vic.

An even greater danger was the possibility that the Greater London Council, led by Ken Livingston since Labour's victory in the 1981 GLC election, would withdraw its financial support. The new Labour administration had considered withdrawing all grants to national arts institutions based in London, in order to redistribute the money to community-based arts programmes. The new policy was led by Tony Banks, who chaired the GLC arts committee. In 1981 the GLC relented, but in 1982 it again considered a complete withdrawal, once more relenting only at the last moment.

With that background, ENO could ill afford a clash with the GLC over race. As soon as he heard about the *Rigoletto* problem, the GLC's new arts chairman, Peter Pitt, immediately stopped its grant which, at a million pounds, was the largest to any arts organisation in London. Questions of race were already very much in the news as a result of the decision by the Prime Minister, Margaret Thatcher, to admit the white South African runner, Zola Budd, to instant British nationality in the hope of celebrating a medal for Britain in the 1984 Olympics. The GLC had already made a stand on that question and was certainly not going to pay a huge sum of money to an organisation exhibiting, in Pitt's words, "blatant racism.....wholly outrageous, insulting and unacceptable."

White was shocked but kept his distance and his dignity, saying, "I must retain my backbone and stand up to it. I don't think it is ENO policy – it can only be one person's idea. I know I cannot work for certain companies because of my colour." One of the oddities of the situation was that the Chairman of ENO at the time was the same man who had heard White sing in the USA and had arranged for him to come to the ENO, the Earl of Harewood. The matter was resolved by ENO agreeing to submit its casting policy to the GLC for approval as a condition of continued grant.

Later a singer playing the part of a young peasant girl opposite him in *Eugene Onegin* said that such a character would not fall in love with a black man in Russia in the nineteenth century. It was too unnatural. White's position was that she was entitled to her view but that all opera is make-believe. Given the number of times that grossly overweight consumptives die in *La Boheme* and famous tenors well past middle-age play young lovers and generals, it is not difficult to see his point. When White returned to his role of Timur in Puccini's *Turandot* at Covent Garden in 2001, he, like all the other singers, was so heavily disguised as Chinese, that skin colour was irrelevant.

White is London-based and British although he may still have his Jamaican passport as well, not being sure whether it has been renewed. In reviews of his performances he was for a time called American. Jamaica is no longer a natural home for him. When he visits he sticks out as a foreigner. On one visit two men were talking very loudly about him, saying, "Here comes an Englishman". Typically he challenged them to explain why they had said that, and the answer was that he was clearly not local. It showed in the cut of his trousers. White adds that it is also a question of the effect on skin of living in a cold climate, for he says that the climate does affect skin tone. More generally he has commented, "I do not blend very easily", teasingly leaving it to the hearer to decide whether he is talking about colour or personality. There is just a hint that he likes being thought of as a little prickly.

What does White consider himself to be? Quietly and poignantly he mentions the final line in Schubert's *Der Wanderer,* "Ich bin ein Fremdling überall", "I am a stranger everywhere."

He felt this strongly at one time, but no longer. Now he is established. Whilst still travelling the world and spending months at a time in France, he is a Londoner.

A decade after the *Rigoletto* problem, the black face of a *Flying Dutchman* appeared on posters all over the London Underground, advertising the ENO production in which White was to triumph. White has sung much Wagner in London, Edinburgh, Glasgow and San Francisco. But not at Bayreuth.

❖ ❖ ❖ ❖ ❖

Whilst White talks about our freedom to make choices, he is also quite fatalistic. Things happen to him and he then makes the choice about what to do, whether, for example, to accept an invitation to appear. "I go where things take me. Exploration is the university of life." He works with people who like what he does and then they call him up, sometimes years later, with offers of collaboration on a new production. There are also regular trips to France, for performances at the Chatelet and Opera Bastille in Paris and repeated summers at Aix-en-Provence and Orange in the south.

He has often had calls from Peter Sellars, the San Francisco academic and director, and these have taken him to California, Amsterdam, Salzburg and Paris. Sellars likes White's open attitudes when rehearsing. It was he who suggested White as the male lead in *El Niño* and Adams wrote the part with White's voice in mind, very much as Britten wrote many of his parts in opera for a particular person's unique voice. Adams's compositions are often called minimalist. They are certainly sparse. Sellars's productions have the same quality, intended to shock (successfully with some critics and audiences) but as often as not thin and boring. White rises musically and dramatically to the occasion. His realisation in *El Niño* that his supposedly virgin wife was pregnant was as terrifying as anything he has done.

Mark Elder, now conductor of the Halle Orchestra but musical director at the English National Opera in the eighties, is another musician with whom White often works. The association started at ENO's London home, the Coliseum, and continues. White was one of the soloists in Elder's Verdi concert performances with the Halle in Manchester in 2001 to mark the centenary year of Verdi's death. The year certainly started strongly in the Bridgewater Hall, for Elder is regarded by many as our foremost Verdi conductor. With a full symphony orchestra, instead of the usual opera orchestra in the pit, and Willard White singing excerpts from *Don Carlos* and *Aida*, the sound was magnificent. As one observer wrote, "A vast operatic monster with Willard White at the front and eight double basses at the back is an exceptional sonic experience."

White also enjoys singing regularly with Simon Rattle. The closeness of their association was forged during their country house season together at Glyndebourne in *Porgy and Bess*. They have often appeared together in concert halls. The trio of Rattle, White and Sellars collaborated on *Pélleas et Mélisande* in Amsterdam in 1991. Rattle and White's Aix-en-Provence Festival work together in 2000 was Janacek's *The Makropoulos Case*, sung in the great open-air theatre. Whilst the production was generally not liked, Rattle's orchestral work and White's magnificent singing were widely applauded.

Perhaps an unlikely collaboration, but only for those unfamiliar with White's openness to various kinds of music, was with Paul McCartney for the premiere in Liverpool Cathedral of the former Beatle's *Liverpool Oratorio* in 1991. The work was not well received, despite the contributions of Carl Davis to the composition and Kiri Te Kanawa to the singing. White, with Sally Burgess, had to sing an assortment of vicars, teachers and nurses, and also to receive some vocal advice from McCartney on television. But it was new work, that White is keen to do, and a grand occasion.

WILLARD WHITE

❖ ❖ ❖ ❖ ❖

Now in the second half century of his life, White is very fit and works hard. He practises daily – "sometimes in my mind", he adds with a barely perceptible smile. When on *Desert Island Discs*, he was asked by Sue Lawley how he would get on alone. The prospect appalled this gregarious man, but he quickly added, "I am a survivor."

The voice remains strong and true, perhaps not as smooth at the very bottom as once it was, but as good as ever in the baritone range. White still enjoys using it and audiences still love hearing it. He recognises that he has a gift, considers that he is lucky to have it, and is happy to share it. Denying a religious belief again, he says that every time he goes out on to a stage he just opens himself up to the powers that be, and if he touches people, so be it. He usually does.

BILL ALEXANDER

Hunstanton is an unlikely breeding ground of great theatrical talent. A small seaside resort on the north Norfolk coast, it has never been fashionable like its neighbours, Blakeney and Brancaster. It is divided into two parts by a large grassy clifftop: the western edge of the town has the usual seaside mix of amusements, funfair rides and fish and chip shops, whereas the eastern part is older, more picturesque, with quaint houses and narrow lanes. It was in this part of Hunstanton that Bill Alexander, born in 1948, grew up. His parents, the Patersons, had moved there to run small shops and, later on, the Lighthouse Cafe. The young William Paterson (the change of name came later) spent a happy early childhood there, crabbing in the rockpools that appeared at low tide, and attending the local primary school. The businesses run by his parents – typical seaside places selling gifts and haberdashery – generated enough income to send their son to a private boarding school in Kent for his secondary education.

Ramsgate, a small, seasonal holiday town, in which St Lawrence School was located, would have been a familiar setting to the boy from Hunstanton. This was not one of the great private boarding schools of England; indeed, Bill Alexander was later to describe it as "a very obscure place". His time there, whilst entirely happy, was unremarkable but for one influence which was to point him in the direction of his later career. That influence was his English teacher, John Binfield.

Good English teachers are special people. They appreciate the evolution of language whilst defending it against corruption; they love language for its clarity, subtlety and rhythms; they appreciate its power to convey complex and simple ideas, to render the obscure meaningful and voice universal truths. A good English teacher will generate excitement in his pupils, will encourage discussion and debate, and foster curiosity in the world of ideas through the medium of literature. John Binfield was in some ways unorthodox. He would dangle a text in front of his students and tell them that it was much too difficult for them to tackle, that they would not appreciate it. To a group of adolescent boys, this challenge to their maturity and intellect was irresistible and they would grapple with the piece until they had understood it. His approach to poems was to acknowledge that they needed to be read by the young more than once over the years before they would be appreciated fully, but alongside this belief was the conviction that schoolchildren could gain access to the most difficult texts. It is possible to see in this early experience of literature the beginnings of an approach that was to lead to some of Bill Alexander's most notable theatrical successes. His respect for the text of a play is at the heart of his productions such as *Richard III*, but this sits alongside a belief that an understanding of the words can be expressed visually to illuminate meaning and make it accessible to a wide audience.

English teachers traditionally have responsibility for the annual school play, more often than not a Shakespeare, and John Binfield was no exception. His were no toe-curlingly awful efforts appreciated only by the relatives of those performing. In the 1960s, his pupils tackled plays as demanding as *Othello* and attracted the attention of reviewers in national papers such as *The Times* and *The Times Educational Supplement*. Bill Alexander gained his first acting experience under the direction of Binfield, and taking part in these productions rapidly became the most important feature of his school life.

In fine Tudor tradition, all the female parts were taken by boys, a decision driven less by artistic or historical rectitude than by the fact that the cast was drawn from the pupils at this then all-male school! Alexander recalls with some amusement his first role as Perdita in *The Winter's Tale*, which necessitated the wearing of a short Greek skirt and a good deal of stage make-up. He admits that, as a young boy, he made a more than passable female to play the romantic lead. Unfortunately, such was the construction of the acting area that there was no backstage space along which the actors could move. Any exit followed by a re-entry from the opposite side of the stage required the hapless boy to run the gauntlet of stares and comments from local youths as he made a 100 yard dash along a public street to be on time for his next entrance, clad only in diaphanous chiffon and lipstick. This element of farce clearly escaped the notice of *The Times* reviewer who was charmed by Alexander's performance.

Subsequent roles included Marullus, one of the tribunes in *Julius Caesar*, and Lodovico in *Othello*. The part for which Alexander has most affection, and which must surely have been the most demanding for a teenager, was that of Prospero in *The Tempest*. His performance earned special praise from *The Times Educational Supplement* reviewer for its dignity and the noble contrast he achieved with the sprightly Ariel in a production that was "a triumph". It is difficult to imagine a better early preparation for entry into the professional world of the theatre than a school career steeped in the study of texts led by an inspirational teacher and the realisation of the written word on the stage in a series of acclaimed productions. Unfortunately, school is also about more mundane matters such as passing exams and, at the time of Alexander's triumphant Prospero, he was just three months away from taking his A-levels.

Binfield did his best to help Alexander to win a place at Oxford. Alexander was attracted to the ancient universities by his reading of *Brideshead Revisited*. Romantic visions of endless summer days punting, picnicking off strawberries and quails' eggs, or declaiming *The Wasteland* in stately college rooms took precedence over academic considerations when he made his application. During his seventh term in the sixth form, he applied to St John's College. When that failed, Binfield tried to exploit a connection at St Edmund Hall, but all places had been filled. In those days, entry to read English at Oxbridge was dependent upon proficiency in Latin, which Alexander says he did not possess, being "rotten" at the subject, and this was a contributory factor in his failure. With hindsight, it is possible to say that his subsequent acceptance of a place at Keele University, with the wide opportunities it offered to students to participate in all aspects of theatre from classical to contemporary, gave him the best possible grounding upon which to base his future career.

In the late sixties and early seventies, Keele was making a name for itself as the preferred choice of students who wanted a progressive higher education. It suited Alexander very well. All students followed a four-year course: a general course in the first year, four subjects in opposing disciplines across years two and three, and two specialisms in year four. Besides enabling students to discover where their real academic interests and talents lay (Alexander specialised in English and politics), it also gave them time in which to pursue their extra-curricular interests. Alexander worked hard enough to achieve a creditable degree, but flung himself into acting and directing, becoming a member of the dramatic society, and also founding not one, but two drama societies of his own: Guerilla Theatre and the Keele Performance Group. Both were notable for the physical nature of their work.

For the moment, the influence of John Binfield and his respect for the text was subsumed by that of an American off-Broadway company called Living Theatre. Two of their New York productions – one using improvisation about drug addiction, the other about life in a US Marine Corps prison – were seen in London in the early sixties. Their influence on drama was immense in two ways: their work often included improvisation and audience participation; it also made texts with timeless messages relevant to contemporary audiences. An example of this was a performance of *Antigone* that justified civil disobedience as a means of opposing the war in Vietnam. These approaches, experimental at the time, where the performance contributed at least as much as the text to the production and its impact, were a major influence on Alexander at Keele, and echoes of them reverberate through his later work.

This was all a big step from the meticulously-prepared, annual boarding school performance of Shakespeare. It is easy to imagine how appalled John Binfield might have been by this departure of his protégé from the theatrical straight and narrow. Only the arrogance and hubris of youth could conceive a dramatic interpretation of *Paradise Lost* in which there were precious few of Milton's words, but plenty of hot action. The Keele Performance Group did just this in a performance which was, perhaps mercifully, left unrecorded!

Like many people looking back on their formative years, Alexander was later to condemn his life at this time. On reflection, he was more aware of what he called the "fascistic" nature of the group, deriding it as a "rice-and-nuts-and-guru theatrical commune" which sent its women out to do the laundry.

At the time, however, the communal life must have retained its appeal, for he moved from Keele to London and joined Inter Action. This was an archetypal sixties group, led by a Harvard-educated American called Ed Berman who had come to Britain as a Rhodes Scholar. He was an extraordinary man of great energy and diverse interests. The two constant features of his work were the commune approach for those contributing and a commitment to community activities. Members, usually about sixty in number, drawn from the arts, education and community work, were paid £1.50 a day with a room and dinner. Berman's activities, based at Kentish Town in north London, are still remembered with affection by residents. He took ponies, circuses, clay-modelling and many other novel activities to inner-city communities, involving local people in their organisation. He even set up a farm at St Pancras, hardly the most rural of locations. He campaigned to defend London against planners, including demonstrating against changes to Piccadilly Circus, and he submitted a planning application to turn Buckingham Palace into flats with public recreation space.

Founding the Union of Father Christmases and setting up a Dial-a-Santa line in competition with the Post Office are examples of just how far his interests reached.

As was forecast by an *Evening Standard* columnist in 1977, when a new and costly headquarters for Inter Action was opened in Kentish Town by Princess Anne, this phenomenon of the sixties did not long survive respectability. The *Standard*'s writer warned that this first step towards institutionalisation would encourage the natural distrust that people have of temples of culture for the initiated. His words had a prophetic ring, not only for Inter Action, but also could refer to that existing Palace of Culture in the Midlands, The Birmingham Repertory Theatre, which struggles to fill its auditorium from amongst the local population. Its struggle is part of Bill Alexander's later history. In the seventies he was enjoying himself on the Fun Art Bus, living in various squats and having a marvellous time.

The Fun Art Bus was a product of Berman's fertile creative mind. It certainly takes an imaginative leap to transform a standard red double-decker London bus into a cinema on the lower deck and a theatre on the upper deck with a puppet theatre on the side. It was described at the time as "the smallest theatre on wheels in the world". Alexander was an actor in the theatre (his last ground-breaking role as an actor before becoming a director was as Inspector Knacker of the Yard), and recalls with amusement how entrances and exits were made via a hatch by the driver's cabin. It was a far cry from the chilly sprints he made as Perdita while acting at school or indeed the cavernous stage space in Birmingham Rep's main auditorium.

If the concept of all this dramatic activity in such a small space were not bizarre enough, the bus had a surreal quality too. Its floor was covered in simulated lawn and the basket for used bus tickets had a new sign on it: "for used poems". The Fun Art Bus lived up to its name for both audience and actors, but after a few months Alexander's career took a more serious turn.

It is perhaps appropriate at this point to ask why the young William Paterson became Bill Alexander. The answer lies in the strange rule of Equity, the actors' union, that there cannot be two actors of the same name holding an Equity card. While Bill Alexander was working to gain his card there was, and still is, another actor called Bill Paterson. Alexander was invited by Equity to use any combination of his three names – William Alexander Paterson – and Bill Alexander was born.

Alexander owes a big step forward in his career to the enlightened approach of one of the then new television companies. In our own time, whilst Channel Four, the BBC and some ITV companies still see the need to develop new talent, there is greater reliance on game shows and other low-cost schedule-fillers. When the first independent television companies were established, the fear was that the break in the BBC's monopoly would result in competition for a mass audience and therefore satisfy only the lowest common denominator of viewers' preferences. This fear was not generally realised, in part because the Independent TV Commission prevented it. There were also some thoughtful and enlightened people running some of the new companies. One of these, Thames Television, was amongst the leaders in seeing that good drama attracts a big television audience and that television directors and producers benefit from a grounding in stage work. It therefore ran a bursary scheme for trainee directors. Alexander spotted the Thames Television advertisement in *The Stage* and, as a result of his success, was appointed as a sponsored assistant director at the Bristol Old Vic in 1973.

The Bristol Old Vic was run at that time by Val May, but he was coming to the end of his work in Bristol before moving to the Yvonne Arnaud Theatre in Guildford. During Alexander's two years in Bristol, May directed a variety of plays (Shakespeare, Stoppard, Bolt) and allowed Alexander an ever freer hand. Alexander became the *de facto* and in some cases the acknowledged director of a wide repertoire of plays. His directing was mainly for the New Vic, with an emphasis on modern works. In a three-month period in the spring of 1974 he directed Pinter's *Old Times*, three years after its first performance, a solo performance based on Dostoyevsky's novel, *Notes From the Underground*, and a translation of a very obscure German play, *The Ride Across Lake Constance*, by Peter Handke.

His Keele experience and the later development of his craft at Bristol led to the first of Alexander's professional triumphs. He had moved from Bristol to London as an assistant director at the Royal Court Theatre in Sloane Square. By early 1978 he was coming to the end of his two years working for the English Stage Company, which had brought in a new era of writing and performance in its main auditorium, and even more so in its experimental auditorium, the Theatre Upstairs. This pioneering group had given Alexander the task of producing *Class Enemy* by Nigel Williams.

The play was about the "burning issue of education in our cities" at a time when education was in a state of flux with the arrival of the comprehensive system. A class of boys in a south London school find themselves in a state of isolation. Left to their own devices, and waiting for the arrival of the ideal teacher who never comes, each boy finds that he can feed on the imagination of the others. Their contributions to each other's learning vary from instruction on how to make a vandal- and cat-proof window box to racist outpourings and humbling confessions. The boys also see a hierarchy developing amongst themselves. Together they create their own tutorial, without the presence of a teacher. It would be charming to believe that the boys who took the roles in *Class Enemy* were drawn from the local community and untutored in the dramatic arts. Certainly they were all *bona fide* north London lads with the accents to prove it, but they had attended Anna Scher workshops and had therefore learned to exploit their acting abilities. Much of the script was written in strong London dialect, which the boys could not read. It would have to be translated for them and they would then proceed to speak it as written! Thus 'aincha' as printed was translated into 'aren't you' for them, only for the light to dawn: "Ah, aincha! Why didn't you say so?" This arduous aspect of the direction process paid off and the reviews were terrific:

> "No praise is too high for Bill Alexander's brilliantly cast and superbly directed production" *The Financial Times*
> "blazes with life and force" *The Guardian*
> " a new play to remember" *The Times*

The production made a tremendous impact and was the first in a now impressive line of new works to transfer from the Theatre Upstairs to the main auditorium. At the age of 29 Bill Alexander had had his first hit. He won an award which carried a prize of £350 for the most promising young director outside the West End. The drama critic *of The Guardian*, Michael Billington, was one of the judges.

Class Enemy illustrated Alexander's skill with a good script which is being realised on stage for the first time and his talent for working with people whose youth and background ensure open-mindedness. Alexander found the young actors a joy and a release. The play was angry and Williams found it appropriate that few people left the theatre smiling. A few years later it played to packed audiences in Berlin and was revived for the Royal Shakespeare Youth Festival when Alexander was at the Royal Shakespeare Company.

It was a natural progression to be in at the birth of The Warehouse, a branch of the RSC being established at this time in London by Howard Davies. Alexander had met Davies whilst at the Bristol Old Vic and they had worked together on two plays, both about Bristol itself and both with a political and social dimension. One was about Concorde, which was at that time being manufactured in Bristol, and the other was called *Bristol Ring Road*. Alexander welcomed the chance to forge a new approach to theatre. This was an important period in his development.

Alexander had become doubtful about the Royal Court's approach to new work. It was an approach that he was to meet later at the main theatres of the RSC, but was quite different from that being developed at The Warehouse. At the Royal Court the approach was to seek out a good script, whether from a well-known or unknown writer, reach agreement that it was indeed a good script ('yes' or 'no'), choose the right director and then cast it. The Warehouse approach was, of course, still to start with promising writers, more than a dozen, but then to develop ideas and scripts together – a commune, in fact.

The plays were mostly about working class or power struggles and suited Alexander's broadly left-wing views. Among the plays he directed were: *Factory Birds*, where a group of young workers, led by Roger Rees, saw the effect of years in a factory on older workers; *Shout Across the River*, about urban desolation; *The Hang of the Gaol*, about the evils of the English ruling class system; *Captain Swing*, about a rural uprising in the 1830's; and *Bastard Angel*, a story of broken dreams of social change, seen through the eyes of an ageing rock singer, played by Charlotte Cornwell. Alexander found such work, including his work on *Class Enemy*, exhilarating and hard precisely because the outcome and impact upon the public were uncertain. He later commented that, when bringing a new play to the public for the first time, he was never certain that the piece was of quality. He always thought it would be, indeed hoped that it would be, but, until it was on a stage before an audience, he could not be sure. The times were both exciting and daunting. References were made in the press to the 'Warehouse Mafia' and to their "unimpeachably working class and often lurid plays". The plays were not, however, strongly didactic, more revelatory and challenging, with the modest enough ambition that audiences might see the possibility of things being better than they were, both for individuals and for society. This itself was unusual to the point of being revolutionary in the West End of that time.

By now Alexander was already doing some freelance work, for example at the Nottingham Playhouse, and this continued for several years, taking him around Britain and to Israel, New York and Washington. The Israeli experience was a strange one: directing a Pinter play in Hebrew, with Alexander not understanding Hebrew and the actors not understanding Pinter. Pinter himself would probably approve!

In 1984 he became an associate director of the Royal Shakespeare Company at Stratford-upon-Avon. Thus began the happiest period of his professional career to date, the "blissful" times when creative energies were high and shared with other great directors and designers. He had already won his RSC spurs with four plays, mostly modern, and a touring production of *Henry IV*. It was as he was about to begin the *Henry IV* tour that he acknowledged the point that he would not be taking Shakespeare to the masses, only to middle-class audiences beyond London and Stratford. Alexander was rather sceptical about the motive for touring and certainly did not see it as theatrical evangelism. He was providing a convenience for the provinces and did not expect to reach new audiences. The fact that he considered the matter at all indicated his recognition that drama has something to say to all people, but that some is not immediately accessible to all.

Nonetheless, a tour of twenty-two towns with Alfred Marks as Falstaff was quite an undertaking. Locations varied from major cities such as Edinburgh to lesser known venues such as Wath upon Dearne. Belfast, well into its latest period of turmoil, welcomed its first major touring company in ten years.

This was one of the RSC's earliest tours, later to become a feature of the company's work, and arrangements were often unsatisfactory or uncertain. Even the venue was not always settled. In Portsmouth a technical college was considered unsatisfactory, the Guild Hall had been previously booked by another company and in desperation the Royal Navy's HMS Nelson Theatre was considered in the search to find somewhere to perform. A sports centre served in another town. The logistical problems, including taking the company's raked seating and limited scenery, not to mention the eighteen players and technical staff, from place to place were formidable. Financial underwriting was also withheld by some hall owners, for example Grimsby Council. This experience of Shakespeare owed nothing to hushed and reverent worship of the Bard in his birthplace.

Despite Alexander's expectations about the likely audience, many people, especially young people, were seeing Shakespeare for the first time performed live by a good cast. The *Henry IV* plays were required examination reading for many young people. The comedy is strong and this particular cast was impressive. Apart from Alfred Marks himself, Barbara Jefford, who had already played thirty-three Shakespeare roles and toured in thirty-nine countries, and the young David Rintoul, who had just been seen as Mr Darcy in a BBC *Pride and Prejudice*, were well-known faces. The cast also went out of their way to foster local interest, for example with all the men appearing in full miners' gear when in a mining area. There were pioneering educational and promotional aspects of the tour.

Back in Stratford, Alexander embarked upon a series of productions that were to become famous and began an exhilarating and dynamic association with Antony Sher. Their work together consisted of a play by Molière, a play about Molière and three Shakespeares. Alexander has a great regard for Molière: "Molière is like no other comic writer." The humour of this seventeenth century French jobbing playwright – most of his work was for the court of Louis XIV, the Sun King – is all there in the text. It is unlike the comedy of that other jobbing playwright, Shakespeare, which can be a foil to tragedy and needs to be performed to be funny. Molière uses comedy to expose human foibles, and it leaps from the page even before theatrical interpretation on stage.

In the 1983-4 seasons at Stratford and the Barbican in London Alexander directed Molière's *Tartuffe* and a play called *Molière*. The latter, by the Russian dramatist Bulgakov, was linked with *Tartuffe* through the idea of censorship. *Tartuffe* had been attacked by the court censors because its theme was religious hypocrisy. Bulgakov's play is on one level an historically inaccurate account of Molière's popularity at the court until he fell foul of the Church and was destroyed by it. Written as it was in 1936 in Russia it is also a thinly-veiled metaphor for Stalinist persecution, using the familiar way of getting round censorship by telling a relevant tale from a different country and period. Throughout Alexander's production a huge bust of Louis XIV loomed at the rear of the stage like Orwell's Big Brother. Given the subject of censorship, the resistance of Stalin to its original performance is not surprising.

Alexander's production had its own difficulties: Sher snapped a tendon, David Troughton had to have a knee operation and the actor playing Louis XIV died.

It was in this first collaboration between Alexander and Sher that the tensions - sometimes sensationally productive and at other times less so - first emerged. These were not personal but about style and method. The actor is flamboyant with a great stage presence that hypnotises audiences. The director respects the essence of the work being performed and resists theatrical distortions which are not part of his artistic interpretation of the text however much they win over audiences. Reviewers admired Alexander's fine and dashing production. The *Birmingham Post*, ten years before Alexander's arrival at the Rep, noted his skill as a director. There were, however, slight worries about the lack of balance between the comedy and the menace. Whereas this was attached mostly to the translator and re-writer of Bulgakov's work, actor and director did not escape.

The conversations about *Tartuffe* between the director and the star illustrate Alexander's views about the importance of the author's words and intentions. Clearly his task was to contain this most flamboyant and physical of actors, although he did not succeed to the extent of preventing Sher from baring his backside as Tartuffe. Sher did not immediately see Alexander's point. He found himself playing up to the audience's laughter and adding to his role some farcical touches of business – actions which raise a laugh but do not necessarily have any justification in the text. This approach worried some observers who noted Sher's dominance of the stage despite the presence of other well-known actors, notably Nigel Hawthorne and Alison Steadman. *The Sunday Express* turned one of the play's lines – "You go too far" – into a piece of advice to Sher. Trevor Nunn, the then head of the RSC, thought Alexander got a perfect balance between domestic naturalism and black farce, but as performance followed performance the quota of 'business' crept up.

A timely adaptation for television had the effect of toning down Sher's performance to the smaller scale required by the more intimate medium of TV. Alexander was able to convince him that the words themselves were the source of the comedy. "I can feel the power of the words doing the work.... without all the business", Sher acknowledged in his diary.

These recordings of *Tartuffe* and *Molière* for television were Alexander's only diversions from theatre work (apart from a brief foray into the world of radio using the famous Archers studio in Birmingham!). His method of working - taking the empty space of the stage, creating a world from it in which the audience will believe, presenting a concept to the actors and working the production up over a six-week rehearsal period with ample opportunity for reflection and development - is at odds with the pressured timescale of TV. Perversely perhaps, Alexander is rather scornful of the idea of being able to retake parts of the film to come up with the right end product. It lacks skill and finesse. Perhaps anyone can do it. Alexander found his first day ever in a TV studio "scary". His inexperience was not helped when the BBC technicians went on strike.

Trevor Nunn's admiration for Alexander's work, and perhaps also his understanding of how Alexander was getting the best out of the talented Sher, led to his suggesting another collaboration. Nunn gave Alexander his first chance to direct Shakespeare in the main theatre at Stratford, with Sher in the lead role. The play, *Richard III*, was a brilliant choice for both men, showing the insight that has made Nunn such a powerful influence on British theatre for several decades. The production was to become a world-wide success, remembered long afterwards by audiences in Stratford, London and throughout Australia.

Given that the Alexander-Sher relationship was based upon creative tension, many hazards were to lie ahead before success was achieved. Sher had already noted during their earlier collaborations that they complemented each other by pulling in opposite directions. The long rehearsal period allowed at the RSC gave them ample scope for discussion. The fundamental style and image of the production came about through the interaction of three independent spirits – Alexander, designer Bill Dudley and Sher. If Sher's relationship with Alexander thrived on tension, the two Bills worked easily together. Alexander suggested that he wanted to emphasise the religious element of the play and Dudley designed the huge, light-flooded set, inspired by the interior of the Chapter House at Worcester Cathedral. This was decided before Sher became involved. An abiding image of the production and the themes of the play is of the 'bottled spider' crouching on a gigantic tomb, its shadow elongated and dominating the entire stage. Sher contributed the idea of Richard using crutches, not as a pitiful cripple but as the principal way of propelling himself like some fearsome springing insect virtually from one side of the stage to the other in one movement. It was a moment of breathtaking theatrical originality. Alexander had enlarged upon the crutches idea, suggesting the agility of the performance. Then Sher, well into rehearsals, had doubts about the entire idea, which was of course his own, and suggested cancelling the crutches. Alexander, horrified at the complete change of direction, gently persisted in their retention.

Another aspect that caused debate was the 'hump'. For Sher it was the key to the character and he embarked upon some painstaking research into the nature of back deformity. For Alexander a hump was a hump and he wanted to concentrate upon Richard's character. The words, the characters and the relationships were the important things. Ultimately the hump, when revealed on stage, was a distraction, obviously manufactured and only just escaping the dreaded inappropriate laughter from the audience.

The greatest danger was that Sher was speaking increasingly of the play as a comedy. It says much for Alexander's force of character that this potential disaster was seen off. A strange difference between the two men was that Sher was haunted by the Olivier film of *Richard III* and even suggested dropping the opening lines – "Now is the winter of our discontent..." - because they were so well-known through Olivier's definitive performance. Alexander had not seen the film.

One of their creative disagreements was about cuts. This time Sher rightly won the argument, but only at the eleventh hour. For a man who now cuts Fortinbras and a good deal more from his latest production of *Hamlet* and suggests that Shakespeare needed a good editor at the time of writing, Alexander was shy of making any cuts at all in *Richard III*. He did, however, invite the cast to suggest cuts in their own lines as they went along. He denounced "lazy cutting" and "careless butchery". For Alexander it was an extension, albeit with a well-known Shakespeare text, of the Warehouse approach. Directors and actors would work on cuts as they went along and as they developed their understanding of the play. The problem with this approach is that *Richard III* really is a one-man play: all other parts are small by comparison, and, with actors as notable as Patricia Routledge and Brian Blessed in the cast, Sher could see that there would be few offers of self-mutilation! In the end, after some tinkering, an 11.05pm finish at one of the previews, where the audience was almost too tired to clap, prompted more drastic measures. Large parts of the play were cut, but with care not butchery.

The tensions were creative. Sher commented that the two men "thought as one", which the record does not confirm. He was right, however, in noting the excitement that they generated in each other, a fact known throughout the Company.

The outcome was a vindication of Alexander's way of working. His insistence that the action must not be kept going at the expense of the texture and structure of the play prevailed. There were many differences and discussions, and final accord. Shakespeare's text was respected. Sher shone. It was a triumph. Celebrities came from afar to see performances, Peter Brook, Douglas Fairbanks and Michael Caine amongst them. Sher's parents came from South Africa to see a performance. Charlton Heston was in the same audience and had tea with them afterwards. Sher senior, a Jew, rejoiced at having had tea with Moses!

The British critics recognised that the play was hardly Shakespeare's subtlest and applauded Alexander's presentation of it in the grand manner. This main feature of the show, determined by the set, had been decided by Alexander and Bill Dudley before Sher had been committed to the role. The critics also admired Alexander's attention to detail. One specifically noted that this was not a "one-man show".

This was a pivotal production for Alexander, perhaps the most important of his career to date. The point was made at the time that, despite the glamour, the theatre is like most other jobs: "You keep your nose clean, make yourself useful within the organisation and, with a little luck, you'll be allowed some of the icing." Whilst Alexander has been a pioneer at The Warehouse in London and The Other Place at Stratford, there is still some fairness in the analogy. Big companies like the RSC have their hierarchies and other features of businesses. It had been noted that Alexander was not an ambitious man, but this confuses extroversion and ambition. Alexander's shambling appearance and self-effacing manner belie the strength of the man beneath, driven to better his own achievements in the theatre. With *Richard III*, Alexander was made an associate director and his reputation grew.

During a moment of particular closeness during the preparation of *Richard III*, Alexander and Sher had a simultaneous thought that they should collaborate again to do *The Merchant of Venice*, which happened four years later at Stratford. Whilst Sher again gave a performance judged to be "a spectacular and thrilling conquest of the role", it was Alexander's production that impressed. The obvious problem of the play – an apparent paradox between the Christians' blatant anti-semitism and Shylock's own unattractive trickery – was resolved in Shylock's favour. Some dubbed the performance anti-Christian because Alexander made it clear that the play is about the persecution of a minority community by a bullying majority. Shakespeare is a generous master in allowing Alexander to exercise his desire to highlight contemporary issues through great works of the past.

Sher and Alexander worked together once more - on a production of *Twelfth Night* with Sher as Malvolio. It was not a success. The two men remain good friends, acknowledging that at the time of their professional association, there was a lot at stake for both of them. The collaboration with Bill Dudley continued for productions of *The Merry Wives of Windsor* and *A Midsummer Night's Dream*. Dudley followed the ideas of Alexander and when the latter said he conceived of *The Merry Wives of Windsor* as having a parallel with the decline of the ruling classes in 1950's Britain, Dudley took off on a flight of retro fancy. He decorated the set with old-fashioned hood hairdryers under which the women gossiped, dressed his men in plus fours and even had a Morris Minor on stage to complete the fifties feel. The result was hilarious and entirely appropriate: the text was not compromised and the underlying themes enhanced. *A Midsummer Night's Dream* was less successful and when the production transferred to the Barbican, Alexander rethought the set and Dudley's name was no longer on the credits.

It would be wrong to assume that Alexander was totally immersed in Shakespeare in the 1984-1992 period. He directed a significant number of new plays and forged an association with the playwright Peter Whelan which was to last throughout his time at Birmingham Rep. Alexander directed Whelan's *Captain Swing*. Its broadly left-wing theme, about the struggle of agricultural labourers in the days before trade unionism, was congruent with Alexander's own vaguely left-wing non-party political views. The partnership continued with *The Bright and Bold Design* which was essentially a study of an old-style socialist, a "loud lumbering dinosaur" and foreman of a pottery factory in 1935. After the plaudits received for *Richard III*, it must have seemed like damning with faint praise to have a reviewer say "Bill Alexander's production builds up a nice atmosphere", but mixed reviews are accepted as part of the director's lot. Whelan treads very close to didacticism in his plays and it is to Alexander's credit that he can translate an earnest tract into watchable theatre. Whelan's play, *The School of Night*, an Elizabethan thriller about the murder of Christopher Marlowe, was the last that Alexander directed for the RSC before making his next significant career move.

BILL ALEXANDER

The progress from Stratford to become Artistic Director of the Birmingham Repertory Theatre had its beginnings in the early nineties, when Bill Alexander was approached by the Bristol Old Vic to become the artistic director there. He declined on the basis of having no administrative or financial experience, but the seed of an idea had been planted and he later paused to reflect on whether he had made the right career decision at the time. Thus when he was subsequently approached by David Edgar, who was on the Board of Birmingham Rep, to undertake the same job in Birmingham, he thought, why not? He was aware that there was very strong support for the arts from the council in Birmingham, which matched the Arts Council grants, something very rare, and which would fund his endeavours.

There is no doubt that, although Stratford and Birmingham are geographically close, they are in every other respect worlds apart. Anyone returning to Birmingham now after many years away is astounded by the transformation of England's second city. The massive planning blunders of the sixties and seventies, which built the inner city ring road and effectively isolated the centre from the rest of the city and deadened it after dark, have largely been neutralised. City centre streets, once congested with traffic, are now attractive pedestrian precincts. The canals and their footpaths, formerly hidden behind industrial squalor, now offer a pleasant environment in which to eat, drink, walk and generally relax. Central to the revival of Birmingham have been the three pillars of Symphony Hall, the Birmingham Royal Ballet and the Repertory Theatre.

Bill Alexander left Stratford the day after his last production there, *The School of Night,* opened and joined Birmingham Rep on November 5th 1993. Beginning any new job is a daunting prospect, but for Alexander the change was initially traumatic. Having enjoyed the camaraderie of a close group of directors, designers and actors working successfully and to national and international acclaim with the RSC, he was set down in an environment where he knew no-one. Not wanting to remove his family from Gloucestershire, where his children had reached a crucial stage in their schooling, Alexander lived in a flat in the theatre during the week, returning to Gloucestershire at weekends when his work schedule allowed.

In addition to his known skills as a director, he now had to acquire the business skills that would make the Rep profitable. This was no easy task. The main auditorium was playing to 50 per cent capacity audiences when he arrived. Unlike Stratford, which drew its audiences from across the country and, indeed, the world, Birmingham was catering for a local population: it was not a national theatre. With a smaller potential audience and a large theatre to fill, it was vital to discover what would draw in the people of Birmingham and establish a regular theatre-going public, what would, to put it crudely, put bums on seats. The acting space was a problem. A vast stage did not lend itself to the kind of four-handers with a realistic set put on in London, but needed, rather, a cast and a set on an epic scale. The word 'epic' was to appear many times and in many contexts during Alexander's time at the Rep. Tackling these difficulties required artistic ingenuity and creative skill, both of which Alexander successfully applied to the problem.

With hindsight, Alexander says he would not now have an artistic policy when running a theatre, but would do what "felt right" at the time as Sam Mendes did at the Donmar Warehouse. When he arrived at Birmingham, however, it was with a very definite artistic policy. He aimed to present works chosen from one of three areas: acknowledged classics of world drama, great plays that are almost never done, and new writing. He could be criticised for being rather too highbrow in his choice of plays for that first season – Ben Jonson's *Volpone*, *Othello* and Patrick Hamilton's 1920's thriller, *Rope*. Indeed he appeared somewhat disdainful of 'safe' audience pleasers such as Alan Ayckbourn and Willy Russell.

His production of *Othello* tackled the challenge of the huge stage space by foregoing the traditional notion of set, opting instead for a space that had, apparently, no enclosing boundary at the rear of the stage. Black square paving stones vanished into the gloom. From the shadows the actor playing Othello, Jeffrey Kissoon, emerged on to a stage that used lighting to define the geometry of the space. The lighting rig was forty feet above his head, emphasising the vastness of the area. Rather than finding the yawning emptiness daunting, Alexander revelled in it. His basic premise that the themes and issues of *Othello* are timeless and universal suited the abstract design. To this he added almost sculpted groups of actors to support the protagonists. A substantial number of the cast of thirty-two was drawn from the local community in an association that Alexander was to continue throughout his time at the Rep and which he found hugely exciting.

It was a production conceived on an epic scale and it received critical acclaim, particularly for its design, one writer commenting: "it is the visuals that stay in the mind." This was not, however, to be the production that married artistic with commercial success. It was the beginning of a long and difficult search by Alexander to find the crucial mix upon which his future depended. In one of his first interviews after having taken up the post of Artistic Director, he commented: "Rightly I will be judged by the Board on box office and if after eighteen months there has been no significant improvement the Board would be absolutely right to think about sacking me." He remained in post until 2000.

Alexander's production of *The Snowman* in 1993 could not have been further removed from *Othello* in every respect. Based on the now classic cartoon book by Raymond Briggs, which itself spawned a TV film version screened annually at Christmas time, the stage version looked set to be a crowd-pleaser. Alexander worked on the concept with Howard Blake to create a magical show. Full of tricksy special effects and ingenious lighting, actors flying through the air on wires, with music, dance and mime replacing dialogue, the production made full use of the space and put on a spectacle which was rated "10 out of 10" by children in a *Sunday Times* round-up of Christmas shows in 1997. The show played several Christmas seasons in Birmingham and transferred for a London season in 1998. It is due to be staged in London again over the Christmas period of 2001. Its regular revival points to its critical success: " a remarkable production", and its popularity with children: "the roar of delight from a very young audience when the second act began said it all", and would logically point to its commercial success, but it, too, did not fill the theatre in Birmingham and did not make any money. The production looks likely to be the best-remembered of his time at Birmingham, an idea he greets with some exasperation, referring to "The Bloody Snowman!"

A desire to continue using the cavernous space of the stage to positive effect, creating epic theatre, was continued in his 1995 production of *Macbeth.* He had noticed that the back wall of the stage with its bare brickwork and metal fire escape had something of the urban war zone about it and he used this idea as part of his broader conception of the play, dressing the set with iron walkways, shutters and staircases. *Macbeth* is often designed along militaristic lines, with quasi-Nazi uniforms, reflecting the play's themes of war and the search for power, which ultimately corrupts, but this must surely have been the first indoor production where army Jeeps crossed and recrossed the stage. More than once in his Shakespeare productions, Alexander has used his design and direction to echo twentieth century preoccupations. Thus his *Merry Wives of Windsor* became suburban housewives of the fifties gossiping under the hairdrier, while the class war raged around them. It was noted that this *Macbeth* had allusions to Bosnia in the form of a hanging woman, the Gulf represented by a carbonised skeleton and a terrorist massacre of Lady Macduff and her children, leaving only the TV blaring in the corner amidst the carnage. The production was a personal favourite of Alexander's and he was bewildered by the reaction of the critics. He had one superb review from Charles Spencer, "one of the best of my career", but the others were not particularly good. The more uncharitable of the critics saw his artistic licence as a way of attracting younger audiences, most notably the GCSE English Literature set. Alexander refutes the claim and notes that the production has had its imitations. If it had been deliberately designed to draw the exam crowds, it did not do so, and Alexander was left looking for other ways to entice the people of Birmingham into the theatre.

Not all of the productions at Birmingham at this time were Shakespeare or interpretations of other people's work. Alexander rekindled his successful association with Peter Whelan to create a play, *Divine Right*, in 1996. It is a 'what if' drama set in the year 2000, imagining a Royal Family in which the Prince of Wales is about to remarry and renounce his claim to the throne. The play plots the progress of his 18-year-old son as he slips away to mingle anonymously, Henry V-like, with the public to discover their views. The second strand of the play has a Labour government in power and a strong republican element in that party gaining support. The idea for the play was Alexander's. Whelan was casting about for a subject for a new play and Alexander, a friend as well as a colleague, suggested: "Write about the end of the monarchy and the beginning of a republic". Whelan and Alexander felt that they could not have chosen a better serious issue, likely to capture the public's, and more pertinently, the theatre-going public's attention. The monarchy was an explosive subject at the time. Princess Diana, in a TV interview with Martin Bashir, had told the world about her disastrous marriage, about her affair with James Hewitt and her desire to become the 'Queen of People's Hearts'. In April 1996 she received her decree absolute and the split with Prince Charles was complete. The Queen had had her *annus horribilis* in 1992, and in 1996 the Conservative government was in its death throes. In an interview just before the play's opening night at Birmingham, Whelan told an interviewer why he had written the play as a republican and avoided the gossip surrounding Diana and Fergie: "If I did the latter I would be going over ground already covered by others. Anyway, because I set the play four years hence, I was anxious to keep the Fergies and Dianas out of it. In four years' time, I hope, people will be saying 'Diana who?'" The dramatic irony of these words is almost painful now. Diana has become an icon to some, a goddess who was sacrificed on the altar of a crumbling monarchy; to others her life and death are now the most potent point in the argument for electing our Head of State. The debate continues.

The play received mixed reviews. The seriousness of its approach was queried by some and compared adversely with contemporaneous satires on the subject, notably Sue Townsend's *The Queen and I*, where the Royal Family is exiled to a council house in the Midlands, and Michael Dobbs's *To Play the King* which attracted large TV audiences. Alexander was applauded for putting the play on in Birmingham, thereby providing a platform to air the crisis in national identity of which the crisis in the monarchy was but a part. Peter Whelan gained his own accolade when he received an award for Best New Play from the TMA Theatre Awards that year. As for Alexander, he had remained true to his own personal belief in the need to provide the public with thought-provoking works on matters of topical concern and to the artistic vision he had outlined on his arrival at the Rep which was to stage new works. Still the people of Birmingham did not turn out in significant numbers to see it and Alexander says of the production: "It emptied the place."

In 1997 the Rep received a huge shot in the arm in the form of £5.7 million of lottery funding as a stabilisation grant, to consolidate the artistic plan for the theatre and make it a going concern. It cleared the theatre's £2 million deficit and doubled its annual subsidy. For Alexander, it was artistically liberating. It would enable him to refresh his original vision, although in essence it remained the same: to put on six epic productions a year suitable to the size of the auditorium, which would tour nationally and abroad; £1 million to be put aside for commissioning new work; big name actors to be attracted with the offer of better pay; a permanent group of eight actors performing new plays in the intimate studio space; staging of 'discovery plays' – great works rarely performed. It was the opportunity to challenge the National Theatre and the RSC as a flagship company, bringing theatre to the Midlands and the North. It was also Alexander's last chance to make the Rep pay. If he could not boost audience figures now, he never would.

It did not work. How dispiriting to put on play after play which received national acclaim - *The Cherry Orchard* with Janet Suzman, *Old Times* with Tim Piggott-Smith, and productions of *The Tempest* and *The Merchant of Venice* to name but a few - and consistently see houses 30 per cent and 50 per cent full.

The production of which Alexander was most proud during his time at Birmingham was *Frozen*, a new play by Bryony Lavery. It dealt with the topical issues of paedophilia and child murder and starred Anita Dobson of *EastEnders* fame and Josie Lawrence, the comic actress who at the time seemed to be on every TV comedy show. Discarding their familiar personae for this gripping three-hander, they played the mother of a sexually abused child and an American psychiatrist, with Tom Georgeson making up the trio as the paedophile, Ralph. Alexander described the play as "the most brilliant new play I have ever done", and the critics agreed that it was a major work. It played to 25 per cent houses in the main auditorium.

The greatest box office success of Alexander's time in Birmingham came about almost by accident. Richard Eyre of the

National Theatre was to put on a co-production of *The Alchemist* with Sheffield, which pulled out at the last minute. He rang Alexander and asked if Birmingham would like to take Sheffield's place. Alexander agreed and the play, a busy and crowded production, was duly staged. On reflection, Alexander thought that it was the NT tag that drew the audiences, along with familiar names Simon Callow and Josie Lawrence in the major roles. The irony, that he had been trying to create a national profile for Birmingham, was not lost upon him, nor the irony that the play he was least happy with did the best business.

Alexander tried everything. For his Christmas production on the eve of the millennium, he put on *Nativity*, once again in collaboration with Peter Whelan. He thought, not unreasonably, that this was an appropriate juncture in history to put on a play about the birth of Christ. Despite a plethora of miracles, a real, live, flying Angel Gabriel and moments of humour, it lacked the appeal of the traditional pantomimes showing elsewhere in Birmingham at the time. Five months later Alexander was directing another interpretation of the story of Christ. *Quarantine*, about Christ's forty days in the wilderness, was conceived as a promenade production, although in the 150-seat studio it was on a far smaller scale than the National Theatre's interpretation of the medieval mystery plays. Alexander termed it less a promenade for the audience and more a pivoting on their heels and coming face to face with Jesus! By the time he came to direct *Twelfth Night* it is possible to speculate that Alexander's growing frustration and depression at the failure of his policies to bring box office success bled into his interpretation of this normally jolly play. One critic commented that it was unrelentingly gloomy and the first production of the play he had seen without laughter.

In the Spring of 2000, Alexander announced his resignation as Artistic Director of Birmingham Rep and a decision to take six months' sabbatical with the words: "I don't know what to do". In truth, it seemed as if he had tried everything to make theatre in Birmingham pay. It is easy, with hindsight, to pick over the reasons why, despite putting on productions which artistically have cemented his reputation as one of the nation's leading directors of the theatre, the audiences did not come in significant numbers. Perhaps the 'Catch 22' of a large stage that needed expensive epic productions, which were not to an audience's liking, who therefore did not come, and therefore did not provide the income to put on expensive epic productions, was insoluble. Perhaps the indefinable link between the theatre and the community was lacking. Perhaps Alexander's decision not to move his home to Birmingham prevented him from entirely understanding the people who lived there. Perhaps there simply was not the appetite for theatre when there were so many competing leisure activities available in the area. Theatres nowadays need to diversify to survive and a theatre complex which could make more contact with the public through community-related activities, going out to the local population, would have more chance of success. Perhaps Birmingham needed a Fun Art Bus.

Certainly Alexander was very much concerned, for the very laudable reason of wanting the theatre to achieve national status, that the plays put on in Birmingham should be reviewed in the national papers. This had the effect of alienating the local press. A hostile local press can be a dangerous beast and cannot have helped Alexander's cause in Birmingham. There was even a hyena-like dispute that broke out among the Birmingham journalists about which one had given Alexander most trouble. When Alexander accused one, Fred Norris, of having a negative influence on the Rep, Norris was delighted and fuelled the dispute with a vituperative article about Alexander, but another journalist, Bill Hayward, was inflamed that he too had not been accused of the same negativity. In a strange way, the parochialism of this spat vindicated Alexander's view that the

Rep needed to broaden its horizons if it was to be successful.

Was his artistic vision too highbrow? A look at the programme for the Spring and Summer of 1999 would suggest not. It was a lively mix of music, dance and drama, of crowd-pleasers such as *The New Rocky Horror Show* and *The Pajama Game*, 'serious theatre' such as *The Birthday Party* and *Jumpers*, and new works such as *The Four Alice Bakers* by Fay Weldon. One trend which Alexander was not happy to accept was the growing practice of provincial theatres being receiving houses for successful London productions. He noted with sadness the fact that the Everyman Theatre in Cheltenham had gone along this route and it looked likely that others would follow. He thought the movement was in the wrong direction and gave provincial theatre a bad name. He put down to his own pride and vanity the fact that he believed someone should be producing the new plays to feed London theatres, and Birmingham under Bill Alexander was the place to do it. The old dichotomy between artistic integrity and commercial success was not resolved by Alexander. As he ruefully admitted: "I was never any good at sums". What is indisputable is his artistic talent, and he emerges from his sabbatical revitalised and eager to pursue new projects. One should not be too gloomy about Alexander's time at the Rep. Once he got used to the business of running a theatre and was putting on plays of his choice, he found the work exciting and enjoyable. Within the profession there was a strong sense that he had enhanced the reputation of the theatre.

Bill Alexander is currently in talks with the Ambassadors Group to front a new company, The London Shakespeare Company, which would put on a major Shakespeare production each year at the Albery Theatre beginning with *All's Well That Ends Well*. In the summer of 2001 he took his acclaimed Birmingham Rep production of *Hamlet* to Elsinore. The Christmas season will see a revival of *The Snowman*. There are plans to work abroad in Europe, America and Tel Aviv. He has no plans to diversify into TV or film work. He is essentially a 'theatre animal' who loves live theatre for its difficulty, the challenge of filling an empty blank space in real time, which the director has to animate. What drives him is the belief that he still does not know how to do it, that the craft has not been mastered. What he does know is that text and the visual aspect of a play must complement each other, that the text must be energised. It is the realisation of this idea that has been at the heart of his best work throughout his career to date. He is hungry to work, and now free from the shackles of having to second guess what will make the economy of a regional theatre turn over successfully. The future looks bright for Bill Alexander.

JEREMY DIXON
and
EDWARD JONES

Whilst some architects were helping us to celebrate the millennium by building PVC-covered domes and wobbling bridges, others were at work to give us longer-lasting pleasures. Foremost amongst the architects who are extending and renewing some of the landmark buildings of London is the partnership of Jeremy Dixon and Edward Jones. It was established in 1989 to complete the redesign of the Royal Opera House although the two men had known each other since their student days and had previously worked together in the 1970s.

Dixon and Jones, with others (like the architects of Tate Modern, the British Museum's Great Court, the Gateshead Millennium Bridge and the London Eye), have done something remarkable. They have got us to look at buildings and structures again for their beauty and functions. It is demanding on the neck muscles but does wonders for the spirits. Architects are in the news in a way that they have not been for many years. Not as figures of obloquy for erecting dull, rain-stained, concrete slabs nor as architectural caricatures for designing futuristic creations that bear little relation to their function - even the otherwise wonderful Sidney Opera House cannot stage grand opera because its pit will not take a full orchestra - but as admired artists.

What are the buildings in London that have attracted hugely increased numbers of visitors and given great pleasure in recent years? The Royal Opera House, now visited by almost as many non-opera and ballet-goers as people who see the works on stage. The National Portrait Gallery, where the older works that were previously neglected are now attracting crowds and where tables in the restaurant have to be booked well in advance. Somerset House, once the home to records of births, deaths and marriages, but now a splendid public building with a riverside terrace, and an open space for the public to enjoy, with imaginative fountains that are replaced by outdoor skating in the winter.

Dixon and Jones have made these buildings important again and enabled them to function properly for our time. Theirs are not simply works of restoration. They are new buildings created as part of the opening up of old buildings, carried out sympathetically and with great flair by two imaginative architects. They cannot say, as Christopher Wren could, that their monuments are all around them. But then they did not have the benefit of the Great Fire before they got started.

Their work is itself carried out in an old building, part of a former industrial site and, on the outside, a rather gaunt building amongst the otherwise elegant Victorian terraces of Gloucester Avenue in London's Primrose Hill. It was in the nineteenth century the factory and stores of the postal telegraph service, presided over by a civil engineer and surveyor.

Once past the entry phone, the only external concession to modernity, and having climbed the stairs that look unchanged after a century and a half, you reach the architects' studios and enter a different world. A long uninterrupted loft with a high ceiling, flooded with daylight, original wood floors, a mezzanine open floor at one end where the partners work and can survey their staff much as their Victorian predecessors might have done, and a little library and interview room partitioned off at the other end. The old has been largely kept but made to work for a new purpose. Its origins are obvious and valued for their quality but it feels entirely modern. The work place that they have created for themselves illustrates, on a small scale, their sensitive transformation of an old building for contemporary use.

Before their recent work in London, Dixon and Jones had already made their marks, individually and in partnership, in Leeds (Henry Moore Institute), Aberdeen (student housing at Robert Gordon University), Toronto (Mississauga City Hall), Portsmouth (a new science building for the University),

Cambridge (Darwin College) and Plymouth (a Sainsbury superstore). All of these works won awards. Their current projects are taking them to Oxford, Salisbury, Norwich and Belfast, whilst they also start on a major, prestigious building for University College, London. Meanwhile they are the master planners for the development of the National Gallery in Trafalgar Square and for the continued development of Somerset House.

Jeremy Dixon and Edward Jones met as students, although they were not professionally close at that time, and they later worked together as employees before setting up separately in private practice. Their present partnership was not formed until thirty years after they first met. They have worked apart for longer than they have worked together and they still do some things separately. Jones spent a significant part of his earlier life as a teacher at the Royal College of Art and in some of the most prestigious North American universities, and cannot quite give up doing something that he enjoys and at which he excels. He still travels to the USA for short periods to give lectures and has a regular engagement teaching American students in Florence four or five times a year. He is the joint author of the standard work on the buildings of London, acknowledged as his favourite on the subject by Richard Rogers. Dixon also lectures, assesses students and judges competitions.

Their way of thinking is crucial to their success. They do not have one style that makes their buildings immediately recognisable, as for example does Norman Foster. They are not signature architects. Nor do they belong to the clan that Deyan Sudjic, the architectural reviewer, calls "the ones licensed to be weird." In Dixon's words, they are "more a Picasso, responding in different ways to new challenges, than a Matisse who found his individual style early and spent his life honing it."

They would not have put the "carbuncle" on the end of the National Gallery that was once planned before the Sainsbury wing was built, not because of a hostility to modernity, but because it was not right for the site or sympathetic to what was already there. They could not have built Pimlico School, where the concept of the ocean liner in the architect's mind imposed itself, without regard to the way in which schools operate and with little understanding of the difference between a glass-sided sun deck and a classroom. But equally they have no truck with the neo-classical pastiche favoured by royal amateurs. In the thinking that precedes their designs they assess the needs of the users and the opportunities of the site, follow certain principles – "connections", "opening up", "geometrical" are words that recur in conversation with them – and use materials with an understanding of their effect. They think conceptually but diversely. It is an effective partnership between two quite different people.

Both men are knowledgeable, thoughtful and imaginative. Otherwise they are a contrast with qualities that complement each other and which are the basis of the successful collaboration. Jeremy Dixon speaks quietly and reflectively in a deceptively languid manner belied by a record of having successfully brought off some very complicated grand projects. Edward Jones is the more extrovert of the pair, using an eyebrow like a conductor's baton to emphasise a point. They can both explain architecture lucidly to those without professional knowledge. Both men are humorous, but again in quite different ways, the one almost imperceptibly so, the other naturally jolly.

Although they had worked together previously, the Royal Opera House was the project on which the present Dixon-Jones partnership was founded. Dixon was already working with his architect wife, Fenella, and Bill Jack, of the Building Design Partnership, on the opera house project. In this fraught undertaking, almost the only constant factors were the architects and the sponsors, principally John Sainsbury and later Vivien Duffield. Government ministers, directors of the ROH and the board of governors came and went. It took sixteen years from start to finish, with the total money actually to build becoming finally available only in the last few years. So there was no certainty that this early work would bear fruit. By 1989 the Dixons had already been working on the project for five years.

In that year Jeremy Dixon's personal and professional world fell apart. Fenella left him and architecture. Other people were also leaving the practice, because there was still no certainty that their efforts would ever bear fruit. The most important constant, the design team, was now itself falling apart. Jeremy, needing to find a professional collaborator in place of Fenella and shore up the dwindling team, decided to telephone Edward to see whether he was available.

Meanwhile, Edward Jones had been working and living in Toronto. He had been commuting by air to teach at Harvard and Princeton. In 1989 he reached a big decision with his wife Margot. Having spent a large part of his professional career teaching at universities and having enjoyed it, he had accepted an offer of a full professorship with tenure at Princeton, a prestigious appointment. The couple were already house-hunting in the area when it became clear that Margot was unhappy at the prospect. As Jones says, few Canadians relish the prospect of living in the States. As Margot herself says, she was not particularly attached either to her native Toronto. They found themselves not wanting to go back to Toronto or forward to New Jersey. Where, then? London? Edward telephoned Jeremy.

In an extraordinary occurrence after a long gap in their professional association, the two men called each other simultaneously and found each other's telephones engaged. "Spooky" is how both describe the remarkable coincidence. The result was the present partnership. As the two men say, one with a grimace, the other with a grin, a new partnership was founded by a couple of wrinklies, although they were both only 50. In 2001 it was still only twelve years old but has enormous combined experience.

Two years after forming the partnership, the pair won the prestigious Gateway to Venice competition at the Venice Biennale in 1991. Their victory over 270 other competitors was a commemoration of their coming together. The task was to design a bus station in the Piazzale Roma, and, as in so much of their work when planning a new building with the advantage of a large, empty site, they chose a geometrical form, in this case a circle, with a hint of the colosseum. Despite having held the competition, the Venetian authorities decided to abandon the project and the bus station was not built. The £7,000 prize money did little more than cover the costs of their model.

As Jones comments, with the mock innocence of one who not only participates and succeeds, but at the same time wonders at the absurdity of the competition itself, "Architects must be slightly mad." They put up with a tendering system that requires so much expenditure of time, effort and money in such competitive conditions and with no guarantee of building ever taking place and little prospect of even covering their costs. But winning the prize cemented the partnership and enhanced its reputation. Without monetary value at the time, it was an investment for the future.

❖ ❖ ❖ ❖ ❖

Meanwhile work was continuing on the Royal Opera House project. It dominated their lives for a decade, for it was a mammoth task, conducted against a background of financial, political and artistic uncertainty. Everybody had an idea on what to do for the best. Even the Culture and Arts Minister, Chris Smith, a stout fighter for the project, lobbed a hand-grenade into the debate at a very late stage by suggesting that the building should house both of the two major opera companies based in London, with the English National Opera moving from its home at the Coliseum in St Martin's Lane to co-habit with the Royal

Opera. Bernard Haitink, the opera's distinguished musical director so admired by his musicians and audiences, resigned but was persuaded to stay. Anthony Dowell, the director of the dance company, soldiered on and lost some of his best young dancers in a conspiracy that took them to Japan. More than two hundred people came and went in the architects' office during the long gestation period. Not an inspiring backdrop for architectural endeavour.

After years of doubt, sufficient lottery money suddenly became available to complete the finance and enable work to begin on the ground. Then it all had to be finished in two years. During its construction, it was one of the most attractive building sites ever seen by tourists, neatly bordered with mock hedges, all trim and tidy. During these two years, £5 million were being spent every month. Miraculously it was completed on time.

For Dixon and Jones the design principles which they had evolved remained valid, despite the shenanigans going on between the financiers, politicians and managers, and the turmoil amongst the Opera House creative staff. The triumphant outcome that is the new Royal Opera House building illustrates their thinking and why they have been so good for the capital city.

One of their principal aims was to draw the ROH back into its surroundings. Previously it was a huge building dominating the narrow Bow Street, unconnected with the Covent Garden from which it takes its popular name. Specifically they wanted to connect Bow Street and the Covent Garden piazza, which is now achieved at street level. Vertical routes were just as important and they have achieved a connection between the front entrance, up the original grand staircase, then left through the Floral Hall and up a long, dramatic escalator to the new open-air loggia looking down on the piazza and all the bubbling life of the old market place. This route also achieves, in building terms, the egalitarian objective of reducing the stuffy and elitist image of the previous theatre. The amphitheatre bar at the top of the escalator, there to serve those in the cheapest seats, is a major attraction – "a rooftop village" with direct access to the open-air loggia and its unexpected glimpse of Nelson's Column, and a clever indoor window looking down on the Floral Hall.

Dixon and Jones have also met the requirements of what is a city within a city. The ROH houses not only performers, both singers and dancers with their different needs, but also a wide range of craftspeople, caterers working on a scale to match a grand hotel, and the administration needed for such a large enterprise.

The building itself now generates excitement and pleasure. The Floral Hall, sun-lit during the day, magical at night, is simply a wonderful place to spend time. Although much structural and detailed work was done on the auditorium, it feels just the same as it always did. This itself is a characteristically brilliant touch, for the auditorium was always the best, perhaps the only good, part of the original. The new building that makes up one corner of the Covent Garden square is a fine example of urban renewal, simple in style and not dominating the former fruit and vegetable market buildings that it faces. Technically the building has moved forward by two centuries. An additional auditorium, the Linbury, is in a very modern style, suitable for smaller-scale productions, lectures and performances by outside companies, such as Pegasus Opera, dedicated to bringing in new audiences. The new construction is sympathetic to the old. The entire building compels attention and invites exploration.

Along with other landmark buildings created around Britain at the turn of the millennium – the Lowry Centre at Salford, the Walsall Art Gallery, the successful Millennium Bridge at Gateshead and many others - this combination of creation and re-creation by Dixon and Jones has made us look at buildings again, and not just take them for granted. 'Gawping' at buildings has returned to London. Buildings now get reviews like films, plays and music in all the main newspapers. It would be quite proper for the new ROH to put notices outside, such as "magnificent" - *The Times*, "wonderful, wonderful, wonderful" - *The Observer*, "a Garden of earthly delights" - *Sunday Times*. They would not be comments about a production on stage, for they are verdicts on the building itself.

Not everybody likes it, but then not everybody shared Dixon and Jones's wish, and that of Chris Smith, to make the House more accessible. Typical of some board members and their attitudes to the artists, let alone the public, was that of an old Etonian banker. He thought that one of the directors working at the theatre at the time, was a "bastard" who needed to be "kicked." The person deserving a horse-whipping was Trevor Nunn, who had brought his celebrated Glyndebourne *Porgy and Bess* with Willard White to the House, before going on to become director of the Royal National Theatre. The comment was the more ludicrous because *Porgy and Bess* was intended to reduce some of the Royal Opera House's huge deficit, which it did with an extension of the run to satisfy the demand for tickets.

Some rather more sophisticated people considered that the aim of greater access dictated the style. "As popular as a taxi cab, it's been revamped in an easy modern-shakes-hands-with-soft-classical styling, courtesy of that charming and talented architectural duo Jeremy Dixon and Edward Jones." It is, in fact, a typical Dixon and Jones triumph, blending the existing with the new and with "endless short cuts and back doubles through the building that retain plenty of the eccentricity of the original", as one architectural reviewer notes. The new building, for that is what it is, is much valued by those who work in it, those who go to performances, and those who use it just as an amenity - part of Covent Garden and a good place to meet friends, eat and browse.

A large architectural project usually takes about five years from inception to completion. The Royal Opera House took sixteen, with the two men working together for the last eleven of those – a substantial part of anyone's professional life. Dixon, who was in at the beginning, was 44 when he started on it and 60 when it was complete. Their experience confirmed the view, widely held in their profession, that the quality of the client is an important ingredient in the relationships that enable buildings to proceed imaginatively from initial meetings to completion. The old adage that a camel is a horse designed by a committee rings true. Their constancy overcame the difficulties and there were always people on the inside with whom they could work, not least Jeremy Isaacs whose contribution to the triumph they greatly value.

The long, demanding and anxious period spent on the project made both men ill. Jones had pneumonia and was in hospital for some time. Dixon had broken his Achilles tendon and spent the last four months hobbling over the building site with his leg in plaster. Nonetheless they enjoyed the opening night. Jones, still far from well, was released early from hospital for the occasion. Jeremy Dixon, not a naturally flamboyant man, cut something of a dash by painting his protruding toes midnight blue to match the dress of his partner, Julia Somerville, the ITN newscaster. The Queen was said to have been amused. Indeed, "tickled pink" by one account.

The next London client was very much of the quality valued by architects. As Jones says, "A good project has a good client, not a committee." Dr Charles Saumarez Smith was a resident of London Docklands, and one of the buildings there that he most admired had been designed in dark brick by Jeremy Dixon. He was also the Director of the National Portrait Gallery and an imaginative person who knew and could articulate his objectives and who recognised a good idea. Moreover, he was complemented by a similar Director of the National Gallery next door in Neil MacGregor.

Most people, having turned the corner from Trafalgar Square into the Charing Cross Road, did not realise that the 'east wing' was in fact the start of the National Portrait Gallery. When the Treasury had granted the site to the National Portrait Gallery in 1896, it had stipulated that the existing classical style of Wilkins's National Gallery had to be continued round the corner. The new gallery was appropriately described by the writer Henry James soon after its opening as "a bustle attached to the padding of the National Gallery's posterior."

There was a rear courtyard between the two institutions owned by the National Portrait Gallery. The lower levels of the National Gallery had their daylight from this space. Dixon and Jones's proposal was to give the east wing of the NPG to the National Gallery in exchange for bricking up these windows and, as a result, giving to the NPG the unencumbered use of the courtyard. The two gallery directors worked together and encouraged their trustees to agree the 'deal'. They 'connected', as Dixon and Jones would put it. The NPG kept its original entrance, and Dixon and Jones were then able to build straight back into the former courtyard.

The building is essentially a vertical structure. When touring the NPG to prepare their design for the competition, the two architects opened a door off the upper gallery and trespassed on to the roof, discovering a wonderful view across Trafalgar Square and down Whitehall – a vista that nobody knew or remembered existed. What a location for a new restaurant! Similarly, at the bottom of the building there were damp and rat-infested basement vaults that could be turned into a bookshop and small café with a glass ceiling giving a view up to the passers-by in the street above and connecting with the bustle of Charing Cross Road. Between the top and bottom are the portraits.

The need for building arose from increased visitor numbers but also a wish to get more people to the top of the building where the earliest portraits had been neglected. There was also a need to get more natural light into the galleries and this could come only from the top because there were no light sources from the sides until the highest point of the second floor. This light source needed to be made available to the lower floors. The answer was structural. Put a single column with a beam at the top and hang all the floors from it, not covering the entire floor area, so that light can bounce off walls. Put in an escalator to take visitors straight to a higher level, where the previously neglected Tudor portraits are shown, and they then work their way down chronologically. Put the restaurant at the very top above the galleries, not only for the newly discovered vista but also because passing the exhibitions on the way down is then inevitable – there is no down escalator. The Tudor Gallery had to be illuminated for conservation reasons by fibre optics, with the result that the faces now take on a ghost-like appearance in their gilded frames.

The third commission that has brought new life to an old building was Somerset House. Dixon and Jones, with other architects, have provided for the first time in recent years an attraction at the junction of the Strand and the north end of Waterloo Bridge, an area previously regarded as an 'off-pitch' corner of London. The 'connections' that they wanted to make here were between the Strand and the Thames, and between the bridge and the Somerset House courtyard. The 'opening up', craved by the Director, Duncan Wilson, was to give public access to a building previously (and still in part) occupied by the Inland Revenue. What is now a splendidly restored courtyard was until recently a tarmac eyesore for the parking of ministry cars.

The work was a combined effort by several architects. There is now a direct entrance from the Embankment at street level, with the old water entrance preserved and visible under a glass floor as a reminder of the building's former river and naval roles. At the level above, with direct access from Waterloo Bridge, is an existing terrace with splendid views across to the South Bank and, thanks to the meanders of the Thames, to many other important buildings up and downstream. In the large courtyard, which the visitor from the Strand sees on entry to the site, fifty-five fountains in a geometrical grid spurt direct from the cobble stones, and the area is given over to open-air ice skating at Christmas and the New Year. Somerset House is now a public facility – "a palace for the people" as one architectural reviewer has named it. Dixon and Jones's contributions were the bridge connection, the fountains and the canopies.

Following Dixon and Jones's principles of 'connections' and 'opening up' it is now possible to take a walk from the South Bank, across Waterloo Bridge, turn right from the bridge on to the Somerset House terrace, through the courtyard by the fountains, out into the Strand and across Aldwych into Covent Garden.

❖ ❖ ❖ ❖ ❖

Dixon and Jones have remarkably similar backgrounds. They were born in the same year, 1939, both had artistic parents, went to public schools and trained at the Architectural Association School. They are quite different characters.

Edward Jones was born in St Albans. His mother, Margot, was a portrait painter who exhibited at the Royal Academy. David, his father, had been a gifted sculptor and had been taught at the Royal College of Art in the 1930s by Henry Moore and Jacob Epstein. Unlike them, he could not make a living from sculpture, so he went to the USA to design cars for General Motors. He was a leader in initiatives to 'style' cars rather than just engineer them, using his sculptor's eye and becoming Vauxhall's director of styling at Luton for more than thirty years until 1971. He died in 2000, aged 90. Edward Jones remembered his father in the same year by going to see Maggie Smith in *Lady in the Van*, for the vehicle that Miss Shepherd's had parked in Alan Bennett's garden was a Dormobile, one of Jones senior's designs. By another coincidence, Bennett's house and the location of the

Dormobile were in the street where Jones now lives and from which he walks along the canal towpath to work in the partnership's offices.

The influence of both parents on Edward was considerable. Family holidays were usually to those parts of the French countryside most associated with the Impressionists. Art was one of his most important school subjects, although he did not find in the Hertfordshire countryside – "soporific and romantic, but not powerful" - the same stimulation as that of France or other more dramatic regions of Britain.

School was also in Hertfordshire, at Haileybury, the boarding school near Hertford founded originally by the East India Company for the sons of its staff stationed in the East. The school's buildings had been designed by Wilkins, also the architect of the National Gallery and University College, London, where the partnership now have two of their major commissions. Such historical "connections" are important to Jones.

Life at boarding school seemed at the time to be "all right", neither better nor worse. In retrospect it seems "monstrous", all male and much bullying, with chapel three times on Sundays. Survival for an artist was made possible by Jones's skill at rugby and boxing, which made labels such as 'pansy' hazardous to offer and difficult to make stick. There was, nevertheless, something in the values of the school that was admirable. Albeit couched in terms of 'king and country', there was a view that public service had status, and many pupils headed for the church and government. Being an artist was not respectable, but architecture was half-way there. He could rise to the school's expectation that its old boys should contribute to the common good.

After Haileybury, the Architectural Association School (AA), which Jones joined in 1958, was "a magical place." Occupying three houses in Bedford Square, its students of both genders were able to enjoy London whilst working hard at their studies. The students saw themselves as making a contribution to the building of the welfare state and had a strong belief in the improving effects of well-designed schools and public housing. Jones's thesis towards the end of his five years at the School was about designing a training college for teachers at Swindon. Dixon, who was a year ahead of Jones, designed a comprehensive school for his thesis.

Almost a decade as an employee followed, some of it in America. Jones declares himself to be in love with the American dream, not naively for he sees its essential hollowness, but he admires the energy of the country and prefers the notion of being a citizen to that of being a subject. He worked there between his third and fourth years at the AA, in Detroit, and on the Lincoln Centre in New York, student housing for Yale University and the TWA bird-like building at Idlewild (now JFK) Airport, New York.

On his return to Britain he met Dixon again. Although they had overlapped at the AA School for four of their five years there, they had not been very close as students. They now came together, with two other architects, all of them still employees, to work on public housing in part of the new town of Milton Keynes in Buckinghamshire, close to the M1 motorway. They were an office within an office, four architects in their thirties and known as the Grunt Group.

He now considers that their project was planned on too big a scale, too quickly and that their ideas were too sophisticated for the overall plan. They all believed then that architecture would triumph against the odds, but it did not. Many problem families were moved in together and architecture proved to be no more effective in solving concerted social problems in isolation than is education. Both Jones and Dixon drove through the area some years later and were shocked by what they saw.

The two men first worked in private practice together just up the motorway from Milton Keynes in Northampton. To win competitions, which is the key to successful private practice, architects have to be in private practice, or at least to have the trappings of it. Dixon had already won the first stage of a competition, with his wife Fenella, when Jones joined him. Their design for the county council's new offices won the competition but, like the Venice bus station some years later, it was never built. Quite reasonably, as the two men now say, although they were rather sore at the time, the county council changed its priorities and decided to spend money on school buildings instead. Their design, as is often the case with them when working on an empty site, was geometrical, in this case a huge, glazed pyramid. This early and short partnership ended and Jones became an almost full-time senior tutor at the Royal College of Art.

The following year, Jones married the second Margot in his life, a Canadian. Jones travelled frequently to America to lecture at Harvard, Yale and Rice Universities as visiting professor, whilst maintaining a small private practice in London. For seven years teaching was the focus of his activities.

The big break into private practice came when he won first prize in a competition to design the Mississauga City Hall in Toronto. Jones made his name in North America with this building, with Trinity Gardens, another Toronto project, and with teaching at Toronto University. Whilst his designs for Mississauga were being realised on the ground, he was able to check on progress from the air on his way by plane to teach at Yale.

After his long period of tutoring at the Royal College of Art in London and at North American universities, Jones seemed destined for an academic career when he was offered and accepted the full professorship at Princeton but, as we have seen, he and Margot decided that they preferred to return to London.

❖ ❖ ❖ ❖ ❖

Dixon's mother was a painter but largely gave up her career to bring up the children. His father in a sense did the opposite of Jones's, being an engineer first but being more interested in porcelain. More important than either of his parents' professions was the environment in which they decided to bring up their children. Soon after the start of the war in 1939 they moved from Bishop's Stortford to Penn in Buckinghamshire to join an informal artists' colony. The main contingent were leaving London to escape the expected bombing of the capital, and included Herbert Read and several curators of the Victoria and Albert Museum. Read was a strong advocate of the view that architecture would be the salvation of the arts. "He was proved wrong, of course," comments Dixon sadly now, but that was the basis of the group and it had a big influence, vicariously through his parents, on the teenage Jeremy. It enabled his parents to see and they were able to let Jeremy see that architecture was the right career for him. Music also played a big part in the life of the group, with recitals and concerts in the Mayflower Barn at Penn. Dixon is sure that he heard an early concert by the Amadeus Quartet there in the late 1940s.

He became a boarder at Merchant Taylors' School where he had "a pretty poor school life". The school emphasised the academic to the exclusion of other skills, whereas Dixon's aptitude was for making things. Making models gave him the greatest pleasure and he still believes firmly that making model aircraft is the best way to learn about structure and the achievement of strength. So he was good at woodwork, metalwork and art in a school that rated other subjects more highly. Reflecting on his early education, Dixon now thinks that he was probably dyslexic before the phenomenon, let alone the term, was recognised. Even now he dislikes writing – "Writing a letter is a nightmare." – although he claims to be good at dictation. The other feature of school life that made for misery was his sadistic house-master. He left school feeling a failure.

Capping his rather miserable time at school, Dixon's parents split up. His mother was his saving grace. After Herbert Read, whose ideas reached him through his parents, she was the second great influence on him, in particular by taking him to London during school holidays to look at buildings. She did for him, as part of his education, what he now does for us in making buildings important things at which to look.

A career using art, not considered a proper subject at Merchant Taylors' but the one at which he excelled at A-level, was where his future lay and architecture held out at least the prospect of being able to earn a living. His arrival at the Architectural Association School, a year before Jones, gave him an enormous sense of liberation after public school. The School was a very important place for both men. Founded in the nineteenth century, it was independent and democratic. Its students appointed and could dismiss the principal. Staff were not permanent, but were changed frequently with many visiting teachers, in order to ensure a breadth of current practitioners. Whilst Dixon and Jones were there people like John Summerson, Furneaux-Jordan and Reyner Banham were everyday lecturers. Having left school, Dixon was entering a new and exciting world. He was free to be himself and gain confidence.

Admission to the AA was by talent rather than examination qualifications. Dixon's strengths were in the things that he had made and his ability to demonstrate his eye for form and for buildings. Dixon states boldly, and doubtless to the chagrin of many other architects, that, "Architecture is not an academic subject." He is not, of course, denying that there is a body of knowledge to be mastered, a past to be studied, and much technical support needed from other specialists such as engineers, but he is saying that architecture is primarily about imagination and having a good eye.

There was a consonance between the AA's approach and the sense of great change in society, engendering much creative energy. The students worked late into the night with enthusiasm, feeling part of a special era and seeing themselves as important in the development of a new and better country. Students' desks were placed in alphabetical order by surname, which put Dixon next to Fenella Clemens. They worked together as students, married and then worked together professionally.

Whilst still an employee, Dixon had a valuable and instructive experience. In 1971 he was a leading member of the team that constructed a forty feet high tower on London's South Bank as part of the *Art and Revolution* exhibition at the Hayward Gallery. The others were Christopher Cross, Sven Rindl (an engineer), and Christopher Woodward (later the joint author with Jones of the *Guide to the Architecture of London)*. This was an after-hours activity. Every evening he would go to the South Bank and work on first the designs and then the construction to the sound of blaring pop music. By contrast, his much later choice of music on the BBC Radio 3 programme, *Private Passions* and on Classic FM's *Tonight at 11* included more chamber music than loud pop, although his musical tastes remained eclectic.

Tatlin's Tower, more correctly the Monument to the Third International, was so called because it had been designed by the Russian, Vladimir Tatlin, who was neither an architect nor an engineer but an artist. His drawings suggest a wildly impracticable undertaking. Building his tower was an odd experience for Dixon, "like a musician interpreting someone else's composition, liberating because we could get on with the task in hand without inventing everything from first principles." Architects are supposed to design structures for others to build, not build the designs of artists, and this was an unusual, rewarding and educative experience. It was also an opportunity to work on a very prominent site.

The next important and formative work was on a housing development in London. The most important of his developments, now that he was in private practice, was in St

Mark's Road, North Kensington, described in a millennium retrospective on the architecture of the 1970s as neo-classical, which is hardly an accurate label. Dixon was agonising with Fenella at the time on the role of architects, and coming to the view that "the city was being destroyed by the very profession to which I belonged." He has his own tale of two cities, seeing Paris as taking its charm from its formality and public buildings, whereas the glory of London is its informality and low density dwellings. "It is essentially a city of houses and the existing streets are a wonderful model." This was not a fashionable view at the time when public money was used mainly to clear sites and build tall blocks of flats. Dixon's task was to relate his new conviction to the twentieth century, so, taking the Queen Anne model, he built a street of houses that were domestic in scale but realised in modern terms and materials.

❖ ❖ ❖ ❖ ❖

The partners' ways of thinking become clear when they are describing their two buildings for Darwin College, Cambridge, founded to bring together post-graduate research students and academic staff from a wide range of disciplines. Both edifices bear the partnership's plaque, Dixon taking the lead on the Study Centre and Jones on the student accommodation.

The college buildings front the busy Silver Street and back on to the Cam as it flows past the islands owned by the college. Across the river are the rows of punts for hire below the weir at Silver Street. If you have ever hired a punt or stood on the bridge nearby you will have seen the Study Centre, modern yet sitting comfortably in its surroundings.

Dixon describes how he approached the Study Centre project and this gives insights into how he designs: "Firstly, you obviously think about the project, read the brief, but you withhold from trying solutions until a significant moment, usually visiting the site. At this moment the brain works incredibly quickly, ranging back over previous ideas, fitting shapes to functions and projecting forward to fresh ideas. This happens in a flash and the bones of the project, both in shape and content, are there as if by magic. It is a process that I don't understand and has something to do with the subconscious." The process that he describes is mysterious, and the outcome at Darwin College has beauty as well as practicality. He uses an interesting phrase about "the connection between the architect's social wisdom and his knowledge of how materials work."

The Study Centre is a good example of the way in which the design of a project is influenced by parallel concerns. Functionally, it had to provide a good working environment. Formally, the interaction of the street curve with the straight water edge resulted in a three-dimensional curved roof. The existing college buildings were long and narrow and the Study Centre is at the very end. To reach it, you have to thread your way through corridors and go outside to a courtyard before arriving at an anonymous door in an old external wall. Opening the door, you see the dramatic interior of the Study Centre, constructed in oak of different kinds, overlooking the river. The pleasure is in the unexpected sight at the end of this journey from the college entrance. You have no idea what is behind the door. It is a surprise and a delightful revelation.

The design uses the curved road front as a solid wall at street level, lined with books, thus insulating the students from the noise and sight of the road outside. Opposite the book stacks are several computer rooms, not one large distracting room as is so often provided. These are divided by staircases to the upper level. Here, built above the computer rooms, the individual study places have splendid views of the river in one direction and out, above the bookstacks, to the 'backs' on the street side. It is light and airy. The judgement of the users is the acid test. Interviewed in the spring of 2001, two students were warm in their verdict on the Centre as a place in which they enjoyed studying. Even the faint noise of people excited by their departure in newly-hired punts, drifting across the water in the summer when the windows were open, gave the students a pleasing sense of human contact.

The student accommodation, known as Frank Younge House, is a short distance from the main college buildings and is in an entirely different style. Jones describes it as the stern section of a cruise liner, and the concept is both apt and functional. Unlike Pimlico School, a building less than thirty years old that needs to be pulled down because the ocean liner concept came first and the needs of a large school nowhere, Jones's thinking starts from the needs of the students. The ship concept comes later. The difference is that a cruise liner is a good model and starting point for student accommodation precisely because both need to cater for everyday needs in a compact space. In this case there is also the equivalent of the open sea in the form of green playing fields, a natural visual focus.

The building is entirely new and all white, both inside and out. It is built on three sides of a square around a large wooden deck. The two side wings slope backwards, with reducing numbers of rooms on each floor. High quality kitchens for students are in the central joining block. Each floor has an outside balcony overlooking the deck and the playing fields, being much enjoyed by the students on a warm, sunny May day. Every part, including the built-in furniture, has been designed by the architects. There is a single, pervasive concept that is also functional. It works.

A resident who was doing a PhD in architecture in the summer of 2001 liked the building very much. Her only criticism was that even the window coverings are white blinds, and the floodlighting of the building outside makes it impossible for her to achieve darkness – she sleeps wearing an eye mask and longs for black-out. The only criticism of the cleaners was that there are no cupboards for them above the ground floor, and you cannot cart vacuum cleaners up four floors. They noted, however, that another college residence has no cupboards for cleaners at all, so Dixon and Jones have done rather well!

❖ ❖ ❖ ❖ ❖

Whilst working on their three big millennium-related projects – Covent Garden, the National Portrait Gallery and Somerset House – Dixon and Jones had other commissions on the stocks. This biggest of these was the Said Business School in Oxford. This was both politically and architecturally controversial. The politics embraced the university (and few arenas are more political than academia), the city council and the government. The project was briefly exposed to a wider public as a footnote in the Hinduja passport affair, the cause of Peter Mandelson's second going. Neither the building nor Dixon and Jones had anything to do with any of these events. But, in the hunt for other examples of ministers leaning on public authorities in the interests of wealthy foreigners, for that is how it was portrayed, it was revealed that the prime minister's office, no less, had enquired about planning permission for the Oxford building.

The site itself was the first object of controversy. Oxford University accepts huge donations with hauteur and usually on its own terms. It has occasionally rejected multi-million pound offers if the donor has been held to be wanting. More often it accepts with nervousness. As Simon Jenkins has written, "Dons grab any money going, but instantly plunge themselves into doubt and guilt." In this case the site itself was disputed, with the donor, Wafic Said, threatening to walk away with his £20 million. The compromise was that he should have a prime site next to the railway station, neither in the green belt nor affecting the 'dreaming spires' part of the city, with Said paying for the planting of mature trees and re-paving the station forecourt to improve the area.

The importance of the client for architectural success has already been noted. Oxford University rarely speaks with one voice: disputation is its lifeblood. Wafic Said himself wanted something classical. The City Council wanted something imposing for this important site. In reality there was not a single client, but many interests, all with some power.

No surprise, therefore, that the ideas of Dixon and Jones met opposition, even though they won the competition. They themselves ruled out any suggestion of imitating the 'romantic silhouette' associated with Oxford. In the completed building, their basic geometrical idea remains intact and appeals by its simplicity. The need is for lecture and other teaching rooms with the social amenities that go with them. Very importantly there is a strong emphasis on creating conditions that promote informal discussion. This was one of the main outcomes of Dixon's and Jones's visits to American business schools, where they observed the daily work of the occupants, noticing in particular the effective mingling of professors, students and business people. Two cloistered arcades encourage this approach whilst also alluding to (or 'connecting with' in the Dixon and Jones lexicon) the medieval Oxford college format. The library and information centre has a vaulted reading room and open browsing area that also encourage contact.

The principal south-facing façade went through various versions. The final scheme has a tall and minimalist steel portico, acting as a sunshade to the fully glazed elevation. Without this large-scale *brise-soleil*, the barrel vault roof to the reading room had been earlier criticised as being too akin to a 'roll-top' bread bin!

The glazed entrance façade encourages the idea of accessibility. Not a question of opening up old buildings, as in London, but of constructing a new one in the heart of Oxford without the tiny doors that in colleges say "keep out" whatever the rules on admission say. For people arriving in Oxford by train, the new

Said Business School makes a statement about Oxford, that it venerates the past but also looks to the future.

❖ ❖ ❖ ❖ ❖

Suddenly, as the first year of the new millennium was ebbing away, the partners realised that they were running out of work. Very prominent commissions do not guarantee continued work. A 'full order book', as manufacturers call it, cannot be assumed as a permanent feature, even for applauded architects. Contracting, whatever the sphere, is an uncertain way of earning a living. The pleasure and excitement that come from not being another's employee has its grit of uncertainty. Twice in the 1990s they were short-listed to redevelop the South Bank area around the Royal Festival Hall, did all the preparation and then were runners-up. So, in the autumn of 2000, they had to go out and win new business, just as they had in their earlier years. Of course, their high reputation made it easier, but nonetheless there was grafting to be done in the architectural market place and no certainty of success. Yet success they have had and the order book is full again.

Their current major projects take them all over the country. The copy of Magna Carta owned by Salisbury Cathedral is kept in the chapter house but is soon to have its own building which Dixon and Jones will design. In Norwich they are working on a building to join a large shopping complex to the city centre, and in Liverpool on a large urban development on an important site. In both these cases, they are the specialists bringing their skill at giving new life to old cities that need sensitive handling. They won a competition to build for Queen's University, Belfast a student centre to be used by staff, students and the community, 'connecting' them in what Jones has dubbed the "Good Friday Agreement building".

In London their recent work gives hope that London University, once a great patron of architecture but in the second half of the twentieth century a desecrator of Bloomsbury, may recover its reputation. Dixon and Jones will create a new building at the back of University College. The imposing classical façade built by Wilkins in the nineteenth century as its front entrance in Gower Street will be complemented by a second entrance at the rear in Gordon Street, with a new building to house the Egyptian collection of Flinders Petrie.

Wilkins was the builder of Haileybury College that Jones had attended, and the National Gallery with which both Dixon and Jones were associated when working on the National Portrait Gallery. Their understanding of his work could hardly be deeper. University College was founded in the early nineteenth century, as the first college of what was to become London University, specifically to provide university education for people who were not communicants of the Church of England, a requirement for attendance at Oxford and Cambridge at that time. It was shortly followed by King's College, to ensure that anglicans would keep their end up in the capital, in a building that shares premises with Somerset House. Dixon and Jones even stumble on connections.

The task ahead for them will require all their imagination and skill in connecting with the old buildings whilst creating something that is new and of quality. Their work is to be next to the College's modern, glass-fronted Bloomsbury Theatre. The other college buildings in the street and square are either dull, functional, modern and probably irretrievable or attractive but soot-blackened and neglected Georgian and Victorian terraced houses now used by college departments. The present leaders of the College have had the vision of their founders in commissioning architects who have proved their ability to handle sensitive sites with flair. Gordon Street will start to look up.

At the same time they have been appointed master planners,

overseeing all extensions and renovations, for both the National Gallery and Somerset House. London, Liverpool, Belfast, Norwich and Salisbury should feel both safe and excited in their hands – a rare achievement for architects.

And when they have finished those projects? Godfrey Smith has noted in the *The Sunday Times* that, with the Said Business School complete, the remaining subject not yet admitted to respectability at Oxford is architecture itself. He has suggested that a neat decision would be to build an Oxford School of Architecture and to invite Dixon and Jones to build it. Now, there's a thought.

MARGARET TYZACK

Margaret Tyzack has been acting on the stage and in television and films for the past half century. Her face and voice are distinctive and immediately recognisable when she is performing, but without restricting her range of roles, for she has had a pioneering career as an actor, particularly in helping to create the format of the television drama series, and also in creating parts in new plays. For half a year she appeared on television screens every week in *The Forsyte Saga*, following that with more weekly appearances in *I, Claudius*, *The First Churchills* and *Cousin Bette*. These were the pioneers of long-running drama series on television, shown many times in Britain and around the world.

Along with television, she has performed regularly in theatres throughout Britain, including both the Stratfords (Warwickshire and Ontario), and has had several long runs in New York. On the stage she has taken leading roles for the Royal Shakespeare Company in each of the last three decades and created many roles in new works by writers such as Tom Stoppard, Brian Friel and Alan Bennett. Few have matched her experience and range. The hundreds of reviews on her performances are unanimous in praising her gifts, sometimes in productions that otherwise fail to find favour. She is always striking on stage. You notice her whatever her part.

2001 was the fiftieth year of Tyzack's professional career and the seventieth of her life. Her last ten years have been as varied as the first forty. The London stage has kept her busy, creating the role of T S Eliot's mother-in law in Michael Hasting's *Tom and Viv*, performing another mother in Stephen Daldry's celebrated and long-running production of Priestley's *An Inspector Calls*, playing Miss Prism in *The Importance of Being Earnest*, creating on stage in Tom Stoppard's *Indian Ink* the role played on radio by Peggy Ashcroft, and appearing as one of Alan Bennett's *Talking Heads*.

At Stratford, Newcastle, London and New York she played the

pivotal role of Amy in T S Eliot's *The Family Reunion* for the Royal Shakespeare Company in the 1999-2000 season. Another key role was that of Mrs Clemmens in the radio serial of Dickens's *Little Dorrit*, narrated by Ian McKellen, in the summer of 2001. There were many other stage roles during this period, and also roles in films such as *The Young Indiana Jones* and in television such as Lady Tippins in Dickens's *Our Mutual Friend*, and guest appearances in series such as *Dalziel and Pascoe* and *Midsomer Murders*.

❖ ❖ ❖ ❖ ❖

The Forsyte Saga made her a familiar face, but was by no means the start of her career. It was because she had already done so much successful television drama, performed and shown live in the 1960s, that the BBC wanted her for the role of Winifred, sister to Eric Porter's Soames. She had shown many times that she had the subtlety needed for the small screen. The saga covered several generations of the Forsyte family. Winifred and Soames were in the first and the last episodes. There were twenty-six in all. Tyzack was in all but three. This was planned to be a prestigious series, scheduled for the main Sunday evening slot. It was pioneering television. The BBC was taking enormous risks. Would people follow this family story once a week for half a year? *The Forsyte Saga* was serious drama from another era, just occasionally as sensational as modern soaps – there was marital rape – but an entirely different kettle of fish.

The programme turned out to be a phenomenon. It was transmitted in weekly episodes about an hour long, taking half a year. It attracted 16 million people to each episode when first shown in 1967, reaching 18 million for the final episode when it was re-shown in 1969. Churches were emptied and had to re-schedule their Sunday evening services so as to avoid the clash with the programme. The magnitude of this achievement for a drama series is shown by the audiences reached by some more expectedly popular programmes being shown at the same time: 15 million for *Morecambe and Wise* and for *The Rolf Harris Show*, 14 million for *Dad's Army*. *The Forsyte Saga* figures are rarely reached today with a much bigger viewing public. The top-rating television show at the beginning of the twenty-first century, the quiz programme, *Who wants to be a millionaire?*, rarely matches the audience figures for *The Forsyte Saga*. To reach 18 million viewers, *EastEnders* had to have Phil shot and keep the suspense about the culprit going for many weeks to build the size of audience for one night that was routinely achieved by *The Forsyte Saga*. Such has been its impact on the psyche of programme-makers that Granada television is re-making it, with Amanda Root playing Tyzack's part of Winifred.

The series was part of a wider revolution in television. In the early 1950s transmissions had been for limited periods and even by 1960 there was no day-time television. The day was for work and study. The night was for sleeping. Viewing was an evening activity in between, with a close by bedtime. Tyzack's distinctive face made her a natural recruit to this new, intimate medium.

Based on John Galsworthy's novels, the series told the story of the business and social ambitions of Soames Forsyte, and the impact of his ambitions and his character on his relationships and family. The novel would today be regarded as a 'blockbuster'. Almost 800 pages long, it traces the story of the Forsyte family through six generations and more than a century, with a family tree at the beginning, parts with headings such as 'The Man of Property' and chapters with the breathless titles found in old children's stories such as 'Val hears the news', 'Timothy stays the rot'. Wilson regarded it as a masterpiece. David Giles, the main director, regarded as quite a good, second-rate novel. It made excellent television because it was about relationships.

Giles recalls two crucial contributions made by Tyzack to its success. First, there was her experience of acting live in television drama, much greater than any other member of the cast. All the actors had stage experience, whilst some, like Kenneth More, were principally film actors. None had Tyzack's television acting background. The method of making *The Forsyte Saga* was to rehearse for ten days before moving into the studio and then to record an episode, just short of an hour in length, almost in one go. Only two and a half hours of camera time were allowed. All the sets for each episode were in the one studio. Costume changes and moves from one set to another had to be encompassed in that time. Five minutes were allowed when they all had to change into mourning clothes for a funeral, and the same for changing back again for the next scene. It was not quite live, but almost so. Retakes were rare. 'Out-takes', the muffed lines and shots of actors larking around, which are the staple of so many television programmes now compiled from the cutting room floor, were unheard of then.

For stage actors, used only to giving a live performance with an audience and the opportunity to develop the play over several performances, this was a new and alarming experience. For those used to film, with the opportunity to make mistakes and do it again, it was terrifying. The countdown to the start of recording was tense, with anxiety usually dissipated by some outrageous joke shouted out by Kenneth More from the 'room' next door. It was Tyzack who had the experience of the medium to reassure and guide the others. This was particularly necessary towards the end of the run. When the first dozen or so episodes had been recorded, transmission started. With transmissions taking place weekly and episodes being recorded fortnightly, the clock was ticking. Experience and calmness were invaluable qualities.

Her other major asset, as recalled by Giles, was her contribution to the very happy working atmosphere that prevailed. Whilst other actors arrived, as younger members of the Forsyte family, or left as their characters died, Tyzack was always there, welcoming the newcomers. She struck up a close friendship with

Susan Hampshire. Frantic as recording time approached, but without a feeling of rush - ten days' rehearsal for each scene - it was a very happy time for everyone.

Giles comments that live television sorts people out. Tyzack and Porter had to age from about 19 to their seventies during the series. Not just a question of make-up. All the skills to convey changes in relationships as people grow old together were needed. Giles admired the way in which Tysack conveyed the ageing process so well. The first thing this young actor said to him when they met, with a twinkle in her eye, was, "I do not like too many moves." In fact, as the young Winifred, she moved about all the time to create a contrast with the older Winifred that was to come.

Giles remembers moments that show the strength of her acting. In one episode, her husband Montey (Montague Dartie, 'man of the world') has left her. Everybody is advising her to divorce him, but she still loves him. He returns to their house during a social gathering without her knowledge. The others get him out of the room before Winifred knows that he is there, but she recognises the smell of his cigar and knows that he is back. The script did not mention that she was aware of his visit. It had to be done subtly by facial expression. Would the audience get the point? Could she convey this without words? Giles says that she did it perfectly. As he comments, when drama is going well, actors can be free to take risks because the audience is with them and they do not have to make everything explicit. When Porter and Tyzack were playing Soames and Winifred in old age, tension and some comedy were achieved by his being made long-sighted and her short-sighted.

An American described the performance as "Peyton Place with class." Another commentator said that Tyzack "made Queen Mary look common."

With the exception of America, where television was already solely in colour and there was little taste for a programme made in black and white, the BBC sold the series worldwide, including Russia and, even more of a coup, to the culturally defensive French. It was a global success, and the first of its kind. The series was very important to the BBC, for it launched its long and successful role in the commercial world. 'Auntie' the BBC may be dubbed, but it has always been able to show other entrepreneurs a thing or two. The appointment of Tyzack to the OBE was as much a recognition that the BBC was now a global force in broadcasting as it was a tribute to her work in *The Forsyte Saga.*

❖ ❖ ❖ ❖ ❖

In conversation, first after a performance of *The Family Reunion* overlooking the Avon on a summer evening in Stratford and later in London, Tyzack talks easily and modestly about her achievements. With no illusions about her profession and refreshingly free from the pretensions that beguile many of its members, she draws attention to a remark by Paul Schofield: "I have found that an actor's work seems to wither away in discussion and become emptily theoretical and insubstantial." Avoiding this trap, she converses easily but always on the premise that acting is something that you do, and when it is done, it is over. It is by its nature short-lived. Done well, of course, it shares with writing the power to enlighten and transform as well as entertain us.

This is something that she understands whilst dismissing attempts to analyse how it is achieved. Her point can be appreciated by anybody who has listened to the pretentious attempts on radio and television to analyse the work of great comedians. Much better to see their work. She dislikes all the "bullshit" written about acting. Her use of this word is uncharacteristic and its effect alarming. It shows the strength of her belief. These observations would have been conveyed as a diatribe in the mouths of others. They lose nothing of their force by being expressed gently. Everything is expressed gently. References to people with whom she has worked are mostly admiring and generous. When they are otherwise, they are strictly off the record, for she is without malice.

She has sometimes been compared to Flora Robson and Edith Evans, mainly because, alongside her frequent appearances in comedy, she has often played queens, dominatrixes and other grand ladies. She is in life nothing like these characters. Those who know her well say that she is hilarious company, reducing a room to hysterics. In personal conversation both her voice and her face, compelling when in a performance, seem quite different, even ordinary, as if to confirm her point about acting. Her feet are firmly on the ground. When the performance is over, it is over, and it is time to get a drink, do the washing or go to bed.

It is only when she speaks of some directors that the eyes roll upwards, although even then she is quick to say that she personally has rarely been asked by a director to do anything of consequence that she thought wrong for the part. Directors with whom she has worked have fond and admiring memories of the experience. The words that recur are 'professional', 'sensitive' and 'convincing'. David Giles, the main director of *The Forsyte Saga*, who spent a year of his life working with Tyzack in rehearsal rooms and studios, followed by several months on *The First Churchills*, attributes much of the congeniality of the entire experience to her personality and her knowledge of her craft.

In her private life, which she is scrupulous to keep private, she is content, living in Blackheath with her husband, an improbable engineer turned university mathematics teacher whom she has known since they were 15. She is a grandmother and the proud mother of a psychiatrist son. A noted sender of cards to her friends, fellow actors and directors, she maintains many warm friendships forged during her acting career.

Tyzack's skill as an actor is difficult to capture because it is in part intuitive. It was revealed, almost without her noticing it herself, when she was still at school. One of her teachers at that time, Elizabeth Pursey (then Watson), describes it as a gift that others just had to help her to discover. At school she played the part of a 90-year-old miser. Pursey was amazed at the ability of this young girl to capture the essence of the character, with "an astonishing look in the face of a 16-year-old." The deputy headteacher at the time, Sister Benedict, now 90 years of age, can still recall that miser's face of more than fifty years ago.

The gift is not that of theatrical histrionics, although she can thunder and menace with the best of them, but of subtly portraying human feeling and in that way convincing the audience about the author's words. Tyzack can look and sound stern, and indeed has played parts such as T S Eliot's witheringly disapproving mother-in-law and Arthur Clemmens's twisted mother in *Little Dorrit*, more often than comedy. She has been convincingly caustic, bitter and wild in *Who's Afraid of Virginia Woolf?*, and herself comments that she has played more than her share of emotionally crippled women. But, as Pursey observes, "that is not her soul". She needs to know the author's intentions and then goes deep into the psychology of the character. It sounds trite in a profession that invites scepticism, but she seeks truth, not as a conscious quest but naturally. She would never make such a claim herself.

❖ ❖ ❖ ❖ ❖

The origin of Margaret's surname is 'du Thisac'. The family came to Britain from France in the sixteenth century, having lived at Lichecourt in Alsace-Lorraine. They were fleeing from the Catholic persecution of Protestants – the asylum seekers of their day. Escaping from France was a crime resulting in 'condign punishment'. French Protestants arriving in Britain in the sixteenth and seventeenth centuries were strong-minded and hard-working. If they had been otherwise, they would have conformed and stayed at home. They were not poor. The du Thisacs were gentlemen with a coat of arms. Many brought new skills to Britain, in the du Thisacs' case an improved method of glass-making. Tyzack's ancestors seem to have settled in Sheffield before moving to Newcastle, the north-east being a major centre for glass-making. Sunderland had cornered the medieval, monastic market for stained glass long before the Tyzacks arrived and has remained a centre of glass-making ever since, now having the National Glass Museum. The Tyzacks were part of a long history of manufacturing in the north-east.

By the time Margaret was born, the family had long left its Huguenot and glass-making past and was well established in the Plaistow area of east London. Most of the family, including Margaret's father Thomas, were workers in the local Tate and Lyle sugar depot. As with many of her generation, it was education that lifted her sights and led her to be more adventurous in her choice of career than her family background might have allowed. Born in 1931, her primary education was initially at an all-age, elementary school. At that time most children in England attended the same school between the ages of five and 14, the years of compulsory education, before leaving school for work. Tyzack was in a mixed-age class at a school in West Ham, some of this during the Second World War. She learned very little. Only the lucky minority transferred to secondary school at the age of 11. Tyzack was one of them. It was when she went to St Angela's Convent School at Forest Gate in east London in 1942 that school became interesting. Her parents were not Catholics but wanted something better for their daughter than the all-age school.

Tyzack recalls St Angela's with unalloyed pleasure. She had "a gloriously wonderful time". She was not and is not a Roman Catholic, but is grateful for what she experienced. She admired and adored her teachers who were very well educated and enlightened women, liberated rather than confined by their religious vocation. Above all they were kind and understood that her imagination was in conflict with the requirements of examinations. She can now accept the wisdom of the teachers' standard advice to examinees to read the question and give the examiners what they want. At that time she did not. She went into the secretarial sixth form, almost for lack of an alternative, since her inclinations towards the disciplines of typing and shorthand were no greater than towards those of academic studies. Sister Benedict recalls a time when Margaret got another girl to do her secretarial homework so that she could concentrate on drama.

St Angela's was remarkable at the time for its emphasis on drama. Novel in the 1940s and 1950s were its curriculum policy of drama for all and its specialist course for a small group of pupils. There was also one very big production a year, when examinations were over in the summer, and Tyzack took to the stage twice, in the chorus of *The Mikado* and as a 90-year-old miser. Without all of these, Margaret might never have discovered her gift. As Pursey puts it, "She found herself in a special way in speech and drama."

It was also a special time in education. After the war the prevalent idealism and hope affected schools. They were intellectually stimulating times and St Angela's was a very special school, enlightened and with a binding philosophy that valued all pupils across the entire ability range. It embraced the comprehensive principle with enthusiasm. This was again crucial to Margaret's development. Pursey explains Tyzack's claim never to have passed any examinations: "She felt that she did not shine as a scholar and that made her very at home when her talent was unlocked. She did not see herself as a scholar because she had a great gift that she did not know immediately at the time." Of course, if she had not attended this school with its inclusive values, the gift might never have been revealed.

One of Tyzack's hallmarks as an actor has been her clear

enunciation. She is always willing to receive help from voice coaches. She recognises, as some younger performers did not in the depressing Stratford seasons of the early 1990s, that even experienced performers may need guidance from experts on the rhythms of verse and to ensure audibility in all parts of large theatres. It says much for the dynamism and worldliness of a small school founded by a religious order that two women - her teacher, Elizabeth Pursey, and one of her fellow pupils, Catherine Fleming, now dead - went on to become voice coaches, respectively at the Royal Academy of Dramatic Art (RADA) and the National Theatre.

Tyzack herself went to RADA. Although she left before Pursey arrived to teach there, Tyzack has sought Pursey's guidance throughout her career. Pursey dislikes the term 'teacher' as inappropriate for her work with Tyzack. As she says, "You can discuss a play and a role intellectually and artistically with her, and then her gift takes over and you have to stand back. With gifted people, you have to stand back and let it go."

At the age of 17 and with her one-year secretarial sixth form course ending, Tyzack was without a clear idea of what career to follow. She vaguely assumed that she might teach, more out of admiration for Elizabeth Pursey than any idea of what it entailed. Without the required academic qualifications, this was never a serious prospect. Acting and an application to RADA emerged. What she had gained from Pursey was an understanding of texts, how to enunciate clearly and to modulate the voice in response to meaning.

Despite her claim to have no scholastic strengths, she clearly gained a good knowledge of literature and drama at St Angela's, and the ability to comprehend and perform a text, because one of her test pieces for RADA entry was as Shakespeare's Juliet. The other was an extract from Shaw's *Pygmalion*, in which she played all three leading parts, demonstrating her versatility and ability to convey character as she moved easily and convincingly between Eliza Doolittle, Professor Higgins and Colonel Pickering. It was her success in switching between the male and female roles, with their different pitch and tone, which won her the place. Tyzack herself put this rather differently: "I just think that they were bowled over by this 17-year-old slip of a girl doing deep, men's voices, and decided they'd better let me in." *Pygmalion* was to crop up twice more in the next few years at key moments in her career.

With typical modesty, Tyzack says that it was not at the time as difficult to get into RADA as it is now. It is true that in this period, not long after the war, many girls saw RADA as a kind of finishing school. Well-to-do girls, often poorly educated, went to various schools and colleges to be 'finished'. The girls' need was to acquire poise, confidence, good manners and grooming, and to learn the conventions of 'society'. Switzerland was the favoured location for this conditioning, but not all of the aspirants had the cash to match their status. Catering, hotel and art colleges fulfilled the need less expensively. For a short while RADA contributed to the pool. One student in Tyzack's year was a Jewish girl who went home at 4 o'clock every Friday afternoon because of the Jewish Sabbath and was obviously not considering a career in the theatre.

A few of the girls went on to small parts in films, following the J Arthur Rank starlet route, never to be heard of again. The only other girl in Tyzack's year to achieve celebrity initially took that route, before finding stardom in American television. Her name was Joan Collins. The men on the course were usually more serious about their careers. Some were GIs, American solders still 'over here' after the war, usually older than the British students and financed by the US government as part of its demobilisation package.

One crucial element in Tyzack's training at RADA was the support of West Ham Council. It paid her tuition fees and fares. Without that she could not have gone to the academy.

RADA had its own theatre, the Vanbrugh, next to the academy in Gower Street in the Bloomsbury area of London dominated by London University, but it had been bombed during the war and had not yet been rebuilt. The students therefore had no place in which to perform in true theatre style before public audiences. Nonetheless, the training gave Tyzack important parts in thirteen different productions, often doubling up on small and leading parts in the same play. In Shakespeare's *Twelfth Night*, for example, she played both the second officer and Sir Andrew Aguecheek. One big opportunity to play in front of audiences arose when *The Taming of the Shrew* toured open-air venues around London. Those who remember the performance say that, with her long, fair hair and her huge temperament, she dominated the production. Tyzack herself has a more prosaic view: "One of the venues was Russell Square. I think they chose me because my loud voice could be heard above the traffic!" Her final role at RADA brought her back to *Pygmalion*. She played Eliza before her departure as she had before her arrival.

As important as RADA was to her development as an actor, Tyzack's first job – two and a half years at Chesterfield Civic Theatre in Derbyshire – was crucial. This theatre, still flourishing and now called the Pomegranate Theatre, was one of many throughout England where young actors could learn their craft, performing in a wide range of works and many different parts alongside experienced practitioners. As repertory theatres, they put on a different play every week. With music halls, variety theatres and the burgeoning cinemas they were an important part of popular entertainment. The Chesterfield Civic was in Tyzack's day a fine example of civic enterprise with a mission to bring good drama to local people.

Tyzack was one of the RADA students whose qualities had been recognised by an agent on one of his talent-spotting visits and it was he who got her an audition that led to the job. Another member of the same agency, Joyce Edwards, is still Tyzack's agent today. Following the practice of the day, Tyzack was put into a category to aid those looking for performers - 'juvenile character' - but this did not restrict her roles for long. She was one of the lucky ones who went straight from RADA to paid and regular work. Not that the pay was much, £4.10s a week, with the actors having to provide their own clothes on stage except for period costume. This was before the 1950s' revolution in the theatre, sometimes known as 'kitchen sink' because it dealt with working class lives and took audiences beyond the usual Noel Coward range of characters then prevalent in London's West End.

Chesterfield people were down-to-earth. They paid 'good money' to go to the theatre and expected those on stage to be 'well turned out'. The actors' salvation was to borrow articles from local shops in return for a mention in the programme. Older readers will recall that theatre programmes always included, after the cast list, a further list such as, 'Furniture by Whites of Chesterfield. Telephone by GPO. Nylon stockings by Kayser Bondor. Virginia cigarettes by Abdulla.' Tyzack had a particularly fruitful relationship with a milliner. "The company manager was a super-efficient Austrian who ensured that any loaned articles, sometimes expensive items such as fox furs, were always returned in a better condition than when they arrived!", Tyzack recalls. Sponsorship in the theatre is not new. The practice was at a very modest level in Chesterfield in 1951 but crucial to impecunious actors.

Pygmalion again played an important role in Tyzack's life, for it was not only her RADA test piece and the final play in which she had starred there, but also the play in which she first worked professionally. But now she played a bystander. Not even 'the' bystander, for the senior roles of 'the bystander' and 'the sarcastic bystander' were allotted to more experienced performers. Tyzack was one of five 'other bystanders'. The start of a professional career meant a reduction to the most lowly of ranks but, curiously, she was the only bystander who appeared in the publicity photographs. The distinctive face caught the eye.

The extraordinarily demanding 'rep' way of life gave an excellent training. The company was always working on three plays, putting on a new one each week. The morning rehearsal was for the work to be performed in a fortnight's time. The afternoon rehearsal was for next week's performance. The evening was, of course, the current production. At the end of the week one play closed and a new one entered as the morning rehearsal. To keep the playgoer's appetite whetted, each week's programme contained a synopsis of the following week's play. The drawbacks of such a method of working are obvious, but the consequences for anybody who could sustain the workload were overwhelmingly beneficial. The only relief from the relentless weekly schedule came when amateur groups, such as the Chesterfield Teachers' Drama Society, or visiting stars, such as Lupino Lane, took over the theatre for a week. Concerts were given on Sundays, such as that by the BBC Northern Orchestra conducted by the young Charles Groves soon after Tyzack arrived in Chesterfield.

The company had one unusual feature for a 'rep'. It had, for much of Tyzack's time in Chesterfield, a director who also saw herself as a teacher, Chloe Gibson, from whom Tyzack learned much. Gibson had played with the Old Vic company and had directed plays in London, finding directing more exciting than acting. Energetic, with scarlet-framed spectacles usually pushed on top of her head, she took daily rehearsals. Her firm views on the value of 'rep' in training young actors were given in an interview to the *Sheffield Telegraph* soon after her arrival at Chesterfield. "There is still a wrong attitude in dealing with students. Too often they go to provincial theatres to watch acting which is often bad, and for years they are allowed only to look after props and take very small parts." With Gibson, young actors were given training and sometimes played leading roles. The policy allowed Tyzack within a fortnight to take on a lead role in a popular play of the time, *Queen Elizabeth Slept Here.* Just as well that it was a comedy. When the door of the set stuck, she entered through the fireplace. Other young actors with whom Tyzack shared her two-and-a-half-year Chesterfield apprenticeship were David McCallum, later celebrated on television as the *Man from U.N.C.L.E.*, and Joss Ackland.

The other aspect of a 'rep' training that was so valuable to Tyzack was the variety of drama in which to participate. A month after arriving she was playing a speaking part in Pinero's *The Second Mrs Tanqueray*, followed by a small character part in Tennessee Williams's *A Streetcar Named Desire*. She also began what was to become a feature of her career, the creation of parts in the premieres of new plays.

Tysack's last two performances at Chesterfield vividly convey the demands of acting in 'rep'. On Christmas Eve 1953 she opened as Prince Charming in the pantomime *Cinderella,* with Joss Ackland playing the role of Pong, one of the brokers' men (he drew the short straw: the other one was called Ping). The last performance was on Saturday, two weeks later. The following Monday she opened as Portia in *The Merchant of Venice*, with costumes on loan from the Memorial Theatre at Stratford and with David McCallum playing a minor role and doubling as assistant stage manager. In her final performance at Chesterfield, Tyzack was noted in the local press as "an old favourite of the town audience." The "old favourite" was just 23.

Tyzack has successfully woven five strands into her distinguished career: television, work for the two great national theatres (the Royal Shakespeare Company and the Royal National Theatre), comedy, new plays and film. As a spectator, her own preference is for the last of these, reflecting perhaps that it is the medium in which she has worked least. She is rarely in theatres as a member of the audience (busman's holiday?) but frequently in cinemas. At different stages of her career, one of the five strands has dominated to the exclusion of others. If an actor commits herself to the RSC for a season, usually followed by a further season at the RSC's London home, she has little time for anything else. The same is true of long-running television series such as *The Forsyte Saga*. Tyzack's career has been one of quality rather than volume. She is very clear about parts that she will not take.

When asked to outline the stages of her career, she uses Shakespeare's ages of man as the format, skipping the 'muling and puking' period and coming out with four phases: 'rep' when she played "mainly tarts", television playing "emotional cripples", comedy, and finally "frightful old bats". She is, of course, being light-hearted and her career has not been quite as chronologically tidy as this suggests, but it is the case that particular activities, stage or television, have dominated her career in phases.

❖ ❖ ❖ ❖ ❖

Television gave her the big break. It is not surprising that, when the British Film Institute asked professionals and critics in 2000 to choose the best ever one hundred television programmes, *The Forsyte Saga* was in the top twenty. Another television series in this top hundred, *I, Claudius*, also featured Tyzack. This time she played alongside Derek Jacobi in the hugely successful 1976 adaptation of the Robert Graves book. In between, Tyzack performed in *The First Churchills*. For this she was made Actress of the Year and invited by Westminster Abbey to fit a new wig on its effigy of Queen Anne, the role that she had performed in the series.

The television series of which Tyzack herself is perhaps most proud is *Cousin Bette* when she played the title role. Based on the work by Honore de Balzac, this was well received in Britain in 1970-71, and even more so in America, where melodrama is better appreciated. There the performance received much US magazine coverage, including the front page of *Life*, and in 1973 Tyzack was nominated for an EMMY award.

❖ ❖ ❖ ❖ ❖

Performing for the Royal Shakespeare Company at Stratford-upon-Avon and in London and for the National Theatre on London's South Bank has been a regular feature of Tyzack's career. She has acted for the RSC in each of the last four decades.

Tyzack began her work at Stratford in 1972, although she had already worked for the RSC earlier at the Arts Theatre in central London in 1962. Peter Hall, then the director of the RSC, had taken the Aldwych and the Arts Theatres to complement and extend the Stratford seasons. In fact, the Stratford season that year was not a great success, a production of *The Cherry Orchard* in particular being widely regarded as a flop, despite the presence of John Gielgud, Peggy Ashcroft, Dorothy Tutin and Judi Dench. The occupation of the Arts Theatre was to give an airing to neglected plays.

In Tyzack's case this was Maxim Gorky's *The Lower Depths*, a piece written sixty years earlier that had been produced only three times in London, receiving a total of only sixteen performances, despite being regarded by many as a great play. It dealt with drunks and derelicts who are given hope briefly by the appearance of a messianic figure before descending again into depravity. Tyzack's fellow derelicts were Fulton Mackay, Julian Glover, Freddy Jones, Prunella Scales, Nicol Williamson and June Brown, well known now as Dot Cotton in *EastEnders*. The messianic figure was Wilfred Lawson, later more usually remembered for his inebriated performances, but at that time about to attempt *King Lear*. Tyzack admired him "as a wonderful and talented actor." Peter Hall attended performances to encourage his mostly young cast. Tyzack prepared by finding out as much as she could about Gorky. 1962 was an auspicious year not only for Tyzack, making her first of many appearances with the RSC, but for theatre generally, for it was the year in which the Chancellor of the Exchequer, Selwyn Lloyd, agreed to finance the creation of the National Theatre.

A Stratford season has for most actors a little of the repertory experience, albeit at a slower pace. They appear in several plays in the one quite short season, the performances overlap, and the actors mix major and minor roles. Much of the same programme is then repeated in London during the following winter, in all taking over a year. As a member of the company at Stratford and London for the 1972-73 seasons Tyzack had three roles of varied importance: Tamora in *Titus Andronicus*, Portia in *Julius Caesar* and Volumnia in *Coriolanus*. Playing Portia must have seemed like a night off. The three plays, with *Antony and Cleopatra*, were performed in one season to give audiences the chance to see all four of Shakespeare's Roman plays. Tyzack repeated two of them on transfer to the Aldwych Theatre, then the RSC's London home before the Barbican was built. This was for Tyzack a return to major stage work after her long-running television series. 1972 was a vintage year for the RSC, both artistically and financially. The series of plays was directed by Trevor Nunn, later the director of the National Theatre and of such famous productions as *Les Miserables*. The company took £1 million at the box office for the first time, but it still considered itself to be on a financial knife edge, although being only £3,000 in the red.

Coriolanus was, by common consent, an exciting and spectacular production that was also clear and true to the text. As Volumnia, Coriolanus's mother, Tyzack dominated the stage, although in different ways according to who was observing. To Michael Billington, then as now *The Guardian*'s drama critic, she was a humanised Volumnia. To another critic she was a "very tough lady", to another "a woman of undaunted mettle". To *The Times* she emerged as "an exultantly bourgeois matriarch seen at her most typical when computing the number of her son's battle wounds as if they were cricket runs." "Without question, the performance of the night was the Volumnia of Margaret Tyzack, notably in the great scene at the end when she pleads for her son to spare Rome from his anger. 'I was moved withal', said Aufidius afterwards. Indeed, so was I.", wrote *The Daily Telegraph*'s critic. Thus she was tough, humanised, bourgeois and moving. Subtle acting.

The relatively small part of Portia (with Patrick Stewart, later to command the Starship Enterprise, playing a lean and hungry Cassius) was followed by another of Shakespeare's strong female roles, that of Tamora, the Queen of the Goths, in *Titus Andronicus*. The production itself, unlike *Coriolanus*, did not win universal approval, but Tyzack's contribution to it did. "Margaret Tyzack rounds off what has been a fine season for her with the role of Tamora... a rounded figure of vengeance." Disliking the production, *The Times* exempted its "supreme merit" which was "Margaret Tyzack's turning a monochrome villain into an interesting and almost credible figure."

A year later Tyzack was again at the Aldwych with the RSC in *Summerfolk*, the second of Maxim Gorky's plays that she did for the RSC. The general complaint at the time was that Gorky's "provincial professionals and intellectuals, pondering languorously" did not match Chekhov's. With a popular touch, the *Daily Mirror* warned that "it's a grey summer, folks", but the red-tops did at least review RSC productions in those days. The cast was, nonetheless, impressive. "Norman Rodway, Ian Richardson, Sebastian Shaw and the magnificent Margaret Tyzack are in there somewhere." Despite this and other pannings from the critics, the play was well received by audiences and transferred to New York in 1975.

Tyzack's playing of two Gorky works, separated by twelve years, was chance. Not prepared for a question on the topic, she immediately recalls that she found some affinity with the writer, saying that, if she had been in Gorky's position in Tsarist Russia, she too would have been a revolutionary. As when preparing for the earlier play, she read as much as she could about him and understood how his humanity later got him into difficulties with Stalin. He was a kindly revolutionary, upbraiding some demonstrators for poking fun at the Tsarina because of her limp. Tyzack's feelings about playing Gorky reflect her view of the man: "You have to bring something raw to it, simplicity and goodness."

This Stratford season and its London aftermath were followed by a season at the other Stratford in Ontario, Canada, in 1977. It was in this beautiful theatre close to its own River Avon and without the summer crowds and busy streets of the Warwickshire Stratford, that Tyzack met Maggie Smith. The Ontario Stratford had begun life in a marquee, now commemorated on its lawns by a splendid life-size bronze sculpture of men pulling it up with guy ropes, and had grown by this time to three theatres, as in Warwickshire. Three years earlier, amidst a storm of Canadian nationalist protest, the British director Robin Phillips had been appointed to run the theatre and he effectively built several seasons around Maggie Smith. Phillips had directed for the RSC at the British Stratford and followed its approach of repertory casting. Tyzack played the countess in *All's Well That Ends Well*, Queen Margaret in *Richard III* and Mrs Alving in Ibsen's *Ghosts*.

Opening performances were bunched at that time, so that the New York critics could come for a short stay and catch all the first nights. The enormously demanding task for Tyzack was to give the first performance of *Ghosts* in the afternoon and the first of *All's Well That Ends Well* in the evening of the same day. Her performance as Mrs Alving in *Ghosts* attracted rapturous comments from both the Canadian critics and those from New York who had flown up for the opening. After giving a performance with a wealth of meaning conveyed by voice and face, she demonstrated her down-to-earth qualities by commenting, "I always seem to play such respectable parts. I never get fan letters like most of my friends – you know, 'Meet me in Battersea Park and I'll give you a good time'."

Tyzack has rarely been the subject of disputed judgements by critics and audiences, but there was one occasion when some did think that she lacked the fire and energy to play spiteful or anguished roles. Albee's *Who's Afraid of Virginia Woolf?* portrays a ferocious and raw marital relationship. When Tyzack played Martha, the wife, at the Lyttleton (National) Theatre in 1981, one critic admired her "laughing, spitting venom", but thought that she lacked the "boisterous vulgarity" needed to "draw blood". Another (an American living in London) disliked a cast of "such ineffable Englishness". Others, however, welcomed Tyzack's performance in this revival of the play as "a genuinely fresh reading, replete with vicious understatement and all the more effective for suggesting that Martha has not let go of herself completely." She was "wonderfully resourceful in her variations of tone and pace." There was an echo here of a judgement on her performance in the Gorky play at the Arts Theatre two decades earlier, when she had "a quality of brooding menace" that reminded one critic of Flora Robson. As often with critics, one man's meat is another man's poison. What is interesting is that, as with her Volumnia many years earlier, different observers sometimes saw different, even opposite, features in the same performance. That is the outcome of subtlety.

In 1983 Peggy Ashcroft played Countess Rousillion in *All's Well That Ends Well* at Stratford in what was to be her last performance. It was one of those productions, by Trevor Nunn, that acquired a huge reputation and had to be repeated in London and then in New York. Dame Peggy was unable to continue with the production on its transfer and Margaret Tyzack, well known to Nunn from her earlier RSC season, took over Ashcroft's role in both cities. It was the part that Tyzack had played in Canada six years earlier. The production was already two years old. It was a heavy responsibility to assume the role created by the leading female actor of the period, and quite difficult to join a cast that had worked together successfully. Tyzack was grateful for the welcome she received.

❖ ❖ ❖ ❖ ❖

As with many actors, it is comedy in the theatre that gives Tyzack the greatest pleasure. Laughter is an immediate indication to performers of their effectiveness. People can weep quietly in the darkness of the auditorium without the performers on stage knowing whether they have connected with them. Tyzack had shown an early bent for comedy at RADA where she had won the Gilbert prize for this aspect of drama, receiving the award from John Gielgud.

Her happiest time in comedy was with Maggie Smith in Peter Shaffer's *Lettice and Lovage*. At the core of the play is the relationship between its co-stars. Lettice, played by Smith, is an eccentric, intriguing spinster hooked on the past who has been sacked as a tour guide. Tyzack played the part of Lotte, a foil to Lettice's idiocy, but not a subordinate. Lotte is the starchy official who has sacked Lettice. The odd friendship that they portrayed in *Lettice and Lovage* was complemented by a real friendship and mutual respect, begun in the Stratford Ontario season in 1977 and now strengthened ten years later.

Shaffer's play was a great success, running for a year in London at the Globe Theatre (now re-named the Gielgud in honour of the great man and also to avoid confusion with the newer/older Globe on the South Bank). One reviewer saw the Smith-Tyzack performance as "a stage partnership of which legends are made." One nightly outburst of spontaneous applause was occasioned by Tyzack's *tour de force*, describing her attempt to blow up the appalling Shell Building. There was continuous laughter every night.

This was maintained when the work transferred to New York in 1990, playing, for almost as long there as in London, at the Ethel Barrymore Theatre on West 47th Street. The management of the New York theatre had participated in the promotion of the London production, with the intention of transferring it to New York if it succeeded. The Ethyl Barrymore Theatre, one of the last to be built before the depression, had opened in 1928 and had seen the world premieres of works as diverse as *Pal Joey* and *A Streetcar Named Desire*. The theatre, seating just over a thousand, was intimate and ideal for the comedy from London, yet large enough to meet the huge demand for tickets.

The two actors took up residence in neighbouring apartments at the Wyndham Hotel, next to the Plaza. Tyzack made many friendships in the city. A particular pleasure was that she could see her beloved younger sister, Marion, a teacher living in the USA, at weekends. It was a pleasant time socially, but it was also very hard work. Playing a riotous comedy for three hours requires energy and stamina. For Tyzack there was enormous pleasure in acting with Maggie Smith, whom she regards as the greatest comic actor of the age.

Playing in *Lettice and Lovage* was a joyous way of spending two years of her professional life and gave Tyzack two of her many awards – Actress of the Year Award (Variety Club of Great Britain) and Tony Award (New York). The New York award was a particular feather in her cap. Some distinguished theatre people did not spring up from their tables to the applause of their colleagues that year. Dustin Hoffman, nominated for his Shylock, and Andrew Lloyd Webber, for his *Aspects of Love*, went away empty-handed.

Tyzack continued her association with Maggie Smith in comedy when she played Miss Prism in *The Importance of Being Earnest* to Smith's Lady Bracknell at the Aldwych Theatre in London in 1993. The critics and audiences agreed that the two Maggies were good and brought originality to this over-performed masterpiece, but were otherwise unimpressed. The freshness and originality that she brought to the familiar part of Miss Prism was to convey, with subtlety not vulgarity, her lust for Dr Chasuble. One of her friends admired her performance for being so different from the real Tyzack, saying, "If *you* had lost a handbag at a railway station, with or without a baby in it, you would have had the whole station cordoned off until it was found!"

The Aldwych is her favourite theatre. Built in 1905, it has, she says, a near perfect acoustic, with just a little dead spot under the circle needing particular attention from those on stage. She had played all of her RSC roles at the Aldwych, before returning there in 1993. It was a particular joy to be there again in another comedy in 1995, Tom Stoppard's *Indian Ink*. Although the play had been done some years earlier on the radio, this was its first production in a theatre, and Tyzack created the part on the stage that Peggy Ashcroft had played on the radio. Like the best comedy, it was serious as well as funny, exploring what is indelible in relationships between races. Tyzack played alongside Art Malik and Felicity Kendall in a mixed Indian and English cast. Her role was that of a colonial English woman, pottering about the garden in trousers, waistcoat and sensible shoes. Her "alluring performance, all crisp hauteur, was a load of reactionary fun", but it was also a deeply felt play, "acted with enigmatic precision" by its three stars, Tyzack, Kendall and Malik.

❖ ❖ ❖ ❖ ❖

Realising a writer's words for the first time in performance is both a demanding and a liberating experience for actors. The liberating aspect comes from the audience's lack of familiarity with famous portrayals. Antony Sher has written about the terrors of giving the opening lines of *Richard III*, with Olivier's delivery of "Now is the winter of our discontent made glorious summer by this son of York" so well known that it is parodied by popular comedians. By contrast, to be the first person to deliver lines has advantages, but there is no guidance. Tyzack has often been the creator of new roles, for she has combined new writing with her work in the classical repertoire. Some of these new plays, by their very nature, made only modest impact. Others, including *Indian Ink*, had important things to say and were significant steps forward in British drama. Creating new roles preceded *The Forsyte Saga* and continues to this day.

1963 was the year of John F Kennedy's assassination. Like many people Tyzack can recall precisely the moment when she heard the dreadful news. She was playing in *Ginger Man* at the Royal Court, sitting in the dressing room with the large oval window that, before the theatre's rebuilding, overlooked Sloane Square. Susan Hampshire was on the telephone to a reporter when he heard and relayed the news to her. The two actors later heard the cries of shock and disbelief from homeward-bound workers as they read the headlines on the newspaper billboards outside Sloane Square underground station.

Tyzack had worked at the Royal Court several times before this, taking part in Sunday evening 'performances without décor', mostly new plays. Actors were not paid and were therefore allowed to cancel if other work came along. The arrangement also allowed them to do other work during the week. One of her directors then was Lindsay Anderson. The other leading actor in *Ginger Man* was Nicol Williamson, whom Tyzack admired greatly for his "wonderful voice and dangerous acting." With television beckoning, she turned down, now much to her regret, opportunities to do more work at the Royal Court, then as now at the cutting edge of British drama with much new writing.

In 1984 Tyzack returned to the Royal Court to create the role of Rose, the mother of T S Eliot's wife in *Tom and Viv*. In this account of Eliot's tempestuous marriage, Tyzack had to deliver a speech denouncing Eliot. In this she was terrifying. As one critic commented, "It was left to the magnificent Margaret Tyzack to give him [Eliot] the withering dressing down of which only a matriarch, certain beyond a wisp of doubt that her daughter has married beneath her, is capable." Whatever the doubts of some about Tyzack's ability to find true venom as Martha in *Who's Afraid of Virginia Woolf?*, her work in both plays attracted approval from awarding bodies. For her starring role in the Albee play she had won the award of Actress of the Year in a revival from what are now called the Oliver Awards. As T S Eliot's mother-in-law she was nominated for the New York Drama Desk award in Eliot's native country.

Brian Friel's play *Give Me Your Answer Do* in 1998 at the Hampstead Theatre was not strictly a premiere, because the work had already been tried out in Dublin, but unsuccessfully, so this was a second attempt to bring it off. Regarded by many as Ireland's best current playwright, particularly on the basis of *Dancing at Lughnasa*, Friel confronts in this play the worries and confusions of writers themselves. Tyzack played the writer's mother-in-law in a comedy with the serious purpose of exploring questions of integrity and compromise for writers, living with their families and operating in a commercial world. She and her husband, played by John Woodvine, provided, through their marital sniping, much of the comic relief in a play with serious themes.

❖ ❖ ❖ ❖ ❖

Tyzack has worked with many celebrated directors. She has no truck with the actor's view that directors have become too important, but a review of her career indicates that she has mostly worked with directors who respect the author's words, for example Jonathan Miller who directed her in *A Winter's Tale* for television. There is not much evidence in her career of working with 'concept' directors who sometimes seem to wish to impose an interpretation on a work that strains against its words.

She admired and liked Stanley Kubrick. She first worked for him in *2001: A Space Odyssey*, quite by chance. Kubrick wanted Bill Sylvester, an American, for the film, but did not want to return to America to recruit the cast. He hated flying. Instead he watched a film called *Ring of Spies* featuring Sylvester, seeing Tyzack entirely by chance as she too was in that film. She appears in *2001* in a brief but crucial scene on the bridge of the spacecraft. There was also a small role for Tyzack in *Clockwork Orange*. Kubrick did not use a script for this film. Actors improvised. When Kubrick liked something, he had it typed up and the actors then had literally to learn 'their' lines. There was no part at all for her in *Barry Lyndon*, but Kubrick invited her to do the voice-overs for the trailers. Tyzack has good reason to judge Kubrick "a very loyal man, harder on technicians, probably because he understood their craft better, whilst he gave actors more scope." She found him a humane and funny man. When the actors had been sitting around on the set for a long time in the heat one day, Tyzack asked an assistant if there was any chance of 'a cuppa'. Choosing the right moment, the assistant passed the request on to the great man. He glanced in the direction of the actors, saying, with his strong American drawl, "OK. Water the horses."

Directors who begin work on a new production with statements about the cast and the director reaching a view of the play as an outcome of their work together are dismissed by Tyzack. "I expect a director to direct," she says. "His job is to know the play and block the actors' positions and movements on the stage before the actors arrive, so that their important work together can begin. It's not much to ask, is it?" she adds, indicating that not all directors do this. This does not mean that Tyzack is moulded by the director. The role is hers, but she expects directors to have done their homework, as she has done hers, and she seeks agreement from the outset about the essence of the work.

The famous directors with whom she has worked include, in addition to Kubrick, Bryan Forbes (an early Rank film made at Pinewood), Trevor Nunn (four productions, all Shakespeare), Robin Phillips (her Stratford, Ontario, season and again in *Dorian* in 2001), Max Stafford Clark (*Tom and Viv*), Nicholas Hytner (*The Importance of Being Earnest*), Michael Blakemore (*Lettice and Lovage*), Stephen Daldry (the celebrated, long-running *An Inspector Calls*), Peter Wood (*Indian Ink*), Jonathan Miller (*A Winter's Tale*) and Alan Bennett (she was one of his *Talking Heads*). She will not be drawn on which of them, if any, failed to meet her expectations. David Giles, who directed her in *The Forsyte Saga* and *The First Churchills*, has a very special place in her affections.

❖ ❖ ❖ ❖ ❖

Tyzack's biggest recent engagements have been in T S Eliot's *The Family Reunion* in the 1999-2000 RSC season and in the BBC radio serial of Dickens's *Little Dorrit*. In both she played old, twisted women, but both were far from caricatures. The Eliot was particularly poignant for her, having played Eliot's mother-in-law in *Tom and Viv*. That play was about Eliot's relationship with his wife which finished with his locking her away in a mental institution. *The Family Reunion* is a thinly-disguised attempt by Eliot at expiation, based on the *Oresteia*, with Harry the equivalent of Orestes/Eliot and complete with the Furies. A verse-play, it was difficult to act. Nonetheless, the production worked. Tyzack, having acted earlier in the portrayal of Eliot's failing marriage, was deeply conscious of the guilt that lay behind his writing. Now playing the role equivalent to Eliot's own mother, she conveyed her maternal love by a gaze, whilst keeping her secrets and controlling her grief. A formidable portrayal.

Little Dorrit is, of course, a great novel and the radio adaptation in six parts was masterly. Again taking the role of the hero's mother, Tyzack had to convey granite hardness, religious bigotry, stoicism, anger and eventually compassion, with only the voice to convey these emotions. The play was recorded in old buildings around Spitalfields, where the story is set. The final episode, when Tyzack's house collapses, was recorded in the open air at Lincolns Inn. It was a masterpiece of radio.

In the summer of 2001, Tyzack tackled another adaptation of a great work and the creation of another new role in *Dorian*, a dramatised version of Oscar Wilde's *The Picture of Dorian Gray*. Directed by Robin Phillips, it gave her the chance to work again with the man who had invited her to Stratford, Ontario. "He's a wonderfully gifted director," enthuses Tyzack when mentioning Phillips, who had just directed *Ghosts* in the West End. She was also playing again with Alan Bates, a friend with whom she had been able to spend some time when he had been playing Antony to Frances de la Tour's Cleopatra in Stratford whilst Tyzack herself was in *The Family Reunion*. They had taken cottages next to each other facing the green in front of the theatre. The author of *Dorian* is Trevor Baxter, a friend going back to their days at drama college together fifty years earlier. Quite a reunion. With such recent triumphs, Margaret Tyzack is in good shape to go on enlightening and entertaining us well into the millennium.

ROBERT HARRIS

At the age of 44, Robert Harris is one of the country's best-known writers of thrillers. His books, *Fatherland, Enigma* and *Archangel*, have sold more than six million copies in thirty languages. *Enigma* has now been made into a film, starring Kate Winslet and Dougray Scott, with Harris's story transformed into a screenplay by the playwright Tom Stoppard, and with Mick Jagger as one of the producers.

Harris has been writing and editing since his school days. The value of his apprenticeship shows in his novels. They combine the investigations of the journalist, the grasp and judgement of the historian and the style of the literary scholar. English has been Harris's main academic study, but he is a historian at heart. The skills of both subjects are used to great effect in his story-telling.

Harris lives in a beautiful, riverside old vicarage in the village of Kintbury, Berkshire, in the heart of middle England. The picture, when you visit him on a warm June afternoon, is of the family - Robert, Gill and the four children – relaxing on the lawn under a tree planted in Napoleonic times. It is not difficult to imagine Jane Austen paying one of her many visits to the earlier vicarage that once stood on this site. It is idyllic.

But Harris's origins were altogether more humble. In his early life there was nothing to suggest a glittering journalistic and literary career. Born in Nottingham, he moved at the age of nine to Leicestershire because of his father's work as a printer. Father, a largely self-taught man who had left school at 14, was the dominant figure in the family. A strong Labour supporter whose views were clear and frequently conveyed, he was the biggest influence on the young Robert, who very much admired his father's certainty and stature. Father and son talked all the time about politics, as others talk about football, and father passed to son his love of books, particularly and significantly those of Graham Greene, George Orwell, Georges Simenon, Arnold

Bennett and A J P Taylor. *Archangel* was dedicated to Harris senior. Here was the first source of the young Robert's political education. The women, mother and Robert's sister, Glenys, were the less noticeable side of the household. It was not particularly a question of gender, just that father was dominant and Robert gifted.

Not until Harris became a pupil at King Edward VII School in Melton Mowbray, a former grammar school turned comprehensive in the educational changes of the 1960s, did anything remarkable about the boy become apparent. Then it became obvious to his fellow pupils and to his teachers. As they all say, "Robert had a gift". It was not so much a general academic ability as a quite specific capacity to use words to telling effect.

School brought him into contact with a powerful character and formative influence in the person of his headteacher, Bernard Brewster. A Marxist and a conscientious objector during the war, Brewster was not only the headteacher of the town's upper school but also chair of his local Labour Party and the town's first Labour councillor. "A passionate believer in old socialist principles" is how Phil Vincent, former deputy head of the school and now one of its historians, describes him. Brought into the hostile territory of Melton Mowbray to create a comprehensive school, Brewster was the cuckoo in the nest who won over the town by devoting himself to the interests of his pupils, staff and the community. Here was another man whom Harris greatly admired, and whose public political beliefs reinforced those already learned from his father. But Brewster's main contribution to Harris's development was that he let him get away with things that most headteachers would have stamped on. He let him read at a school assembly, not from the Bible as usual, but from Siegfried Sassoon's *The Case for the Miners*, during the 1993-4 miners' strike in what Harris calls "rock-ribbed Tory Melton Mowbray."

It was from Brewster too that Harris began to acquire his interest in the history of the twentieth century, especially the Second World War, the Cold War and the Eastern Bloc, that was to be the focus of many of his journalistic investigations. Harris himself has become convinced as a result of his journalism and his studies of Nazi Germany and Stalinist Russia, the background to two of his novels, that the main conflict of the late 1930s and the 1940s was between Germany and Russia. It is necessary, in his view, only to drop the preoccupation of Britain with its own role in the war to grasp that this was the essence of the conflict. The seeds of this understanding were sown whilst he was at school.

As for many children of blue collar workers, the sixth form was the period of his flowering. In Harris's case, the combination of characters and the mix of different talents, not least his own, made it one of those golden year groups of pupils that most schools can remember, where the sum is so much greater than the parts. It was a piece of good luck for Harris that he was able to write widely and provocatively - and for an appreciative audience.

The main conduit by which Harris's judgements on the school world found their outlet was the weekly magazine, *Memograms*, which had existed for some time (hence its name based on Melton Mowbray Grammar) but which was moribund before Harris and friends revived it. Harris now describes the paper as his own project and all in the school at the time agree that he was its driving force, but there was what a teacher calls "a very talented trio." The other two were Andrew Lomax, quieter and more studious, and John Vincent, particularly good at sport, something which Harris by all accounts used all his wits successfully to avoid. Another frequent presence in the *Memograms* office was Lesley Smith, who was to become a very successful businesswoman. One work that was certainly all Harris's own was a sketch, *The Stately Homes of England.* He wrote it, produced it (with Lomax) and starred in it. His considerable persuasive powers were used to get the practical tasks done by others. The group had its own office over which Harris as editor presided, comparing his status to that of Sergeant Bilko in the American television series – he had his own little operation that was tolerated within the larger organisation of the school.

Private Eye was their model and surviving copies of *Memograms* reflect the style of their inspiration, with 'revelations', lampoons (for example on the local newspaper, barely disguised as the 'Metlon Times') and polemics conveyed with a light touch. Harris's nickname became Horace Rabbit, a sort of pun on his own name.

Given considerable licence, they took more. Teachers, school policies and other pupils were their targets. Some teachers took it on the chin. When a history teacher with a reputation as a stern disciplinarian in the classroom was depicted as Hitler, he laughed heartily for he was in fact very liberal and was perhaps quite flattered by the attention. Other teachers, with justification, were less tolerant and Brewster's indulgence was revealed to have bounds. Challenges to school policies, such as a piece opposing the study of religious education, sailed close to the wind and led to questions about who was running the school. Harris and his friends needed the protection of Alec Johns, the teacher loosely in charge, who says, "My job was to tie down this bucking horse and take the political flak."

One thing caused Lomax disquiet at the time and even now when he recollects it. Their friends often appeared in the magazine in jocular guises and with affection, but other references to pupils were attacks that Lomax thought were cruel. Johns saw these as the price to be paid whilst budding journalists struggled to find the right balance, but acknowledges that, because the boys were talented writers, their comments were sometimes lacerating.

The general election of 1974 was an opportunity to be seized. As the Labour candidate in the school mock election, Harris conducted his campaign with great flair, assisted by Lesley Smith, and was beaten by only four votes in this Conservative stronghold. Lomax was on the Conservative side, and his acknowledgement that the real victory went to Harris is for that reason the more compelling.

Harris's relationships with his collaborators were complex. Fitting rather uneasily into Melton Mowbray, like Brewster but without the older man's experience and charm, he was often uneasy with himself. He was working class from a large village outside this small and conservative town and had something of a hankering for his birthplace city of Nottingham to which he frequently referred and returned. Although he usually sat in class next to Lesley Smith, who copied his notes, Harris showed little emotional interest in girls. When Lomax indicated that he had found in a Dutch girl the love of his life, Harris was appalled, expressing alarm at how this commitment might define Lomax's career. Harris was himself as conscious as others were of his gift for writing, and he intended to succeed without distractions.

Ambition went hand in hand with perplexity and occasionally an unusual degree of insecurity. When Lomax was made head boy with Harris as his deputy, Harris was astounded and could not imagine why it should have been that way round because he was always the more flamboyant and prominent of the pair. When Johns organised a visit to Leeds University, as part of the sixth form programme, he found Harris diffident and rather provincial, for the 17-year-old fretted for days about how he would get home to his village in the evening when left at one of the dropping off points. Even one aspect of the 1974 mock election, acknowledged by all as a personal triumph, disturbed him. Lomax, his close *Memograms* collaborator, was the organiser for the Conservative candidate. During one of Harris's election rallies in the school hall, Lomax and others burst in waving Conservative placards. This commonplace rough and tumble of the hustings shocked Harris who felt betrayed by his friend. The one who expected his victims to be thick-skinned could himself be somewhat sensitive.

This was a young man with a complex combination of reckless confidence in his gift, occasional diffidence, personal vulnerability to slights and sometimes disregard for the feelings of others. He was, of course, only a teenager. "What a pain in the neck I must have been to people," he now realises. Sitting all these years later in the drawing room overlooking the river across the sloping lawn and recalling his own past, none of this is apparent. Relaxed and charming, revealing his sharp intellect and prodigious memory conversationally and modestly, he is now a confident man at ease with his gift who no longer needs to prove anything to anybody.

Whilst first amongst the talented writers of *Memograms*, Harris was not outstanding amongst them academically. He was good in a year of pupils who were good. "Gift" is the word that contemporaries, both pupils and teachers, constantly use about him. That gift was to use words persuasively and compellingly. Brewster's tolerance, which extended further for Harris than for others, is interpreted by some as a shrewd headteacher's recognition that here was a gift that needed to be given its head. This young man was going places. King Edward VII School can be credited with unlocking the first creative energies of Harris.

In common with many young men and women of his age, Harris was the first from his working class family to go to university. His English teacher at school was a former student of Selwyn College and he helped Harris to follow in his footsteps. Harris was offered a place at the age of 17 before he had taken his A-levels. Having enjoyed English literature at school, he decided to continue with it at Cambridge. This was a mistake, for, after studying for his A-level, he found English at university to be more of the same. There was too much writing about other writers and not enough opportunities to write his own material. By the time he came to understand that he should have studied history, it was too late to change, because he would have had to stay for an extra year, something that he neither wished nor could afford to do.

Once he had left Melton Mowbray, Harris acted as though he were putting a phase of his life behind him. Vincent, one of the trio, also went to Cambridge, although to a different college and with his non-academic interest now sport rather than student journalism. Harris and Vincent rarely met at Cambridge. When Lomax, himself at another university, visited Harris in Cambridge, he found him just as he always had been when they were alone, but rather distant once Harris's new Cambridge friends came on the scene. The three have not kept in touch. An invitation from Brewster did get him back to Melton Mowbray to address the arts club there on *Fatherland*, an occasion filmed by a German television crew for transmission on a programme similar to *Omnibus*, and by all accounts followed by a very convivial evening.

When Harris arrived at Cambridge in 1975 student politics were sterile. Nationally and in the local branch of the National Union of Students, factionalism reigned, with hard-fought contests for the national presidency usually won by the candidates regarded at the time as from the hard left, people like Charles Clarke (in 2001 appointed to the cabinet by Tony Blair) and Sue Slipman (then a communist candidate, later a member of the Order of the British Empire and the director for social responsibility of the lottery-running company, Camelot). There were factions but little discussion of ideas and not much sense of reality. This was not a world that Harris wished to enter.

Yet Harris's years as a student from 1975 to 1978 were to see the eruption of politics nationally with strikes and riots as the forces of left and right confronted each other in what can now be seen as a crux in Britain's economic and political history. Events that determined the history of Britain in the last quarter of the century were the context for Harris's student days at Cambridge – Margaret Thatcher had replaced Edward Heath after his failed confrontation with the miners, Harold Wilson had resumed the premiership in 1974 and then promptly retired, and the financial crisis of 1976 under James Callaghan led to the 'winter of discontent', heralding eighteen years of Conservative rule dominated by Margaret Thatcher who won her first election in 1979. They were tumultuous times.

Harris not only eschewed student politics but also showed no obvious interest in national politics until his final year. Student journalism occupied his time, extending his school experience as he edited *Stop Press*, the students' tabloid newspaper. Then in his final year he suddenly became politically active. In the first term he became Chairman of the university's Fabian Society. Largely on the back of his success in that role, he was elected Vice-President of the Cambridge Union in the spring, automatically moving up to the presidency in the summer term, his final at Cambridge. It was a rapid rise, with some indications of careful planning.

The Fabian Society had been founded by George Bernard Shaw, Sydney and Beatrice Webb and R H Tawney to promote moderate socialist thought, taking its name from the Roman general Fabius who was noted for winning victories by slow incremental steps rather than grand flourishes or revolution. It was concerned with political thinking and policy-making rather than the art of politics itself. Thinkers and talkers rather than doers; words rather than actions. This suited Harris. The Cambridge University Fabian Society became, during the one term of Harris's chairmanship, the largest branch in Britain, doubling its membership to 700. Harris showed a flair for leadership and organisation. A small committee met fortnightly and managed a very efficient operation with representatives in all but four colleges. Its vigour attracted increasing attention from the Labour leadership in London, and eventually that of James Callaghan, who took time off from running the country to accept Harris's invitation to speak at a Society meeting.

Callaghan's speech was a disaster. Beginning by saying that he preferred addressing adult audiences was perhaps unwise of the Prime Minister, and he followed this with a brag about his meetings with fellow international leaders. Callaghan's reputation as 'sunny Jim' seemed to be taking over when he described Britain as a nation that, in the words of the reporter from *Stop Press*, no longer edited by Harris, sounded like a country "flowing with milk, honey and North Sea oil". His government was in fact fighting for its life. But none of that mattered. His appearance was a very big feather in Harris's cap. Other speakers organised by Harris were Anthony Howard, the political correspondent (who was later to advance Harris's career), Roy Hattersley, Derek Jameson (editor of *The Daily Express*), Tam Dalyell (now father of the House of Commons), Betty Boothroyd of the Equal Opportunities Commission (later Speaker of the House of Commons), and Lord Longford. His success in organising such a speakers' list for just one term did not pass unnoticed.

More controversial speakers such as David Irving, then a promising historian with a deserved reputation for finding important details in hitherto unknown documents about Hitler, were on Harris's guest list. Irving further stimulated Harris's interest in Hitler and the Nazis. His claim, entirely justified, was that no documentary evidence has been found of Hitler's having ordered the systematic destruction of the Jews, whom, of course, he did nonetheless destroy, along with gypsies, homosexuals, handicapped people, communists, social democrats and trades unionists. Irving's phrase, "There is no evidence that…." may well have sown the seed that would later lead to Harris's novel, *Fatherland*. Even at that time Irving was controversial, prompting a 'Heil and Farewell' headline in *Stop Press*, which gave details of his various writings and speeches, including his belief that Britain had been wrong to "aid Russia" by going to war against Hitler. Here was another insight that may well have prompted Harris's thinking about the Second World War. Harris was attracted to controversy and investigative journalism. The prospect of a future career was emerging.

The newly-resurrected Fabian Society in Cambridge had not affiliated to the local Labour Party when Harris took over the chair but intended to do so, and there were controversies about who could join the society, because membership of the Labour Party was incompatible with membership of some other organisations. Prominent amongst the disputants was a Nigel Vaz, who during Harris's term of leading the Cambridge Fabians became Nigel K Vaz. His chief role on the committee was to organise social events at which he seemed to be rather good, having had the committee's go-ahead on major decisions such as spending £1.78 on balloons for the Christmas party and subsequently reporting a surplus on the event of £1.96. In order to overcome any difficulty over membership of organisations proscribed by the Labour Party, Vaz announced to the committee that he had resigned from the Conservatives.

Harris's activities in the Fabian Society were the springboard for his election as Vice-President of the Cambridge Union and thus the presidency. The Cambridge Union Society (its official name) was a debating society and social club with a membership fee. As now, the programme was a mixture of serious debates on weighty matters, usually chaired by the president and often with distinguished national speakers who were invited to formal dinners before the debate, and light-hearted jousts which only students would find worth holding.

Harris entered the debating lists as soon as he arrived at Cambridge, taking part in the freshers' debates held in his first month there. Twenty debates were held during the day, with eighty speakers in all. Harris spoke for three minutes, opposing the belief that "nothing succeeds like success" and proving his case by losing and not reaching the finals. The election for the vice-presidency of the Union two years later was hotly contested and Harris's candidacy was something of a surprise, for he had not been one of the most prominent speakers at Union debates. There were slates of candidates and Harris was on a broadly-based list that was supported by Conservative and Liberal as well as Labour groups. Whilst still Chairman of the Fabians, Harris had formally denied a story in a student newspaper alleging that abundant Fabian funds had been promised to a Labour alliance in student union elections. The "abundant" was an addition to the original text of the Fabian committee minutes, indicating that some funds had indeed been promised. Horse-trading was taking place.

Whilst Harris's opponent had a reputation as a witty speaker in the Union, Harris could pitch against this his efficiency in reviving the Fabian Society and his impressive power of persuading prominent people to speak at their meetings, a major duty of the vice-president. Harris won. The voters did not follow the slates slavishly, for they elected a student from the opposition, Ed Stourton, later a BBC presenter, to be the Secretary. Harris and Stourton worked closely together.

The controversial in Harris did not make him popular with the university authorities during his presidency of the Union. Quite indulgent in their general approach, they nonetheless associated prestige with dignity. He had already fallen foul of them by calling the new Chancellor of the University, the Duke of Edinburgh, "a stooge" in print. Prince Philip, when asked about it, rather disarmingly agreed and neatly protected Harris! When Harris, now President, invited some of the 'great train robbers' to speak, (not, of course, Ronnie Biggs for he was in Brazil at the time), the authorities were not amused. The event was a flop, with many students believing that the Union had been duped into giving free publicity to the book that the criminals had just published, and only fifty turned up to hear their story, being almost outnumbered by press photographers. The invitation had not been well judged.

The authorities found even less diverting Harris's invitation to George Ward to speak in a debate. Ward was the owner of a company called Grunwick and his aim was to break the power of the unions. Ward had sacked his workers, which had led to a strike, by now in its twenty-first month. He was a highly controversial figure. It was a very big national story that would not go away. Ward's appearance in Cambridge was unlikely to be a calm event.

Tempers rose during the day, inflamed by Ward's boasting that most employers had "not got the guts" to sack workers as he was doing, so keen were they to "worship at the altar of union power." A national controversy had been brought to Cambridge by Harris and had then been inflamed by flamboyant oratory before the Union debate. The proposition for debate deplored the closed shop, the then legal practice to make union membership compulsory so that workers would act as one in their dealings with employers. The undergraduate who led the opposition, the ex-Conservative Fabian, had by this time completed his name change and was a fully-fledged Keith Vaz; he was later the 'Mr Europe in Tony Blair's first government, and became embroiled in the Hinduja affair with Peter Mandelson. Harris suspects that 'Keith' was thought to sound more plebeian than 'Nigel'. He remembers little of Vaz at the time, except that he was very slim.

The students' union, representatives of the Grunwick workers and others demonstrated around the famous round church at the top of Trinity Street, which stands in front of the Union. The police and the university proctors (the university's own disciplinarians) were out in force and the student newspaper, *Stop Press*, took delight in printing the picture of a police photographer who was snapping individual students for his files. The demonstration was in fact entirely peaceful and there were no arrests. The vote was heavily in favour of deploring the closed shop.

As a speaker in Union debates, Harris argued unsuccessfully against secrecy in government, the practice of whipping in the Commons, the right of the National Front to operate freely and a motion of no confidence in the Labour government. The biggest debate during his vice-presidency also saw him on the losing side, but appearing in some impressive company and heard by more than 500 people in the chamber and more still on television. The motion defined left and right in terms of the role of the state and was posed from the right-wing angle that the role of the state should be diminished. The other speakers were Tom King, Roy Hattersley, Keith Joseph and Peter Shore, all of whom were already or soon to be in the cabinet. There was a consistency in Harris's debating, for he always took the left side in any right-left debate and always shared in the left's defeat.

Once Harris became President it was, of course, his role to be in the chair, but, as was the custom, he did speak in two debates as his presidency ended. The theme of one of these could hardly have had greater relevance to the present time. Harris's argument was that "the American dream has become Europe's nightmare". As was his custom, he lost.

In the other final debate of his Cambridge career Harris proposed that "journalism is an honourable profession." The guest speakers included Derek Jameson, Anthony Holden, Desmond Wilcox and William Deedes. Particularly disappointing for a man about to embark on a career as a journalist, Harris lost that debate also, but he had had fun in his last year at Cambridge and made a name for himself.

Like every young person, Harris now found himself in the shocking need of having to earn a living. He had always wanted to be a writer and most of his activities since the age of 16 had been an apprenticeship for a career in journalism. Having lived all his life in the provinces, he wanted to get to London. The National Union of Journalists at the time required trainee journalists to serve initially on a local or provincial paper before applying for a national newspaper. There were only two exceptions to the NUJ rule. Economics graduates could go directly to work on *The Financial Times*, but that was of no help to Harris, and television was also exempt from the rule. There was only one way in which Harris could achieve all his goals and that was to be employed by the BBC or ITV.

Leaving Cambridge with a modest degree was less important than having been President of the Union and having had success in attracting a string of prominent people to the Fabians and the Union. His last year at Cambridge had been well spent. He had contacts. The broadcasters had a small number of traineeships each year, and Harris was offered places by both the BBC and ITV. He accepted the BBC's offer. The decision was to have a major impact on his career for he was to be at the BBC, mainly freelance rather than employed, for most of the next ten years.

Initially not particularly satisfied with the nature of his work with the BBC, which was as a current affairs researcher on the *Tonight* and *Nationwide* programmes, he seized the opportunity to move to *Panorama*. This was much more to his liking. *Nationwide* was concerned too much with briefly topical questions, without the depth of investigation that Harris sought.

There were also many silly items, such as one on skateboarding ducks. It was superficial and tabloid. The programme went out in the early evening and provided a sort of extended news magazine for people just in from work. It fulfilled a need for many viewers, but not Harris's own professional need. Harris was always more interested in analysis and substance in reporting than in topicality. He has never been a newsman by instinct.

Two men were very important to Harris at this time. An editor of *Tonight* was Roger Boulton, later a frequent presenter of radio and television feedback and religious affairs programmes. Harris moved in his wake when he became editor of *Panorama*. Once on the *Panorama* team, Harris met Jeremy Paxman, beginning a professional collaboration that produced many important programmes. Harris and Paxman had similarly iconoclastic approaches, going off in directions that more orthodox researchers would not consider. They were also similarly dogged and persistent. Success in their working relationship led to a friendship that continues to this day, with the two families still taking holidays together.

Panorama was then an even more prestigious programme than it is today. It had a very large budget and the researchers and journalists were given considerable freedom. They could get their teeth into big questions, not least those that governments would have preferred to remain unchewed. This was very much Harris's forte.

Harris and Paxman both had an instinct for a good story. Just after Russia had invaded Afghanistan and raised the stakes in the Cold War, they discovered an old official government film called *Protect and Survive* which gave ludicrous official advice on what people should do when the atomic or hydrogen bomb fell. Such advice had been around in pamphlet form in the 1960s, but most of it was so silly that it had had the opposite effect to that intended. Nobody could take seriously the suggestion that a brown paper bag over your head would protect you from the effects of radiation following a nuclear explosion. The revival of such advice, exposed in the *Panorama* programme that coincided with the Cold War fear that Russia was expanding further into Asia, was a powerful reminder of the assumptions behind the theory of nuclear deterrence. The *Panorama* programme inspired Raymond Briggs to turn his book *When the Wind Blows* into his famous film, a chilling and much more plausible depiction of life for the survivors of a nuclear attack. Harris showed his flair for digging around and unearthing things that others preferred to keep buried.

Harris and Paxman also collaborated on a very detailed *Panorama* investigation of Britain's capacity to conduct germ warfare. Called *A Higher Form of Killing*, it was extended into a book in 1982. They provide a terrifying account of the ways in which governments of all persuasions and on both sides of the then Iron Curtain prepared chemical and biological weapons for use, not just, as is so often claimed, in order to defend their own armies and civilians from the evil doings of others.

This work encapsulated all of Harris's interests and used all the skills that he had been developing. The setting for several chapters was the Second World War and the method was to seek out all possible sources of evidence, piecing them together, cross-checking, and following up new leads until a convincing story could be told and substantiated.

One of the chapters written by Harris tells how the Porton Down research station developed and tested anthrax bombs during the Second World War on the Scottish island of Gruinard. It is the amateurish way in which the ablest bacteriologists in the land conducted the trials that appalled Harris and it is still shocking to read. The science, as science, was very clever, as it often is, but the methods and the lack of concern for the future were reckless.

The book shows Harris's flair for story-telling. Sheep were bought on the Scottish mainland, taken to the island, tethered in concentric circles around an anthrax 'bomb'; the scientists withdrew, 'lit the fuse' and waited for the sheep to die. In another trial, anthrax bombs were dropped from a plane on more sheep, and so it went on. On one occasion when a huge quantity of anthrax was being transported between Dorset and the island, a distance of more than 600 miles, the van containing the world's first biological bomb was left overnight at a Leeds police station in the charge of the duty sergeant who was ignorant of his true responsibility, whilst the army major and his driver went off for a drink in a pub. You can sense Harris's incredulity, despite his dispassionate assembling of cold facts, and almost hear his interviews with the people whose activities he is cataloguing. The reader's incredulity is that he managed to get them to talk at all.

Whilst he was working on the programme and the book, much of Harris's time was spent at the Public Record Office, the British national archives, surrounded by other historians. He had to search documents, make connections, analyse and write – a historian's paradise. One gem that he uncovered was a "most secret" memo from Churchill in July 1944: "......it may be several weeks or even months before I shall ask you to drench Germany with poison gas, and if we do it, let us do it one hundred per cent." It was only strategic considerations and the problems of what is now called 'friendly fire' that prevented the unleashing by both Britain and Germany of disasters for the world. For Harris, research into Nazi Germany, for he also covered the parallel German events, and into the true nature of the 1939-45 conflict was further unwitting preparation for his first novel, *Fatherland*, published ten years later.

Harris's career in television continued until 1989. Four years as a reporter on *Newsnight*, which is still presented by his old friend Jeremy Paxman, were followed by his return to *Panorama* as a reporter and then a year as a political reporter on *This Week*, ITV's equivalent of *Panorama*.

Working for *Newsnight* was an important step forward, for its leader and inspiration was George Cary who encouraged reporters and producers to present their own stories. This gave Harris the opportunity to make his own programmes and he again chose historical themes, basing programmes, for example, on the repatriation of the Cossacks and on a recently-rediscovered colour film of Hiroshima. It was the combination of his own reputation for getting to the bottom of interesting and sometimes truly sensational stories and his association with important editors that led to his move back to *Panorama*. One of his most important pieces of work there, with echoes of his earlier work, was a programme revealing Iraq's secret weapons manufacture. He had access to a French satellite camera that could photograph ground installations in detail. Help in interpreting the photographs was needed – "knowing which way up they went" is how he puts it – and this was willingly provided by the American and British secret services.

In 1987 Harris became for the first time a newspaper journalist, as the political editor of the Sunday newspaper, *The Observer*. Anthony Howard, whom he had first met at a Cambridge Union debate, was the paper's Deputy Editor. When he telephoned Harris with the offer it was promptly accepted.

Although Harris had previously worked on newspapers, at least as an amateur with *Memograms* and *Stop Press*, he found that he did not now enjoy it, whilst recognising that his time on *The Observer* was 'the making' of him. It was terrifying and hard work. For the first time in his career he was not part of a team or a structure, but entirely on his own, having to make something out of a weekly diet of political news. A particular dislike was the parliamentary lobby, the practice of accredited journalists having to hang around parliament to receive the views, official or otherwise, of politicians. Being the parliamentary equivalent, in Tony Benn's words, of a court correspondent was not congenial.

It was now that he first met Peter Mandelson, a work contact, for Mandelson was the Labour Party's Director of Communications and his job entailed courting lobby correspondents. They met in the room of Neil Kinnock, at the time the leader of the Labour Party.

During his time at *The Observer* Harris was invited back to *Panorama* to make a programme marking Margaret Thatcher's achievement as Britain's longest continuously serving prime minister, as she exceeded Asquith's eight years. Thatcher was, of course, to go on for several more years and to hold the title by a long lead. Knowing that she and the American President, Ronald Reagan, admired each other, Harris sought, and to his amazement was granted, an interview at the White House. It was more informative about Reagan than Thatcher. The President of the USA was under several delusions, not least that Queen Victoria had been an exceptionally long-serving British prime minister.

Despite the unwelcome requirement to perform to a weekly timetable, Harris next became a columnist on *The Sunday Times*. The invitation to write a weekly column came from *The Sunday Times* Editor, Andrew Neil, who was aware of Harris's left-leaning views and wanted a columnist who would challenge and probably upset the typical *Sunday Times* readers of that period, mostly Thatcherites. Even with Neale's enticing remit, Harris found the demands of writing a thousand words by a Saturday morning deadline week after week still rather irksome, but it was a good discipline. Harris worked from home and was never again to work in an office. It had one great merit. He now had time to try his hand at writing a novel.

1988 was an important year. Harris married Gillian Hornby, sister of the writer Nick Hornby. The couple had met at the BBC in 1984 when both were working on *Newsnight*. Gillian had worked at the London bureau of the American network ABC and then at TVAM before joining the BBC. They moved into a four-storey house in St Lawrence Terrace, west London, just beyond the Portobello Road, with George Melly, the rakish jazz singer and raconteur as their neighbour. It was also the year in which Robyn Sisman, of the American publishers Simon and Schuster, gave him his first contract to write a novel. That novel, four years later, was to be *Fatherland*. It was not quite what Sisman had wanted. She had already published two spy novels by Tim Sebastian, the BBC's correspondent in Warsaw, Moscow and Washington, and she was looking for something similar from Harris. Her indulgence and particularly her lack of harassment as the months went by, earned her both Harris's gratitude and an absorbing, gripping and best-selling novel.

❖ ❖ ❖ ❖ ❖

Most of Harris's work before he became a novelist was about politics, both British and international. More than once he combined political themes and the iniquities of journalism as often practised. Usually he has pointed out the shabbier side of journalism or its use to create images, sometimes false. His book, *Gotcha!*, taking its title from a *Sun* headline during the Falklands War, is about the way in which news, as gathered by often very brave reporters (Harris lists, with pride in his profession, 33 journalists and technicians who were on board ships engaged in the war), is transformed by editors and newspaper owners into propaganda. His point is that, particularly at times of crisis, information as gathered by honest reporters is "fought over, distorted, buried, managed, mangled, stamped on, twisted, spun, slanted, fabricated and forged."

Selling Hitler is a detailed exposure of how the world's leading newspaper owner, Rupert Murdoch, overreached himself in his ambition to get the scoop of the century, and made a fool of himself in the process. It illustrates how, for commercial reasons, the mighty can publish rubbish. The rest of us can only be appalled that such fiascos do not seem to affect the growth of media empires.

Good and Faithful Servant is the story of Bernard Ingham who rose from being a left-wing columnist, using a pseudonym on the weekly paper of the Leeds City Labour Party in the 1960s, to Margaret Thatcher's press secretary. It was Harris who established beyond denial Ingham's earliest journalistic efforts in a cause very different from that which was later to give him such prominence.

The story of Ingham, as told by Harris, is not that of a politician with aspirations, nor of a Conservative who has forgotten his roots and his previous convictions, although the exposure of these was unwelcome to Ingham. Nor is it that of the *éminence grise* in the mould of Alastair Campbell to Tony Blair. The story is that of a loyal servant to a prime minister. He carried out her wishes. Harris got to the heart of the matter, resisting the temptation to see Ingham as he was commonly perceived to be. Harris corroborated by his detailed research the pithy judgement of John Biffen, the member of Thatcher's Cabinet who had been described by Ingham as "semi-detached", that Ingham was "the sewer, not the sewage". Harris's title is taken from the Gospel of St Matthew, where the reward for a good and faithful servant is that you may "enter into the joy of thy Lord."

When Ingham left 10 Downing Street on Thatcher's fall he was still wincing at Harris's account of his role, taking comfort from the good wishes of the Downing Street press corps, the lobby whose work Harris had found so uncongenial when he had been political editor of *The Observer*. Writing in his autobiography, Ingham quotes Robin Oakley (then of *The Times*, later of the

BBC) and Trevor Kavanagh (of *The Sun*) as balm on the wound that Harris had inflicted. Ingham's view of himself was, in fact, the same as Harris's - that he had represented Margaret Thatcher faithfully.

❖ ❖ ❖ ❖ ❖

Harris has recently expressed something close to contempt for much current political journalism. The occasion was the publication of Andrew Rawnsley's *Servants of the People*, which gives many insights into the way in which New Labour figures operate and relate to each other. Harris abhors the low level of political discussion, particularly in Britain. He sees Rawnsley's book as further evidence of the way in which much political journalism has descended to little more than picking up the tittle-tattle of camp-followers, in this case competing members of the same Labour Cabinet, and to generating stories of disagreements. Harris holds to the unfashionable view that politics is about the discussion of ideas and that controversy is good. The job of journalists, in his view, is to find out facts that politicians do not want to be known and to analyse the policies and decisions of those who run the country.

That makes all the more surprising his leading role as the defender of Peter Mandelson, when the Cabinet Minister and close ally of the Prime Minister was harried for a second time from high office in February 2001. Mandelson's spectacular fall occurred in the late morning and by the early evening Harris was to be seen and heard on every television and radio channel as Mandelson's champion. His response was in part spontaneous "grieving for a friend", as he put it, but there was also a sense of outrage that, on the specific explanation for the dismissal, that Mandelson had lied, an injustice had been done. The key to this episode was the role of Alastair Campbell, to Tony Blair what

Ingham had been to Margaret Thatcher, something which Harris understood very well. It is surprising, nonetheless, that someone as politically sophisticated and historically knowledgeable as Harris should have been shocked by the ruthlessness and unfairness of it all. Perhaps it was because the execution was being carried out by one of his friends, Tony Blair, to another of his friends. Harris was close to both Blair and Mandelson. Treachery within a hitherto close group is particularly shocking.

Harris's initial meeting with Mandelson in 1987 had turned into a regular Thursday evening drink together, an opportunity to exchange political insights and doubtless the kind of 'tittle-tattle', as he saw it, that Harris disliked so much about Rawnsley's book. Mandelson had attended Robert and Gill's wedding and had spent four or five weeks as their house guest in the country in 1995 to concentrate on writing his book. He is the godfather of one of their children and a regular at the Harris's as well as at Chequers, the Prime Minister's country seat.

Yet Harris was not an uncritical friend. He had earlier regarded Mandelson's acceptance of a large undeclared loan to buy a fashionable house in Notting Hill as that of "a bloody fool". Even when accepting the role of Mandelson's chief defender during this second sacking, he honestly stated that part of Mandelson's own explanation for his action did not make sense. Yet he was appalled that the reason for the dismissal was shabby and that his friend had been "browbeaten" into resigning.

Mandelson telephoned Harris early on the morning of his resignation. At that hour he was fed up and seeking the advice and comfort of his closest friend, but he was quite confident, having no hint of what was to come. In Harris's own word, Mandelson was "ambushed" a few hours later. Mandelson's removal amazed hard-nosed reporters as much as it did himself and Harris. Harris's response led him to be dubbed 'Peter's friend' in an allusion to the Kenneth Branagh film. His many appearances on radio and television later on the Wednesday and during the next few days were most effective. Article after article began to appear, expressing not support for Mandelson, still less any liking for him, but concern that he had been unfairly treated.

The Downing Street spinners went into action. Harris received a call from Downing Street staff urging him not to continue with his support for Mandelson. When he did continue, the spinning was turned against him. Word reached the press that he was not really very close to Blair, "having been invited to Chequers only once". In fact Harris had accompanied Blair for much of the 1997 election campaign, being with him in the small plane used to convey the Prime Minister the length and breadth of the country. Even when defending Mandelson, he was equally anxious for Blair who had "lost his chief liege man."

Harris says that he was not much involved in New Labour as a movement, more a personal friend of Blair and Mandelson, its creators. This is born out by his views on New Labour. Harris had been with Blair as the 1997 election results came in and watched the new Prime Minister's concern, even amidst his elation at the landslide victory, on seeing that the size of the Labour majority had ditched the 'Blair project' to bring Paddy Ashdown into a coalition government that would see the creation of a broad centre political party to the exclusion of the Left. For the 2001 election, Harris resumed his *Sunday Times* political column and expressed his disillusionment with New Labour utilitarianism, especially its debasement of education to the role of satisfying the requirements of business. He rediscovered some of his youthful political passion.

A short time before Mandelson's first fall, Harris had considered using some of his wealth to buy *The New Statesman*, allegedly in Blair's interests, according to Andrew Rawnsley in the book so critically reviewed by Harris. In fact, Harris had had a much longer interest in *The New Statesman*. Twelve years or so earlier, when the weekly was in a bad way, he had been involved in talks to rescue it. In the 1980s he had written to the chairman of its board, the Labour MP Phillip Whitehead, offering himself as editor if a vacancy arose. The two men had similar backgrounds in broadcasting and Whitehead had been national Chairman of the Fabian Society during Harris's last year at Cambridge. Nothing came of this speculative approach.

Then in 1998, Nick Butler, a friend of Harris's from Cambridge and now an adviser to BP and a committed New Labour man, let Harris know that the present owner, Geoffrey Robinson, wanted to sell the publication and Harris re-entered the market. Robinson was a Blair minister, the man who had given to Mandelson his troublesome loan, and was thought to be an acolyte of Gordon Brown. Rawnsley's claim that the Prime Minister invited Robinson to Downing Street and urged him to sell *The New Statesman* to Harris is explicit and convincing. The only aspect of Rawnsley's account that may be interpretation rather than fact is that the Prime Minister wished to wrest the weekly from the Robinson/Brown axis and deliver it to his own Blair/Mandelson axis, of which Harris was a part.

Harris met first Robinson's solicitor and then had several meetings with the man himself, but it all fizzled out. Then Robinson fell from office along with Mandelson. Unlike Mandelson, Robinson fell from grace as well as office, in his case with no chance of a second coming. He then seemed to have decided to hang on to *The New Statesman* and that was that. Whatever the truth of all this, and perhaps the most obvious truth is how complicated all these New Labour relationships had become, there is no doubt that Harris was more than an acquaintance of the Blairs.

Harris's return to London political life over the Mandelson affair was something of an interlude. His visits to London political salons are now infrequent. He is very much the country dweller with his family. The house is large and beautiful, a Victorian vicarage with its original bookcases and still largely as when first built. A picture of the vicarage by the house's architect, Talbot Bury, hangs in the hall. The house is one of twelve parsonages designed by Bury, a collaborator of Pugin who was responsible for much of the design work on the Houses of Parliament in the nineteenth century. As a family home it sees many local people come and go. It is also the centre of a lively social life with London friends. London comes to the country.

❖ ❖ ❖ ❖ ❖

Harris's method of writing is unusual. He does not belong to the Jeffrey Archer school, although writing is for both men the basis of their current prosperity, enabling them to live in lovely old former vicarages in beautiful riverside surroundings. (Archer is of course temporarily resident elsewhere.) Whereas Archer follows the more usual method of having the idea, sketching the plot and then working hard to produce a thousand or more words a day to a strict routine that requires something approaching purdah, Harris's approach is initially reflective and ruminative, and this shows in the quality of his work.

Harris is a story-teller. Initially, ideas come and go, with some taking root. A main character develops (Hitler, Stalin, Alan Turig) who is not usually the protagonist of the book once it is written, but whose thinking, character and significance are the background. Incidents and scenes then emerge, sometimes in isolation but all within the framework of the background character and his times or the time created for him. This process is like creating in the mind a scene for a film and then, instead of setting it down as a script to be photographed, writing it so that the reader can share the scene. There is something of a similarity here with Thomas Hardy's writing which often reads like the outline of a film script.

A historian by nature if not profession and trained in research by his experience in television journalism, Harris then ensures authenticity by much reading and visiting. His powerful imagination is the final ingredient and has led to two of his novels having a unique feature – they use our knowledge of the past to create circumstances that are different from what we know happened but which could easily have happened, and they create that world so convincingly that we gain new insights into history and politics whilst enjoying the story itself. There is a similarity here with Frederick Forsyth's *Day of the Jackal* where the reader's knowledge that de Gaulle is not going to be assassinated does not detract from the thrill of convincing events that suggest that he will be.

Once the thoughts, characters and main plot are clear, Harris does sometimes write very quickly. He had already shown this before embarking on his novel-writing, by finishing *Gotcha!* in four weeks, *Selling Hitler* in ten and *Good and Faithful Servant* in twelve. In all these cases the research periods were often long – almost three years in the case of *Selling Hitler* and eight years of watching Bernard Ingham in the case of *Good and Faithful Servant*. But research and rumination were followed by swift composition. Three books with a total of well over 800 pages in half a year's writing time is an impressive rate.

❖ ❖ ❖ ❖ ❖

We now reach a dilemma. It is impossible to discuss Harris's methods further without reference to the content of his books. It is a particular form of cruelty to reveal the ending of a book. With Harris, part of the thrill for the reader is to know or to guess roughly where he is taking you, but to find nonetheless that the journey remains captivating, thrilling and, in the end, not exactly what you had expected. So the warning now is: if you have not yet read the three novels, stop reading this chapter now and return to it when you have.

The longest gestation period of an idea was for *Fatherland*. Reviewing his career it is possible to see how the strands of his work as a journalist and researcher came together in this story. As his first fictional writing it is like every novelist's first work. There is much of his previous experience in it.

Harris himself does not know, but it seems likely that the origin for the idea was his interest in David Irving, one of the speakers whom he had invited controversially to the Cambridge Fabian Society. Irving has since become notorious for his court case against the American author and the publisher of a book on so-called holocaust denial. His case turned on his claim that there was no evidence of Hitler's having ordered or even having been aware of the systematic destruction of Jews. When invited by Harris to Cambridge in the 1970s, Irving was already controversial but was regarded as a serious historian with an aptitude for spotting the significance of documents amongst the mountain of papers facing the historian of twentieth century events. The fallacy of the argument that if "there is no evidence that" something happened, nobody can say with certainty that it did happen, was understood by the man in the street let alone academics. The exoneration of Hitler on the grounds that he left no documentary evidence of his involvement or that historians have so far found no such documents is patently daft. But supposing that such evidence did exist and was waiting to be found.....?

From Irving's argument grew Harris's later thought about what would happen if an incriminating document lay buried in Nazi archives, in a context in which Hitler was not defeated but had conquered much of Russia and eastern Europe, with the war continuing on the eastern front, whilst he reached a *modus vivendi* with the West. In those circumstances, imagined by Harris but historically plausible, the discovery of documentary evidence of his having ordered the holocaust would be dynamite.

The imagined context is Harris's own creation, based on his understanding of what could have happened. Suppose that the Japanese had not bombed Pearl Harbour and that the USA had therefore continued to ignore Churchill's pleas for its participation in the war and remained non-combatant. If then Britain's struggle to survive failed, as it so nearly did when all of the rest of western Europe had already fallen to the Germans or had maintained an uneasy neutrality, might not the British government have had to do a deal? Would not the policy of appeasement, founded as it was on the belief that Britain had no national interest in opposing Nazism and Germany, have had a resurgence, with its advocates willing to run Britain on Hitler's behalf? An alternative history can then be imagined. Britain, defeated on the continent and incapable of continuing the war, accepts a semi-autonomous status within the Third Reich. The USA returns to its preferred neutrality. Germany is left to destroy the evidence of the holocaust in Germany and extinguish the remnants of communism on the eastern front.

Then another strand comes along. In 1986, when working for the BBC, Harris made a television film on the Hitler diaries hoax and wrote *Selling Hitler*, as has already been seen. Harris's research led him into a detailed analysis of what documents Hitler did create and what happened to them. The hoax had started with the 'discovery' of some diaries that were high quality forgeries by a man who knew Hitler's handwriting. *The Times* was informed of their existence and consulted one of its directors, the Oxford Professor Hugh Trevor-Roper, who had many years earlier written an account of *The Last Days of Hitler*. He had with great care put together the evidence about Hitler's retreat to the bunker, reaching the conclusion that Hitler had committed suicide with Eva Braun and that their remains had been burned and dumped in a crater as 6000 Russian tanks encircled Berlin and allied planes bombed the city. He seemed the ideal man to authenticate the 'diaries'. Unfortunately, he got it spectacularly wrong. *The Times* bought a pup, Rupert Murdoch had egg on his face, and Harris had a book giving an account of the events which is both detailed and thrilling to read.

Four months before the false news broke that Hitler's diaries had been recovered, Harris had met Irving again at a party and found him irritated by having wasted time in Munich studying 'Hitler diaries' that he had judged to be forgeries. In this regard Irving was a much better judge of Hitler's writing than Trevor-Roper. As soon as *The Times*' claim became public Harris knew which horse to back. For Harris, unconsciously, an idea was firming up.

His own research into what really happened to Hitler's papers, in preparation for the book and television programme, added spice to the possibility of some papers having survived. It also gave him insights into Hitler's character and ways of working that were valuable background for *Fatherland*. Meticulously piecing together all the evidence, he knew that Hitler had been careful first to save and then destroy his vast archive of papers. Some had been burned in the Chancellery garden in Berlin with Hitler watching. Others had been despatched by air to Berchestgaden from which he deludedly hoped to make a come-back. There are more than enough facts, accompanied by more than enough doubts, to make speculation rife. Another element in the story of *Fatherland* was in place.

So the premise for *Fatherland*, created in a devastatingly convincing and detailed way, is that Germany is allowed by America to continue the war against Russia, having already conquered most of eastern Europe, and thus destroy communism. Britain, facing defeat, instead settles for satellite status with its own quislings in charge. The USA is able to live with the result, even to the extent of its President, John F Kennedy, planning a visit to a still-incumbent and now no longer threatening leader of the Third Reich. Factual details are skilfully woven into the story, such as the fact that Kennedy's Irish-born father, Joe, was the US ambassador in London at the time of the outbreak of war, and was an anti-British, pro-Hitler Irishman, thus making his son's later acquiescence in the planned visit to Hitler seem more of a piece. Harris's meticulous preparation and his journalistic and historical research skills then combine with his imagination (characters, events, action) to create the thriller.

For *Archangel*, once the main idea was clear, he was able again to draw on his journalistic experience. He had been to East Berlin with *Panorama*, and had spent four weeks in Poland in 1985 holding secret meetings with the underground movement led by Lech Walesa whilst ostensibly making a film on the Polish economy. In 1987 he was with Margaret Thatcher on her trip to meet Gorbachev in Moscow when she was mobbed in the street. During these visits he came to understand the appalling way of life in the Eastern Bloc countries – the restrictions, hardships, bureaucracies and cruelty. He has always with him a vast knowledge of history in the second half of the twentieth century, acquired during his time as a journalist and from his own reading.

Then, for *Archangel*, which he found the easiest of the three books to write, he paid two visits to Russia, the first in the company of a friend, Andrew Stuttaford, an expert on the country. This visit was to Moscow and Archangel itself, to become familiar with the terrain and to confirm his knowledge of the new post-communist tensions and politics. The second visit was only to Moscow to check precisely on the addresses of the real people who would feature in the book. Asked why he chose the name *Archangel*, he replies that the crux of the story needed to be in the remote frozen north, the word has the connotation of omnipotence appropriate for Stalin, and he just likes the name. It also fits the pattern of all Harris's novels in being one word.

The two stories similarly mix periods of history, but in different ways. In *Fatherland* the jump is from a fact (Hitler's documents) and a possibility (of their survival) into a vivid alternative history to what actually happened. In *Archangel* the invented element of the story (that Stalin had a son who was brought up in the frozen north and became as great a monster as his father) is then brought forward into the known and meticulously recreated period of the post-Soviet era, with its political uncertainties and corruption.

What *Enigma* has in common with the other two books is the historical setting, but this time the characters act out their story against the known historical background. Even here, though, there are historical facts and allusions to political factors that take the reader's understanding of the period a step further than the history books. Is the American who wants to help the perplexed leading figure of the story really an agent wanting to steal the enigma secret for the US? Might he be trying to ensure the passage to America of secrets that would allow the exploitation of computers to take place across the Atlantic? Harris himself does not ask these questions, but somehow the reader finds himself speculating. The skill is to stop in time for the reader's own imagination to take over.

Lesley Smith, the girl who sat next to him and cribbed his notes when they were 17 in Melton Mowbray, perceptively remarks now that, although there is an important female character in *Enigma*, as there is in *Fatherland*, the emotional relationships between men and women are not a developed feature of Harris's writing. The novels are about events, with people interacting in terms of ambition, political objectives, their response to developments that they cannot easily control and the broad sweep of history. In all the novels, Harris excites the imagination of the reader, conveys much history in an interesting way and provokes thought. It is story-telling of a high order.

There have been two recent mysteries in Harris's life. When an enigma machine was stolen from the museum at Bletchley in 2000, the hot property was returned to Jeremy Paxton at the *Newsnight* studio. Did the thief know of both Harris's authorship of *Enigma* and the Harris-Paxman friendship? Then at the time of the Mandelson affair, an apparently inexplicable burglary took place at the Harris home. Nothing was taken except one computer, and then not even its peripherals, making it a uniquely targeted burglary by a specialist. What was the thief after? A real life enigma.

Dependent, as they are, on the slow germination of ideas and the careful preparation of detail, Harris's books are never going to be produced at a rate of one a year. His current output is three books in nine years. Harris has not written a novel for three years. As in all walks of life, quality has its price. Readers must put their hope in his rueful comment that he will write again, if only because he has four children to support. The sense that he will write three or four more books comes across strongly in conversation with him. It is just that he does not sit around trying to think of a theme and does not know what they will be about. The fourth book is in preparation but Harris, understandably, is giving nothing away. His experience with the Mandelson affair might suggest political intrigue as fecund territory.